Canada's Population Outlook

The Canadian Institute for Economic Policy has been established to engage in public discussion of fiscal, industrial and other related public policies designed to strengthen Canada in a rapidly changing international environment.

The Institute fulfills this mandate by sponsoring and undertaking studies pertaining to the economy of Canada and disseminating such studies. Its intention is to contribute in an innovative way to the development of public policy in Canada.

Canadian Institute for Economic Policy
Suite 409, 350 Sparks St., Ottawa K1R 7S8

Canada's Population Outlook

Demographic Futures and Economic Challenges

David K. Foot

Canadian Institute for Economic Policy

Copyright © 1982 by Canadian Institute for Economic Policy

ISBN 0-88862-445-X cloth
ISBN 0-88862-444-1 paper

6 5 4 3 2 1   82 83 84 85 86 87

Canadian Cataloguing in Publication Data

Foot, David K., 1944-
   Canada's population outlook

ISBN 0-88862-445-X (bound) - ISBN 0-88862-444-1 (pbk.)

1. Canada - Economic policy.   2. Canada - Economic conditions.   3. Canada - Population.
I. Title

HC115.F66   330.971   C82-094477-4

Additional copies of this book
may be purchased from:
James Lorimer & Company, Publishers
Egerton Ryerson Memorial Building
35 Britain Street
Toronto M5A 1R7, Ontario
Printed and bound in Canada

Contents

Tables

List of Figures

Foreword

The economic implications of demographic changes are not widely appreciated. Population growth, aging, immigration and interprovincial migration all have far-reaching economic ramifications in areas ranging from education to health care.

The development of consistent and coordinated national policies requires a consistent view of demographic trends. The institute asked David Foot to provide such a framework, and we hope that the economic policy challenges that he identifies will be actively discussed by decision makers and the public.

Like all our authored studies, the views expressed in this study are those of the author and do not necessarily reflect those of the institute.

Roger Voyer
Executive Director
Canadian Institute for Economic Policy

Preface

This study was commissioned in late 1979, largely carried out during the summer of 1980, and the manuscript revised during the summer of 1981. All of the future projections reflect the preliminary estimated age-sex compositions of the Canadian provincial populations on 1 June 1979. Considerable attempt has been made to ensure that estimated data correspond to actual data for 1979 wherever the latter were available. New figures will become available, not the least of which will be the results of the 1981 census and the consequent revised post-census population estimates for the 1976-81 period. However, although the specific numbers may change, it is unlikely that this will affect the general trends reported in this study. There is something quite inevitable about the fact that "every year we get a year older (or we die)"! The future projections in this study are based largely on this simple premise.

The methodology adopted for this research has been guided by three main principles: first, that the Canada-wide results be an aggregation of consistent province-specific results; second, that it is important to test the robustness or sensitivity of the conclusions to the assumptions; and, third, that it is useful to isolate the likely impacts of population growth and aging on important elements of economic and public policies in future years. The first principle necessitated the use of a multiregional population projection model in which the linkages between the provinces, particularly with respect to interprovincial migration, are made explicit. For this purpose a slightly modified version of the Statistics Canada population projection model was used to generate the future projections reported in this study. The second principle resulted in the development of a series of alternative demographic futures so that the *quantitative* impact of changing *each* of the assumptions can be assessed independently and in combination. The third principle required, among other ingredients, an analysis of projections at *constant* rates (per capita cost, educational enrolment, or labour force participation) so that the impacts of future population change and population aging in Canada can be clearly isolated. The impacts of changing rates can also be examined within this framework, although somewhat less attention is devoted to this.

By providing a consistent demographic framework and outlook, the study should be of considerable use to those concerned with the formulation, development and implementation of economic and public policies in Canada and the provinces. Furthermore, this work explores some of the economic implications and challenges of future population, especially over the decades of the 1980s and 1990s. Many of the findings do not appear in accord with current perceptions and policies. Future demographic developments in Canada will have an impact upon many, if not most, of the decisions in both the public and private sectors in the years ahead, and to the extent that this study provides a useful framework in which to examine the many possible decisions, it will have fulfilled its purposes.

Acknowledgements

In a study of this breadth any author accumulates numerous debts, both intellectual and personal. First and foremost, to the sponsors of the study, the Canadian Institute for Economic Policy, I owe my sincere appreciation, not only for providing me with the opportunity to undertake this work, but also for the considerable encouragement and understanding displayed throughout the duration of the project. The institute's willingness to handle in a personal manner decisions made necessary as new (and not always encouraging) information came to hand was certainly appreciated. In this regard, I feel sure that other members of the institute will not object if I make special mention of my colleague Professor A. Rotstein.

Second, to the numerous persons at Statistics Canada who assisted me with this study, I owe both an intellectual and personal debt. My understanding of demographic data was considerably strengthened (although undoubtedly not perfected) through numerous discussions with members of the staff at Statistics Canada, especially in the Demography and in the Education, Science and Culture Divisions. I am most appreciative of the staff of the Demography Division: its director, Dr. A. Romaniuc; the chief of the population projections section, Dr. M. V. George; and Ms. J. Perrault, who carried out the arduous task of translating my often imprecise instructions into the population projections that form the basis of this study.

As usual, the Institute for Policy Analysis at the University of Toronto provided an excellent environment for this research. I am most appreciative to its former director, Professor J. A. Sawyer, and its current director, Professor R. M. Bird, for the encouragement and advice extended at different times throughout my work on this project. Also, my appreciation goes to Mr. G. Ugray of the institute for his programming assistance and other consultative advice on computational matters. The possible integration of this work with other regionally based quantitative work currently in progress at the institute provided a focus and reason for several very useful discussions with a number of my colleagues. In addition, I consider myself very fortunate in having Ms. S. J. Lane as a research assistant throughout the project and Ms. R. Mollica to type the manuscript.

Finally, this study is dedicated to my friends, whose patience has been tested on many different occasions over the duration of the project, and to all those interested in the interactions between demographic developments and economic policy in Canada and elsewhere.

David K. Foot
Institute for Policy Analysis
and
Department of Political Economy
University of Toronto

Introduction

The interaction between population and economic development, and hence economic policy, was one of the earliest cornerstones in the discipline that is now known as economics. In his pioneering work, Malthus[1] established the linkage between population growth and human subsistence and concluded that the need for human sustenance provided the only check on unlimited population growth. As a consequence, according to Malthus, the object of economic policy should be to restrict the population increase to "manageable" proportions. The two hundred years since Malthus's study have witnessed an explosion in world population in apparent contradiction to his hypothesis. Yet further reflection reveals that the great development in the industrial population in the nineteenth century and the rapid increases in agricultural productivity in the twentieth century have largely reduced the need for the operation of the "Malthusian checks." To be sure, there have been, and continue to be, notable exceptions,[2] but the general conclusion remains: the spectres of famine and death outlined by Malthus almost two centuries ago have been either overcome or, at least, postponed, especially in the more developed regions of the world.

In fact, in recent years in many of the developed countries, the focus has moved from one of expanding population growth to one of declining population growth. This is *not* a new focus,[3] but it is largely unfamiliar to the current generation of demographers and economists, whose experiences embrace the postwar "Baby Boom" with all its attendant and continuing ramifications. It is only recently, after almost two decades of steadily declining fertility rates, that analysts are once again turning their attention to the economic consequences of declining population growth.

This shift in focus is particularly evident in North America, where the populations of Canada and the United States are relatively young in comparison to those in many of the developed nations of Europe.[4] In general, it is the young who are mobile, so in periods of substantial international migration, as in the 1950s and 1960s, the recipient nations, such as Canada and the United States, tend to augment their populations with younger persons. Since these persons often bring families to, or bear families in, their new domicile, they contribute not only to a lowering in the average age but also to a further increase in population growth. The cessation of immigrant flows generally has the opposite effects. Consequently, it is not surprising that in the latter part of the 1970s the focus of demographers and economists concerned with such matters had moved towards one of declining population growth.

In Canada neither the volatility of immigrant flows nor the declining rate of population growth is a new phenomenon. Overbeek, in reviewing Canadian demographic history, concludes that "immigrants to Canada have tended to come in waves. . . . [T]he typical situation so far has been that Canada has known short periods of heavy immigration followed by longer periods of gradual losses, mainly to the U.S.A."[5] Put in this perspective, the experience of the 1970s should hardly come as a surprise. Moreover, the process of the aging of the population that accompanies declining population growth has been a long-run phenomenon. The average age of the Canadian population has been increasing throughout this century, as has the percentage of the population aged 65 years and over.[6]

What is new, however, and will be carefully documented in the pages to follow, is the speed at which this process is projected to continue in the years ahead. By way of illustration, the average age of the Canadian population will likely increase as much in the last twenty years of the twentieth century as it did in the previous eighty years. The same is true of the percentage of senior members in the population. In short, the process of aging can be expected to increase rapidly. This is primarily a consequence of the dramatic decline in fertility that followed the postwar Baby Boom and is relatively insensitive to future demographic developments, including fertility and immigration.[7] Hence the process embodies considerable historical determinancy and, in this sense, is inevitable—a strong assertion in anyone's language, especially that of economists!

Consequently, policy makers (and profit maximizers) should be aware of these trends. The impacts of the aging process on such public programs as health care and education are important and dramatic. Pension schemes (both public and private), housing, the labour force, the unemployment rate, productivity and the growth potential of the economy must not be ignored in this regard. There are few areas of economic policy, both public and private, that are *not* potentially affected by these demographic developments.[8]

Of course, the impact of these developments is by no means limited to the economic sphere. Numerous other disciplines are affected by declining population growth and population aging.[9] To the extent that appropriate policies can be developed and implemented via the political sphere, it is easy to remain relatively optimistic regarding the resolution of the issues raised by this process—politicians get old themselves, and old people vote! But the process is also likely to introduce new challenges in such areas as housing, transportation and health care for which resolutions may not be as easy. Although accelerating, the aging process does occur gradually, which from a policy viewpoint can be both an asset and a liability. It is an asset when it allows sufficient time to develop appropriate resolutions, but a liability when it permits resolutions to be continually postponed. In the years ahead the challenges of this aging process are likely to be numerous. All that can be hoped is that the resolutions will be just as plentiful.

Canada is a decentralized country. The effects of social processes and the policies developed in one region or province are not always the same in another region or province. The impacts of demographic change provide no exception. Population developments have been, and will continue to be, region-specific. However, in developing appropriate responses at this level, it is vitally important that consistent and coordinated policies be conceived and implemented. Thus, it is important, for example, that Alberta be cognizant of demographic developments in Quebec (and vice versa), that education departments be familiar with the impacts of demography on health departments (and vice versa), and that the private sector be aware of demographic pressures on the public sector (and vice versa). If these various policy makers do not incorporate a relatively consistent view of future demographic developments into their respective decisions, the future is likely to contain numerous "inevitable surprises."

Perhaps the most important objective of this study is to provide such a view. A framework that ensures consistency[10] (although no claims to future accuracy can be promised) is used to develop alternative population projections and their associated economic implications for Canada and the provinces to the end of the twentieth century and beyond. Notable features of this study include:

- a careful evaluation of assumptions concerning likely future demographic developments in both an economic and a long-run historical context;
- the presentation of a number of alternative scenarios so that the *sensitivity* of the results to the assumptions can be assessed and quantified;
- a regional orientation that uses the province as the basis for the future assumptions and economic analysis, with the Canada-wide implications being derived as a summation of the provincial results; and
- an attempt to explore beyond the population numbers into the likely *economic* implications of the projections, with particular concern for the implications for public policies in the years ahead.

In many cases, the conclusions are demonstrated to be robust; that is, quite insensitive to a wide variety of chosen assumptions. For these cases the policy maker can proceed with considerable confidence to develop appropriate policies. For those cases where the outcomes are sensitive to the chosen assumptions, the framework for this study permits the identification of the crucial determinant or determinants of the sensitivity. In these cases the policy maker has a clear indication as to where further information is required or where further research should be devoted to obtain a better indication of the most likely outcome. Without such information it is especially important that the policy maker adopt a very flexible approach to policy formulation when the projected future outcome is demonstrated to lie within a wide range of possible results. In these cases it is also important to monitor new information as it comes to hand. Many of the results presented in this study fall into the former group, but even those in the latter group can make a useful contribution to economic and public policies when viewed in this way.

Projections are not forecasts about future events and should only be used as such under a prescribed set of conditions. A projection is conditional on the assumptions that underlie it and can only be expected to be realized if those assumptions turn out to be accurate descriptions of reality. Nonetheless, the choice of a "realistic"[11] set of assumptions does facilitate the use of a projection as a forecast, and the provision of alternative projections enables the user to adequately examine the sensitivity of the results of interest to alternative assumptions. The relative insensitivity of many of the findings in this study to alternative, often quite diverse, sets of assumptions provides a strong foundation for the deduction of the economic implications and policy prescriptions based on likely future demographic trends. The future is inherently uncertain and difficult to predict; yet the inevitable observation that "every year we get a year older" provides considerable solace to the user of the information presented in this study and serves as a *guide* to future demographic trends in Canada and the provinces, at least to the turn of the century.

The study is divided into two main parts. In the first part, a review of the demographic trends in Canada and the provinces is presented, with primary concentration on the aging process. The demographic developments in Canada over the past century or so are reviewed at the national level, and the main components of population growth and population composition are presented and discussed. This is followed by an examination of provincial data and the introduction of information on interprovincial migration in Canada. A detailed examination of the demographic developments over the 1970s shows the emergence of some "new" demographic trends, which are then used as a basis for choosing alternative sets of assumptions to be used in developing the population projections. The characteristics of the various projections are outlined, including a brief discussion of the Statistics Canada model that was used to generate them.

In the second part of the study some of the economic and policy challenges of these projections are explored, beginning with a general overview of the changing requirements of resource allocation in an aging population with the use of dependency ratio calculations. This is followed by two detailed studies of these projected future demographic developments, one on educational enrolment futures and the other on labour force futures in Canada and the provinces. This work concludes with a brief review of other possible applications and the possible policy challenges generated by the findings.

It should be noted that although only a provincial disaggregation is presented in this study, all of the analyses presented herein can, in principle, be extended to sub-provincial regions.[12] Since the study is primarily concerned with the implications of population aging, details on the basis of demographic characteristics other than age and sex (for example, marital status, religion and race) are not considered but, presumably, could be incorporated as based on census data.[13] Similarly, information on occupation has not been presented in this study.[14] These, and other demographically related characteristics, are important for many areas of research but lie outside the primary focus of this study. Others, no doubt, will explore these many diverse aspects relating to the future population in Canada and the provinces.

Part 1

Canada's Aging Population: Past, Present and Future

Population Growth in Canada and the Provinces
1

Population Measurement

The population of any geographical area is the total number of persons inhabiting the area at a given time. As such, a population is both area- and time-specific. In Canada the national boundaries define the area, and a population count is made at discrete intervals, currently every five years. This method of measurement, usually referred to as the census method, differs from a continuously updated registry system in use in some European countries (for example, Switzerland and the Netherlands), where all changes in demographic status are recorded on a separate card for each individual at local registry offices. Decennial censuses (taken every ten years) have been practised in Canada since 1851,[1] and quinquennial censuses (every five years), since 1956. Traditionally, the Canadian census date has been June 1. Canada has used the *de jure* system of enumeration, whereby persons are counted at their regular place of residence. This is in contrast to the *de facto* approach, used in the United States, whereby persons are counted at their location on the census date. For the 1971 census, Canada dispensed with the interview, or canvasser, system of enumeration and adopted a self-enumeration approach, combined with the large-scale use of sample coverage. Approximately one in five Canadians filled out a "long" form of thirty questions, while the remainder filled out a "short" form of twelve questions. Only about 3 per cent of the population (mostly living in remote regions) were enumerated by the interview method. Of course, this new method of enumeration, which was applied again for the 1976 and 1981 censuses,[2] is only possible where the population is highly literate. It has the potential advantages of lower cost, greater speed and perhaps even increased accuracy (through reduced interviewer error or bias).

Table 1-1 presents the results of the Canadian censuses since 1851.

TABLE 1-1
CANADIAN POPULATION AND COMPONENTS OF GROWTH, 1851-1981
(Increase Over Preceding Census, 000's)

Census Year	Population			Births (B_t)	Deaths (D_t)	Natural Increase $(B_t - D_t)$	Immigration (I_t)	Emigration (E_t)	Net Immigration $(I_t - E_t)$
	Level (P_t)	Change (ΔP_t)	Average Annual Growth (%)						
1851	2,436.3	—	—	—	—	—	—	—	—
1861	3,229.6	793	2.9	1,281	670	611	352	170	182
1871	3,689.3	460	1.3	1,370	760	610	260	410	−150
1881	4,324.8	636	1.6	1,480	790	690	350	404	−54
1891	4,833.2	508	1.1	1,524	870	654	680	826	−146
1901	5,371.3	538	1.1	1,548	880	668	250	380	−130
1911	7,206.6	1,835	3.0	1,925	900	1,025	1,550	740	810
1921	8,787.9	1,581	2.0	2,340	1,070	1,270	1,400	1,089	311
1931	10,376.8	1,589	1.7	2,420	1,060	1,360	1,200	970	230
1941	11,506.7	1,130	1.0	2,294	1,072	1,222	149	241	−92
1951[a]	13,648.0	2,141	1.7	3,186	1,214	1,972	548	379	169
1951[b]	14,009.4	2,503	2.0	—	—	—	—	—	—
1961	18,238.2	4,229	2.7	4,468	1,320	3,148	1,543	463	1,080
1971	21,568.3	3,330	1.7	4,105	1,497	2,608	1,429	707	722
1981[c]	24,187.3	2,619	1.2	3,575	1,680	1,895	1,452	727	724

Notes: [a] Excludes Newfoundland.
[b] Includes Newfoundland.
[c] Estimates (see chapter 3 for details).

Source: M. V. George, *Population Growth in Canada*, 1971 Census Profile Study (Ottawa: Statistics Canada, 1976), Tables 1 and 3 with adjustments and updates by the author.

4

It shows that a population of 2.4 million in 1851 has grown to approximately ten times that size over the subsequent 130 years. Between the first nation-wide census in 1871 and the decennial census one hundred years later, the population grew from 3.7 million persons to 21.6 million persons, an increase of 17.9 million persons, at an average growth rate of 1.8 per cent per annum.

This growth, however, has not been spread evenly over the period. The increase in population numbers between 1851 and 1861 was not matched until fifty years later, with the opening up of the Canadian West. And this growth spurt was not matched for yet another fifty years, at the time of the resettlements that accompanied the aftermath of the Second World War. In terms of annual average population growth, these three decadal periods (1851-61, 1901-11 and 1951-61) stand out as the "rapid growth" periods in Canadian demographic history since 1851, all with average annual growth rates in excess of 2.5 per cent. On the other hand, it is interesting to note that in no decadal period over this time has the average annual growth in population fallen below 1 per cent.

Components of National Population Growth

The change in a nation's population stock over a period of time can be conveniently divided into four components. Additions occur as a result of births and immigration, and deletions occur as a result of deaths and emigration. This simple identity can be written as:

$$P(t) - P(t-1) \equiv B(t) - D(t) + I(t) - E(t)$$

where $P(t)$ denotes the stock of population at time (t),

$B(t)$ denotes the number of births over the interval $(t-1)$ to (t),

$D(t)$ denotes the number of deaths over the interval $(t-1)$ to (t),

$I(t)$ denotes the number of immigrants over the interval $(t-1)$ to (t),

and $E(t)$ denotes the number of emigrants over the interval $(t-1)$ to (t).

This identity is applicable to any time period, as can be seen from Table 1-1, in which the interval between time (t) and time $(t-1)$ is ten years. Traditionally, the numerical difference between births and deaths is referred to as the "natural increase" in the population, and

5

the numerical difference between immigration and emigration as the increase attributable to "net immigration" or "net international migration."

The values of each of these components for Canada over the period covered by the censuses are also set out in Table 1-1. From this table it is apparent that much of the rapid growth over the 1851-61 decade can be attributed to natural causes. These account for over three-quarters of the change in population. Although the decadal natural increase did not change much in the subsequent four decades (always being between 600,000 and 700,000 persons), net immigration became negative largely as a result of the opening up of the American West, which attracted many Canadian residents. The rapid growth in the first decade of the twentieth century can also be attributed to a large natural increase, primarily as a result of a substantial increase in the number of births, but the quantitative contribution of net immigration was almost as important. Although emigration continued (even at a higher pace than during the previous decade), immigration to Canada increased over sixfold compared to the previous decade, as people came to open up the Canadian West.

The outbreak of the First World War reduced the inflows and increased the outflows. Population growth declined over the subsequent twenty years in spite of the increasing number of births. During the economic depression of the 1930s, birth rates in Canada and elsewhere declined noticeably. The government virtually closed the national frontiers to flows of people, which resulted in the lowest decadal average annual growth recorded over the entire period since 1851.

The Second World War dominated the activities of the early 1940s, but the cessation of hostilities brought increasing birth rates and renewed immigration flows. The rapid-growth decade of the 1950s witnessed a dramatic increase in the number of births—the postwar Baby Boom—with the natural increase again being the dominant component, accounting for over three-quarters of the change in the population, even though net immigration reached high levels.[3] Subsequently, the decline in the population growth was primarily attributable to a decrease in the number of births and, increasingly, to a decline in the number of immigrants. The former reflects the dramatic decrease in the birth rate since the early 1960s, while the latter reflects the relatively depressed economic conditions that prevailed primarily as a result of international adjustments to increased oil prices since the mid-1970s.

From these data it is apparent that Canada's population growth since the first census has always been positive, has averaged at least 1 per cent per annum between censuses, but has varied considerably. Of the three rapid-growth decades over the period, two (1851-61 and 1951-61) have been dominated by large increases in the number of births, while one (1901-11) was a combination of increased births and increased net immigration.[4] These data suggest that immigrants to Canada have tended to come in "waves"[5] (with a phase of approximately fifty years), followed by longer periods of attrition to the United States. Over the century following the first national census (1871-1971), the natural increase accounted for 82 per cent of the population growth, and net immigration for the remaining 18 per cent.

This brief overview of Canadian population growth suggests a significant interaction between the components of population growth and the associated economic and social conditions of the times. During economically depressed and, in some cases, war-ravaged times, population growth tends to be curtailed by lower fertility, more emigration and less immigration. The reverse holds true during relatively more prosperous times. Thus, Canadian population growth appears to have been stimulated by either depression or war elsewhere in the world, or by relative prosperity at home. When opposite conditions have prevailed, the Canadian population growth has slowed down.

Sex and Age Composition

The composition or structure of a population at a point in time refers to the basic demographic characteristics by which the individuals who comprise the population may be differentiated. Numerous characteristics, both natural and acquired, can be considered, but sex, age, race (or mother tongue), religion, education, occupation and location are the most common. Sex and age are dominant characteristics, since they provide the basis for many of the subsequent changes in the size and composition of the population. Moreover, it is these characteristics that are pivotal to any study of population aging. In a diverse and federated country such as Canada, location may also be vitally important, since many economic policies are regionally oriented and may require significant resource transfers between geographic regions and the various levels of government.[6] These compositional features of the Canadian population are briefly reviewed in this and the next section. They provide the basis for the subsequent analysis of population aging in Canada and the provinces—the prime orientation of this study.[7]

7

In most populations, more boys than girls are born. Since male mortality also tends to be higher, this can be interpreted as "Nature's way" of providing population balance. In Canada there has been between 5 and 7 per cent more boys than girls born throughout this century. An increase in births will, therefore, increase the male proportion of the population. Moreover, since immigrant flows have tended to contain a higher proportion of males than the domestic population, increases in immigration have also tended to enlarge the male proportion of the population. Also, since male mortality tends to be higher at all ages, the ratio of males to females (sometimes referred to as the "sex ratio") or to the total population tends to decline with increasing age.

Until very recently Canada has been a slightly "male-dominant" population, in the sense that the percentage of males has exceeded the percentage of females in the population and hence the sex ratio has been greater than unity (one). From Table 1-2, it is apparent that this ratio increased slightly after the birth-generated population growth of the 1850s and thereafter declined until the birth and immigration-induced population growth prior to the First World War. It reached a decennial census maximum of 1.129 in 1911.[8] Thereafter it has been on a secular (long-term) decline, except for a slight increase in 1931 and a pause as a result of the birth-generated population growth of the 1950s. By 1971 there was an approximate balance between males and females, and it is expected that the interpretation of the 1981 census will record, for the first census date in Canadian history, a slightly "female-dominant" population. As noted above, since male mortality tends to be higher at all ages, this gradual decline in the sex ratio (or percentage of males) suggests that since the 1930s the Canadian population has been aging, although this is by no means the only, or even the best, indicator of the aging process.

The most frequently used summary indicator of population aging is the average (or mean) age of the population. As shown in Table 1-2, the average age in Canada has increased from under 22 years in 1851 to over 30 years in the postwar period. The current average age is around 32 years. Perhaps the best summary measure is the median age[9]—the age that divides the population into two groups of equal size, one half being comprised of younger members and the other half of older members. This has risen gradually from 17.2 years in 1851 to an estimated 29.5 years in 1981. As with the mean, a large increase occurred over the 1931-41 decade when both births and immigration were low. Conversely, there was a decline over 1951-61 when both

8

TABLE 1-2
SEX RATIO, AGE AND AGE COMPOSITION
OF THE CANADIAN POPULATION, 1851-1981

Census Year	Sex Ratio[a]	Age (Years)		Age Composition (%)				
		Mean[b]	Median	0-4 Years	5-14 Years	15-24 Years	25-64 Years	65 + Years
1851	1.051	21.7	17.2	18.5	26.4	20.5	31.9	2.7
1861	1.057	22.7	18.2	16.8	25.7	21.0	33.5	3.0
1871	1.030	23.6	18.8	14.7	26.9	20.5	34.2	3.7
1881	1.025	24.7	20.1	13.8	24.9	21.2	35.9	4.1
1891	1.037	25.8	21.4	12.6	23.7	20.7	38.4	4.6
1901	1.050	26.8	22.7	12.0	22.4	20.0	40.6	5.0
1911	1.129	27.0	23.8	12.3	20.6	19.4	43.0	4.7
1921	1.064	27.4	24.0	12.1	22.4	17.3	43.5	4.8
1931	1.074	28.4	24.8	10.4	21.3	18.8	44.0	5.6
1941	1.052	30.4	27.1	9.1	18.7	18.7	46.8	6.7
1951[c]	1.024	30.3	27.7	12.3	18.0	15.3	46.6	7.8
1961	1.022	30.5	26.3	12.4	21.6	14.3	44.1	7.6
1971	1.002	30.8	26.3	8.4	21.2	18.6	43.8	8.1
1981[d]	0.984	32.0	29.5	7.4	15.1	19.3	48.5	9.7

Notes: [a] Ratio of males to females in the population.
[b] Based on five-year groups and on an average of 80 years for the age group "70 years and over."
[c] Includes Newfoundland from this year on.
[d] Estimates.

Source: Calculations by the author from census results. Data for pre-1901 taken from M. C. Urquhart, *Historical Statistics of Canada* (Toronto: Macmillan, 1965), p. 16. (See also J. A. Narland, *The Age-Sex Structure of Canada's Population*, 1971 Census Profile Study, [Ottawa: Statistics Canada, 1976], Table 12.)

births and immigration were high. The largest decadal increase in both measures occurred over the decade of the 1970s, thus confirming the current importance of population aging in Canada.[10] In summary, these figures show that population aging is *not* a new phenomenon in Canada. There has been a general aging trend in the country since the first census. However, two periods—the 1930s and the 1970s—stand out as significant decades of population aging in Canadian demographic history.

An examination of the changing age composition of the population also confirms this process. Over the period of the censuses, the percentage of the young has been on a secular, or long-term, decline, while the percentage of the old has been on a long-term increase (see Table 1-2). Of course, the birth-induced rapid population growth periods of the 1900s and 1950s represent slight contrasts to these trends, but they did not reverse a process that has been underway since the first census in 1851. This provides further evidence that population aging is *not* a new phenomenon in Canada.

In the middle of the age spectrum, the percentage of the population in the working-age groups (15 to 64 years) has always been above 50 per cent in Canada. From a low of 52.4 per cent in the 1851 census, it rose to a peak of 65.5 per cent in the 1941 census and thereafter declined to 58.4 per cent by the 1961 census. By the 1971 census it was 62.4 per cent, the same as in the 1911 census, but by 1981 the percentage of the working-age group is anticipated to reach a level never before experienced in Canadian history. More than two in three persons (67.8 per cent) in Canada will be of working age.

Underlying this trend are some important compositional changes. The percentage of younger members of this potential work force (15 to 24 years), which generally comprised at least 20 per cent of the total population during the last half of the previous century, declined to a low of 15.3 per cent by 1951. Since then, the percentage has been increasing. However, the percentage of older members of the potential work force (25 to 64 years) was on an increasing trend until 1951 and then declined in the 1950s and 1960s, only to turn around in the 1970s. Consequently, almost all of the twentieth century to date has been characterized by *opposing* trends in the importance in regard to the total population of these two age groups comprising the working-age population. The exceptions are the 1950s, when both were declining in relative importance, and the 1970s, when both were increasing in relative importance. Thus, the very high percentage of the population currently of working age can be described as a reflection of coincidentally increasing trends in the underlying age composition of this group.

A comparison of the population of working age with those of non-working ages (0 to 14 years and 65 years and over) has led to discussions in the demographic and economic literature of dependency ratios.[11] These are population measures that express the relative size of the populations of working age, sometimes called the "non-dependent" or the "productive" population, to those of non-working

10

age, sometimes called the "dependent" or the "non-productive" population. They are used as summary demographic measures of the "responsibilities" towards, or "burden" on a society from, its young and elderly members. Throughout the last half of the last century more than 40 per cent of the population were in the dependent category, while for the first seventy years of this century the figure never dropped below the 1941 low of 34.5 per cent. However, in 1981 slightly less than one in three members of the Canadian population is of non-working age—an all-time historical low.

Once again, this trend masks important compositional changes. In fact, with the exception of the period following the Second World War, this percentage has been dominated by the secular decline in the proportion of the young, which has more than compensated for the secular increase in the proportion of the elderly. This changing compositional mix of dependents has important implications for economic and public policies. These will be elaborated upon in later chapters.

Moreover, these results suggest that in many respects the 1970s represented a unique period in Canadian demographic history, especially from a compositional viewpoint. For the first time, Canada's population became slightly female-dominant, more than two in three Canadians were of working age, and, within the non-working age group, the percentage of young had never been so low and the percentage of old never so high. Whether or not these trends can be expected to continue, or whether they represent a unique situation in both past *and future* demographic history, will be the subject of later chapters.

Growth and Distribution by Province

Currently Canada is a federation of ten provinces and two territories, the most recent addition being Newfoundland, which entered the federation in 1949. Table 1-3 sets out the census population in each province and territory since 1851. From these data it is apparent that Ontario has always been the most populous province, with approximately one-third of Canada's population residing within its borders. Ontario's relative demographic importance waned over the first half of this century, primarily as a result of the development of the Canadian West, but it has increased slightly since the 1950s.

The second most populous province has been Quebec, with between 27 and 30 per cent of Canada's population in censuses since 1901. In 1851 Quebec comprised 36.5 per cent of Canada's population, a share

TABLE 1-3
CANADIAN POPULATION BY PROVINCE, 1851-1981
(000's)

Census Year	Can	Nfld	PEI	NS	NB	PQ	Ont	Man	Sask	Alta	BC	Yukon	NWT
1851	2,436.3	—	62.7	276.9	193.8	890.3	952.0	—ᵃ	—	—	55.0	—	5.7
1861	3,229.6	—	80.9	330.9	252.0	1,111.6	1,396.1	—	—	—	51.5	—	6.7
1871	3,689.3	—	94.0	387.8	285.6	1,191.5	1,620.9	25.2	—	—	36.2	—	48.0
1881	4,324.8	—	108.9	440.6	321.2	1,359.0	1,926.9	62.3	—ᵃ	—ᵃ	49.5	—	56.4
1891	4,833.2	—	109.1	450.4	321.3	1,488.5	2,114.3	152.5			98.2		99.0
1901	5,371.3	—	103.3	459.6	331.1	1,648.9	2,182.9	255.2	91.3	73.0	178.7	27.2	20.1
1911	7,206.6	—	93.7	492.3	351.9	2,005.8	2,527.3	461.4	492.4	374.3	392.5	8.5	6.5
1921	8,787.9ᵇ	—	88.6	523.8	387.9	2,360.5	2,933.7	610.1	757.5	588.5	524.6	4.2	8.1
1931	10,376.8	—	88.0	512.8	408.2	2,874.7	3,431.7	700.1	921.8	731.6	694.3	4.2	9.3
1941	11,506.7	—	95.0	578.0	457.4	3,331.9	3,787.7	729.7	896.0	796.2	817.9	4.9	12.0
1951ᶜ	14,009.4	361.4	98.4	642.6	515.7	4,055.7	4,597.5	776.5	831.7	939.5	1,165.2	9.1	16.0
1961	18,238.2	457.9	104.6	737.0	597.9	5,259.2	6,236.1	921.7	925.2	1,331.9	1,629.1	14.6	23.0
1971	21,568.3	522.1	111.6	789.0	634.6	6,027.8	7,703.1	988.2	926.2	1,627.9	2,184.6	18.4	34.8
1981ᵈ	24,187.3	583.6	125.7	862.6	715.2	6,316.9	8,681.4	1,036.5	983.1	2,147.2	2,669.9	21.5	43.7

Notes: ᵃ Included with Northwest Territories.
ᵇ Includes 0.5 members of the Royal Canadian Navy whose province of residence is unknown.
ᶜ Includes Newfoundland for the first time.
ᵈ Estimates.

Source: M. C. Urquhart, *Historical Statistics of Canada* (Toronto: Macmillan, 1965). p. 14, updated by the author.

that was, like Ontario's, eroded with the movement westward. Unlike Ontario, however, this erosion was halted between the 1930s and 1960s when Quebec's population was maintained at around 29 per cent. Since then, further erosion of the share has taken place.

Besides Ontario and Quebec, early settlement in Canada occurred in the Maritime provinces (Prince Edward Island, Nova Scotia and New Brunswick), which together accounted for over half a million people, or 22 per cent, of the Canadian population in 1851. By the turn of the century this share had been reduced to 16.6 per cent, with Nova Scotia still the most populous of the three provinces. Throughout this century all three provinces have recorded an almost continuous decline in their relative shares. Currently they comprise only about 7 per cent of Canada's population. Even the inclusion of Newfoundland in 1949, which added approximately 350,000 persons to the national population (whereupon the *four* eastern provinces as a group became known as the Atlantic provinces), added only about 2.5 per cent to this total share.

Much of the above-mentioned erosion in relative shares during this century can be attributed to the development of the Canadian West. At the turn of the century the populations of the Prairie provinces (Manitoba, Saskatchewan and Alberta) comprised 7.8 per cent of the national total, with British Columbia contributing a further 3.3 per cent. Moreover, with the gold rushes in the late nineteenth century, the population share of the Yukon and Northwest Territories increased considerably, and by the turn of the century it comprised almost 1 per cent of the Canadian total.[12] As a group, however, these provinces and territories were still less populous than the three Maritime provinces. The major boost to the population of the western provinces occurred as a result of the pre-First World War wave of immigrants, who largely settled in this region. By 1911 the three Prairie provinces accounted for 18.4 per cent of Canada's population, far surpassing the Maritime provinces in less than a decade. The "golden years" continued into the postwar period, and by 1921 the population of the western provinces comprised well over 20 per cent of Canada's population. The cessation of rapid population growth hit Manitoba first. Subsequently, the economic depression of the 1930s contributed to a very hard environment for the farms on the Prairies. Consequently, both the inhabitants of the area and new arrivals found this part of the country less attractive than others. Although population numbers continued to grow, the relative demographic importance of this region began to wane. This trend has not been reversed in Manitoba or Saskatchewan, but was reversed in Alberta in the 1950s, when industrial development associated with new-found energy sources began to take place. After a pause in the 1960s, this trend intensified in the 1970s, so currently Alberta is more populous than the three Maritime provinces combined.

The only Canadian province to show consistent growth in its population share throughout the twentieth century has been British Columbia. Its share has risen rather steadily from 3.3 per cent in 1901 to a current figure approaching 11 per cent. The most rapid growth periods were the 1900s, 1940s and 1960s, although the trend has certainly continued into the 1970s. This relatively steady growth has been primarily associated with the development of a resource-based economy throughout this century.

Finally, after the gold rush of the 1890s, the population of the Yukon and Northwest Territories dissipated and the region has never comprised more than 0.3 per cent of Canadian population since the peak reached in the 1901 census.

By way of a summary, the intercensal average annual population growth rates for each of the provinces are presented in Table 1-4. They underscore the dramatic increases in the Prairies at the beginning of the twentieth century and the subsequent decades of slow growth in that region, except in Alberta. They also underscore the consistently relative high growth rates in British Columbia and the consistently relative low growth rates in the Maritime provinces.

These population movements also reflect, at least since the 1930s, the worldwide movement to urban centres, with Toronto and Vancouver, and, more recently, Calgary and Edmonton, being prime examples.[13] Montreal is the apparent exception, a complete explanation for which would have to encompass an analysis of the role of culture and language in its development. Nonetheless, the existence of a large urban centre in Quebec has not been sufficient to arrest the decline in the population share in that province.[14]

This brief survey of provincial population trends in Canada shows a country that has been continuously, if unevenly, drifting westward. Only the province of British Columbia has shown a continued increase in its demographic share over the twentieth century, while the only decline in Alberta's relative share was slight and occurred as a result of the economic depression of the 1930s. Elsewhere, only postwar Ontario was able to increase its demographic share. Whether or not these regional trends can be expected to continue is also an important and interesting subject for discussion and review. A careful analysis requires a brief review of each of the components of provincial growth and the inclusion of another element in population growth—

14

TABLE 1-4
CANADIAN POPULATION GROWTH BY PROVINCE, 1851-1981
(Average Annual Per Cent)

Period	Can[a]	Nfld	PEI	NS	NB	PQ	Ont	Man	Sask	Alta	BC	Yukon	NWT
1851-1901	1.6	—	1.0	1.0	1.1	1.2	1.7	—	—	—	2.4	—	—
1901-11	3.0	—	-1.0	0.7	0.6	2.0	1.5	6.1	18.3	17.8	8.2	-11.0	-10.7
1911-21	2.0	—	-0.6	0.6	1.0	1.6	1.5	2.8	4.4	4.6	2.9	-6.8	2.2
1921-31	1.7	—	-0.1	-0.2	0.5	2.0	1.6	1.4	2.0	2.2	2.8	0.0	1.4
1931-41	1.0	—	0.8	1.2	1.1	1.5	1.0	0.4	-0.3	0.9	1.7	1.6	2.6
1941-51	1.7	—	0.4	1.1	1.2	2.0	2.0	0.6	-0.7	1.7	3.6	6.4	2.9
1951-61	2.7	2.4	0.6	1.4	1.5	2.6	3.1	1.7	1.1	3.6	3.4	4.8	3.7
1961-71	1.7	1.3	0.6	0.7	0.6	1.4	2.2	0.7	0.0	2.0	3.0	2.3	4.2
1971-81	1.2	1.1	1.2	0.9	1.2	0.5	1.2	0.5	0.6	2.8	2.0	1.6	2.3

Note: [a] Newfoundland excluded prior to 1951 and included thereafter.

Source: Table 1-3.

interprovincial migration. These are presented in the following section.

Components of Provincial Population Growth

Births, deaths, immigration and emigration are four components of growth for each province, as detailed in Table 1-1. However, whereas the change in a nation's population stock over a period of time can be conveniently divided into these four components, an analysis of the change in a province's population stock requires the addition of interprovincial migration. This requires an extension of the previous identity for an individual province (see page 5) to:

$$P(t) - P(t-1) \equiv B(t) - D(t) + I(t) - E(t) + IM(t) - OM(t)$$

where $P(t)$, $B(t)$, $D(t)$, $I(t)$ and $E(t)$ are defined as before,

   $IM(t)$ denotes the number of in-migrants from other provinces over the interval $(t-1)$ to (t),

and $OM(t)$ denotes the number of out-migrants to other provinces over the interval $(t-1)$ to (t).

The difference between these two new components can be referred to as "net interprovincial migration." This can be an important component of population growth for a province and can either reinforce or offset the natural increase and the population change due to net immigration.

Estimates of each of the six components in this identity by province are not easy to obtain, especially over a long period of time. Although adequate data sources exist for births and deaths,[15] considerably less information exists on the provincial distribution of immigrants, and provincial estimates of emigration and interprovincial migration are even more scant and have to be based on secondary data sources. The following paragraphs are devoted to a brief historical review and analysis of these main components of provincial population growth.[16]

Provincial comparisons of births and deaths—the components of the net natural change in the population—are aided by expressing the total number of births or deaths in any province over any time period (usually a year) as a ratio to the relevant source population. The resulting ratios are usually termed the crude birth rate and the crude death rate respectively. These rates, usually expressed per thousand of source population, are presented for the census years in Table 1-5. The overall Canadian data for every year since 1921 are displayed in Figure

16

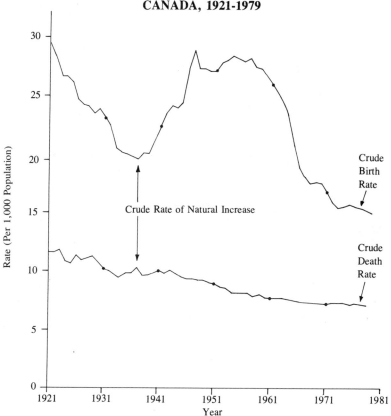

FIGURE 1-1
CRUDE BIRTH AND DEATH RATES,
CANADA, 1921-1979

Crude Birth Rate

Crude Death Rate

Crude Rate of Natural Increase

Rate (Per 1,000 Population)

Year

Source: Statistics Canada, *Vital Statistics*, vols. I and III, various issues.

1-1, providing an indication of the trends underlying the provincial data.

The high birth rate at the beginning of the century was already on the decline by the time of the Depression.[17] Likewise the birth rate was on the increase before the Baby Boom of the 1950s. Its subsequent decline was clearly established by the late 1960s and continued, albeit at a slower pace, through the 1970s, when the crude birth rate reached

TABLE 1-5
CRUDE BIRTH AND DEATH RATES
FOR CANADA AND THE PROVINCES, 1921-1976
(Per 1,000 Population)

Census Year	Can	Nfld	PEI	NS	NB	PQ	Ont	Man	Sask	Alta	BC	Yukon	NWT
CRUDE BIRTH RATE													
1921	29.3	27.2	24.3	24.9	30.2	37.6	25.3	30.3	29.7	28.1	20.3	—	—
1931	23.2	23.3	21.3	22.6	26.5	29.1	20.2	20.5	23.1	23.6	15.0	10.0	15.7
1941	22.4	27.3	21.6	24.1	26.8	26.8	19.1	20.3	20.6	21.7	18.4	14.4	26.3
1951	27.2	32.5	27.1	26.6	31.2	29.8	25.0	25.7	26.1	28.8	24.1	38.0	40.6
1961	26.1	34.1	27.1	26.3	27.7	26.1	25.3	25.3	25.9	29.2	23.7	38.1	48.6
1971	16.8	24.5	18.8	18.1	19.2	14.8	16.9	18.2	17.3	18.8	16.0	27.5	37.0
1976	15.7	20.0	16.4	15.5	17.4	15.5	14.8	16.4	17.3	18.0	14.5	20.6	27.8
CRUDE DEATH RATE													
1921	11.6	12.8	13.6	12.3	14.2	14.2	11.8	8.8	7.4	8.4	8.0	—	—
1931	10.2	13.4	10.4	11.6	11.4	12.0	10.4	7.6	6.6	7.2	8.8	16.5	11.8
1941	10.1	12.5	11.9	12.0	11.3	10.3	10.4	8.9	7.2	8.0	10.4	13.4	25.6
1951	9.0	8.3	9.2	9.0	9.4	8.6	9.6	8.7	7.7	7.6	10.0	9.4	17.8
1961	7.7	6.6	9.3	8.3	7.9	7.0	8.2	8.0	7.7	6.7	8.8	6.4	11.4
1971	7.3	6.1	9.0	8.5	7.8	6.8	7.4	8.1	8.0	6.5	8.1	5.7	6.6
1976	7.3	6.0	9.3	8.4	7.7	6.9	7.3	8.1	8.5	6.3	7.6	5.6	5.0

Sources: Statistics Canada, *Vital Statistics*, vol. I (Catalogue No. 84-204), and vol. III (Catalogue No. 84-206), various issues.

historically low levels. The notable features about the crude death rate are its lack of volatility, or changeability, and its very gradual downward trend, reflecting the improvement in survival rates over time. The difference between the two rates is called the crude rate of natural increase, which, in spite of the gradually reduced death rates, is currently lower than at any point over the past sixty years.

In 1921 Quebec had by far the highest crude birth rate, and British Columbia the lowest. By 1976 British Columbia still had the lowest, primarily due to its relatively older population, but Quebec had the second lowest. The dramatic decline in fertility in Quebec has been one of the notable trends in these provincial data. Newfoundland, on the other hand, moved from a below-average rate to attain the highest birth rate among the provinces by 1936 and has maintained this position ever since. The territories, however, have higher rates, which is attributable primarily to their higher percentages of native population (native peoples have higher birth rates). In general, the Atlantic and Prairie provinces currently have above-average birth rates, while the more populous and more developed central provinces (Ontario and Quebec) and British Columbia have below-average birth rates. Moreover, the range of birth rates has generally narrowed since the early 1960s.

The gradual decline in crude death rates has been experienced in all provinces and territories, although the trend has moderated considerably in almost all provinces—a fact that can be attributed primarily to an aging population. Once again Quebec is notable, having moved during this period from being the province with the highest death rate to one with the second lowest. Also, Newfoundland had moved from an above-average death rate to the lowest rate among the provinces by 1952 and has remained there ever since. By 1948 British Columbia had the highest death rate among the provinces, a position it maintained until the early 1970s, when the Prairie provinces of Manitoba and Saskatchewan surpassed it. Prince Edward Island and Nova Scotia also experienced relatively high crude death rates that have declined only slightly over the postwar period. In general, the Maritime provinces (but *not* Newfoundland) and the Prairie provinces of Manitoba and Saskatchewan have above-average crude death rates, and Newfoundland, Alberta and Quebec have below-average crude death rates.

A consequence of these trends is that Newfoundland has by far the highest crude rate of natural increase among the provinces (14.0 in 1976), and British Columbia the lowest (6.9 in 1976). The rate for Canada stood at 7.9 in 1979, the lowest ever over this historical period from 1921 to 1979.[18] At this point Newfoundland, Saskatchewan,

19

Alberta and the territories are above average, while Nova Scotia, Ontario, Manitoba and British Columbia are below average. There seems to be little in the geographical nature of the country to explain such differences.

One explanation, however, can be sought in the sex composition of provincial populations. Provinces with more males *might* be expected to generate slightly more deaths and perhaps slightly fewer births. The sex ratio for each province is presented in Table 1-6.[19] These data convey a slightly different picture than do the aggregate data (Table 1-2) and do not appear to confirm the relationship suggested above. Although Canada as a whole had not become a female-dominant nation (implying a sex ratio below unity) until the late 1970s, Quebec was the first province to record that position (in the census of 1921 and again in the census of 1951) and has experienced a sex ratio below unity since 1963. Ontario, in 1966, was the second province to experience a sex ratio below unity. Manitoba followed in 1973. British Columbia (which had a dramatic decline in the sex ratio in the 1910s), Nova Scotia and New Brunswick are also expected to have more females than males in their populations by the time of the 1981 census. Of the provinces, Newfoundland and Alberta have the highest proportion of males, while the Yukon Territory continues to contain the highest proportion in Canada. It is interesting to note that over the twentieth century the sex ratios have generally converged on the national mean.

In general, however, there appears to be little correlation between these data and the crude rates of natural increase (see Table 1-5). The most populous central provinces of Quebec and Ontario have below-average birth rates, even though they contain an above-average proportion of females in their populations. On the other hand, Newfoundland has the highest provincial crude birth rate and the highest provincial proportion of females. British Columbia has a below-average birth rate and a slightly above-average proportion of females. With regard to death rates, Newfoundland and Quebec have the lowest death rates; yet Newfoundland has the highest proportion of females in its population, and Quebec the lowest.

There are many reasons why there may not be a strong correlation between crude rates of natural increase and sex ratios. High birth rates increase the sex ratio because more boys than girls are born. Death rates primarily reflect the older age composition where sex ratios may be different from the provincial total. Further, a sex ratio around unity may be more conducive to higher birth rates; after all, only 10 per cent of Canadian births take place out of wedlock. In summary, the

TABLE 1-6
SEX RATIOS FOR CANADA AND THE PROVINCES, 1901-1981
(Ratio of Males to Females)

Census Year	Can	Nfld	PEI	NS	NB	PQ	Ont	Man	Sask	Alta	BC	Yukon	NWT
1901	1.050	—	1.013	1.034	1.038	1.000	1.009	1.087	1.181	1.282	1.770	5.583	1.022
1911	1.129	—	1.009	1.040	1.046	1.020	1.061	1.214	1.454	1.487	1.786	3.248	1.061
1921	1.064	—	1.027	1.035	1.036	0.999	1.021	1.107	1.203	1.227	1.269	2.154	1.135
1931	1.074	—	1.064	1.054	1.045	1.014	1.039	1.108	1.185	1.208	1.246	2.000	1.163
1941	1.052	—	1.074	1.050	1.048	1.008	1.029	1.075	1.141	1.154	1.136	1.778	1.264
1951	1.024[a]	1.050	1.042	1.023	1.011	0.994	1.013	1.034	1.094	1.100	1.050	1.528	1.286
1961	1.022	1.054	1.039	1.031	1.023	1.002	1.011	1.034	1.076	1.073	1.036	1.281	1.255
1971	1.002	1.039	1.015	1.010	1.014	0.987	0.994	1.002	1.033	1.035	1.015	1.172	1.106
1981[b]	0.984	1.027	1.011	0.989	0.998	0.974	0.973	0.977	1.014	1.023	0.986	1.087	1.019

Notes: [a] Includes Newfoundland.
[b] Estimates.

Sources: Calculations by the author from census data (pre-1921) and from Statistics Canada, *Population by Sex and Age, 1921-1971* (Catalogue No. 91-512).

provincial sex ratio data provide no indication of the reasons for the interprovincial differences in the crude rates of natural increase.

Another explanation can be sought in the age composition of provincial populations. Provinces with older populations can be expected to generate fewer births and more deaths, thus leading to a lower crude rate of natural increase. The median ages of the census populations of the provinces for the years 1901-1981 are presented in Table 1-7. These data confirm that the aging trends and patterns outlined above have occurred in all provinces (but not in the territories), with the median age having increased approximately six years in most provinces over the eighty-year period. Population aging has been relatively slower in British Columbia and relatively faster in Quebec, Manitoba and Saskatchewan. Over the 1970s, however, population aging, as suggested by these data, was relatively slower in the western provinces and relatively faster in the eastern provinces.

Clearly, Newfoundland has been the youngest province, with only the Northwest Territories having a lower median age. This would help explain the high crude rates of natural increase in these two regions. The oldest province, not surprisingly, has been the retirement haven of British Columbia, which also has one of the lowest rates of natural increase. The remaining correlations are extremely close, with perhaps the Maritime provinces having lower net natural increases than might be suggested by the median age, and the central provinces—Quebec, Ontario and, in this case, Manitoba—having a higher net natural increase than might be indicated by the median age. In general, however, the relationship is close, confirming the importance of age composition in understanding the interprovincial differences in the components of the crude rate of natural increase.

Once again important compositional differences can be masked by a single aggregate indicator such as the median age. To confirm the above finding, Table 1-8 presents additional compositional detail of the provincial populations by the two age groups that comprise the non-working-age population: namely, 0 to 14 years and 65 years and over. A province may be relatively "young" if it has a high percentage of its population in the former age group, or a lower percentage in the latter age group, or both. The reverse is the case for a relatively "old" province.

In 1901 the provinces with the highest proportion of young people (0 to 14 years old) were the Prairie provinces and Quebec. In each, almost 40 per cent of the population were under 15 years of age, compared, for example, to only 25 per cent in British Columbia. Ontario was next

22

TABLE 1-7
MEDIAN AGE FOR CANADA AND THE PROVINCES, 1901-1981
(Years)

Census Year	Can	Nfld	PEI	NS	NB	PQ	Ont	Man	Sask	Alta	BC	Yukon	NWT
1901	22.7	—	21.5	22.8	21.8	20.5	24.1	20.7	20.5	20.9	28.1	33.1	25.5
1911	23.8	—	23.5	23.4	22.4	20.8	25.8	22.8	23.2	24.0	28.0	35.2	22.7
1921	24.0	—	24.8	23.7	22.3	20.9	26.8	22.8	21.3	23.5	29.8	40.5	20.2
1931	24.8	—	25.0	24.2	22.4	22.1	27.8	24.2	22.0	24.0	30.6	35.3	20.8
1941	27.1	—	25.9	25.9	24.1	24.1	29.9	27.4	24.9	26.3	32.1	30.9	20.6
1951	27.7[a]	21.7	26.2	26.5	24.3	24.8	30.1	29.0	27.4	27.2	32.0	27.2	20.5
1961	26.3	19.3	24.5	24.9	22.4	24.0	28.4	27.7	26.6	25.4	29.8	25.4	21.3
1971	26.2	20.7	24.8	25.4	23.9	25.6	27.2	26.8	26.7	24.9	27.9	24.1	19.1
1981[b]	29.5	25.0	28.5	28.9	27.8	29.7	30.2	29.7	28.8	27.4	30.7	25.3	21.0

Notes: [a] Includes Newfoundland.
         [b] Estimates.

Sources: Calculations by the author from census data (pre-1921) and from Statistics Canada, *Population by Sex and Age, 1921-1971* (Catalogue No. 91-512).

23

TABLE 1-8
THE DISTRIBUTION OF THE NON-WORKING-AGE POPULATION FOR CANADA AND THE PROVINCES, 1901-1981
(%)

Census Year	Can	Nfld	PEI	NS	NB	PQ	Ont	Man	Sask	Alta	BC	Yukon	NWT
						0 TO 14 YEARS							
1901	34.4	—	35.3	33.8	35.6	38.7	31.4	38.3	39.0	39.0	24.8	8.4	22.8
1911	33.0	—	32.7	33.7	35.4	38.5	29.3	34.4	34.1	32.3	23.2	14.0	35.6
1921	34.4	—	32.4	33.9	36.0	38.1	30.2	36.8	39.7	36.3	28.5	20.5	38.7
1931	31.6	—	31.9	32.6	35.5	35.6	27.9	31.3	35.4	32.6	24.6	24.1	38.6
1941	27.8	—	30.1	29.2	31.9	31.9	24.4	26.2	29.9	28.7	21.4	24.7	36.0
1951	30.3[a]	39.1	33.4	32.6	35.6	33.7	27.0	28.7	30.7	30.5	26.1	29.2	36.4
1961	33.9	41.8	36.0	34.8	38.0	35.4	32.2	32.6	34.0	35.2	31.2	36.3	40.0
1971	29.6	37.3	31.7	30.5	32.0	29.6	28.7	29.0	30.3	31.6	27.9	34.8	43.1
1981[b]	22.8	29.1	24.1	23.7	24.9	21.7	22.4	23.3	23.9	24.9	21.8	26.0	35.0
						65 YEARS AND OVER							
1901	5.0	—	6.8	6.7	5.8	4.8	5.5	2.4	2.5	1.8	2.5	0.4	4.6
1911	4.7	—	8.3	7.3	6.2	4.6	5.7	2.4	1.7	1.6	2.2	2.1	4.0
1921	4.8	—	9.5	7.2	6.2	4.6	5.9	3.1	2.3	2.4	3.4	5.9	2.1
1931	5.6	—	10.0	8.0	6.7	4.8	6.8	4.5	3.4	3.5	5.5	9.5	1.8
1941	6.7	—	9.4	8.1	7.1	5.3	8.0	6.2	5.2	5.2	8.3	11.3	2.9
1951	7.8[a]	6.5	9.9	8.5	7.6	5.7	8.7	8.4	8.1	7.1	10.8	5.1	2.7
1961	7.6	5.9	10.4	8.6	7.9	5.8	8.1	9.0	9.2	7.0	10.2	2.7	2.6
1971	8.1	6.2	11.0	9.2	8.6	6.9	8.4	9.7	10.2	7.3	9.4	2.2	2.0
1981[b]	9.5	7.4	11.2	10.4	9.5	8.8	9.7	11.4	11.8	7.7	10.8	3.7	3.7

Notes: [a] Includes Newfoundland.   [b] Estimates.

Sources: Calculations by the author from census data (pre-1921) and from Statistics Canada, *Population by Sex and Age, 1921-1971* (Catalogue No. 91-512).

lowest with 31.4 per cent. Over the subsequent eighty years the situation changed substantially. In general, the Maritime provinces have become relatively younger (and Newfoundland is still the youngest), and the Prairie provinces have aged relatively. Most notable, however, is Quebec, which is now as old as British Columbia by this criterion. This, of course, reflects the dramatic decrease in the birth rate in that province since the early 1960s (as discussed above). British Columbia and Ontario remain relatively old, with New Brunswick and Alberta now at the young end of the age spectrum by this criterion.

At the other end of the age spectrum, the relatively young age of the western provinces and the relatively old age of the Maritime provinces at the turn of the century are apparent from the figures in the bottom half of Table 1-8. However, it is interesting to note that by 1971 Saskatchewan had the highest percentage of population aged 65 years and over, with Manitoba a close second. By this criterion Newfoundland is still the youngest province, and it appears that over the 1970s Alberta eclipsed Quebec as the second youngest.

In summary, the youngest of the Canadian provinces is clearly Newfoundland and the oldest is British Columbia (even though it does not have the highest provincial percentage of persons aged 65 years and over). High birth rates in the Maritime provinces have resulted in an above-average percentage of young people, but they also have an above-average percentage of old people.[20] Quebec is the opposite with below-average percentages in both categories. Ontario and Manitoba are both relatively old with below-average percentages of young and above-average percentages of old persons in their populations. Saskatchewan and Alberta both have above-average percentages of young persons, but Saskatchewan also has a higher percentage of older persons. Alberta has a low percentage of older persons and hence is a relatively young province. It is interesting to note that regional differences in age structure have tended to narrow since 1941. Also, as previously noted, these age compositions are closely associated with the provincial rates of natural increase.

By way of assessing the relative importance of natural increase to the total increase in provincial population growth, Table 1-9 compares the contribution to population growth from natural increases with the total from the remaining sources (net international and net interprovincial migration) as estimated from census information. The data are presented as rates (per 1,000 population) to facilitate comparisons across provinces. It is readily apparent from these data that in all

TABLE 1-9
RATES OF TOTAL INCREASE, NATURAL INCREASE AND NET MIGRATION BY PROVINCE, 1931-1979
(Rate Per 1,000 Average Population of the Period)

Inter-Census Period	Can	Nfld	PEI	NS	NB	PQ	Ont	Man	Sask	Alta	Yukon/ BC	NWT
1931-1941												
Natural	104	—	105	109	132	139	72	94	126	132	46	124
Migration	-1	—	-28	10	-18	8	27	-53	-155	-47	118	99
Total	103	—	77	119	114	147	99	41	-28	84	163	223
1941-1951												
Natural	146	—	121	177	184	194	117	116	107	139	114	211
Migration	24	—	-86	-72	-64	2	76	-54	-181	26	236	177
Total	170	—	35	106	119	196	193	62	-74	165	350	388
1951-1961												
Natural	198	265	157	183	196	222	180	171	186	236	172	304
Migration	64	-29	-96	-46	-49	36	123	0	-80	109	160	96
Total	262	235	61	137	148	258	302	171	106	345	332	399
1961-1971												
Natural	141	237	150	149	172	156	115	167	147	157	140	355
Migration	26	-107	-85	-80	-112	-21	96	-72	-146	43	155	0
Total	167	130	65	68	59	135	211	96	1	200	295	355
1971-1979												
Natural	67	108	42	48	58	64	61	65	66	103	68	178
Migration	26	-14	55	24	41	-22	37	-22	-30	111	93	15
Total	93	94	97	72	99	41	98	43	35	214	161	193

Sources: M. V. George, *Internal Migration in Canada* (Ottawa: Dominion Bureau of Statistics, 1970), p. 76 (1931-61); and calculations by the author

provinces except British Columbia the natural increase has been the dominant factor of population growth from 1931 to 1979. However, during the 1970s both Prince Edward Island and Alberta joined British Columbia in obtaining less than a majority of their population growth from natural increases. These data also confirm many of the previously noted phenomena: the relatively high-growth decade of the 1950s, the relatively high rates of natural increase in Newfoundland, the relative importance of net migration to population growth in Ontario (as well as in British Columbia), the negative contribution of net migration to growth in the Atlantic provinces (until the 1970s) and in the Prairie provinces of Manitoba and Saskatchewan, and the apparent turnaround in the 1970s with regard to the Maritime provinces.

To better understand the role of net migration in provincial population growth, it is necessary to break it down into its international and interprovincial components.[21]

A decennial time series on the provincial distribution of intercensal immigrants is available from census data since the turn of the century. These data (see Table 1-10, top half) show that Ontario consistently has been the principal destination of immigrants, having received more than any other province or region in every decennial period, with the exception of the 1911-21 period when the Prairie provinces received more immigrants. Since the end of the Second World War, Ontario has received a majority (over 50 per cent) of all immigrants to Canada. The province of Quebec generally has been the second most preferred destination, having received more immigrants than British Columbia. The Atlantic provinces have benefitted very little from immigration over this period.

Recently, immigration statistics, which are compiled from information given by every immigrant upon arrival in Canada, have provided information on the province of intended destination. These data are summarized in Table 1-10 (bottom half) for the post-1951 period. They confirm that a majority of immigrants intended to settle in Ontario over this period and that only an average of around one in five were destined for Quebec. Since these figures are respectively above and below the population shares for these provinces (see Table 1-3), it would be expected that Ontario might gain in relative size from immigration, whereas Quebec might lose. British Columbia is the only other province that has consistently received an above-average share of immigrants based on its population share. Consequently, only Ontario and British Columbia have increased their population share as a result of immigration. All other provinces have been relative losers on this account, especially Quebec and the Atlantic provinces.

27

TABLE 1-10
THE DISTRIBUTION OF IMMIGRATION BY PROVINCE OF INTENDED DESTINATION, 1901-1979[a]
(%)

Period	Nfld	PEI	NS	NB	PQ	Ont	Man	Sask	Alta	BC	Yukon/NWT
CENSUS DATA											
1900-11	—	0.1	1.8	0.8	8.8	27.0	12.6	18.9	16.2	13.8	0.0
1911-21	—	0.1	1.7	0.9	10.1	35.2	9.8	13.9	13.5	14.9	0.0
1921-31	—	0.3	2.5	1.4	13.2	41.5	7.6	8.8	12.4	12.2	0.1
1931-41	0.4	0.3	2.9	2.0	16.8	47.3	4.9	4.0	9.1	12.1	0.2
1941-51	0.5	0.2	1.7	1.3	13.7	54.3	5.1	2.8	8.1	12.2	0.2
1951-61	0.2	0.1	0.8	0.5	15.3	57.4	3.2	1.3	7.5	13.6	0.2
1961-71	0.4	0.1	1.2	0.7	17.7	55.7	3.4	1.3	6.3	13.1	0.2
IMMIGRATION DATA											
1951-56	0.3	0.1	1.4	0.7	21.0	53.2	4.8	2.4	7.8	8.4	0.1
1956-61	0.2	0.1	1.1	0.6	21.0	52.9	3.9	1.7	6.9	11.5	0.1
1961-66	0.4	0.1	1.2	0.9	23.2	53.0	2.9	1.7	5.6	11.0	0.1
1966-71	0.5	0.1	1.2	0.7	18.9	53.6	3.9	1.6	6.6	13.0	0.1
1971-76	0.6	0.1	1.3	1.0	15.1	53.9	3.8	1.2	7.1	15.7	0.1
1976-79	0.5	0.3	1.2	1.0	17.4	46.4	4.4	2.5	11.4	14.8	0.2

Note: [a] Row totals may not equal 100.0 due to rounding.
Source: Calculations by the author from census data; and Statistics Canada, *International and Interprovincial Migration in Canada* (Catalogue No. 91-208), various issues.

In recent years (1976-79) there has been a major change in the destination of immigrants—Ontario has been getting less, although still more than its population share, and Alberta has been getting more, now well above its population share. In fact, all of the western provinces have recorded increases in immigration in recent years to levels above their population shares. This westward drift of Canadian immigrant destinations in the latter half of the 1970s, largely at the expense of Ontario, is a major change that has to be carefully considered in developing population projections. However, it should be noted that in terms of population shares the real losers in this period are the Atlantic provinces and Quebec, *not* Ontario—since it is still receiving well above its population share of immigrants.

Very little information is available on the relative contributions of the provinces to emigration from Canada.[22] Total emigration is estimated by the "residual" method[23] and is distributed by province of origin based on information provided by Canadian immigrants to the United States. This is an admittedly incomplete and possibly inaccurate method of allocation.[24] The resulting data, available only since 1961, are summarized in Table 1-11. Perhaps not surprisingly, these estimated emigration patterns are quite similar to the immigration patterns (Table 1-10). The only provinces with emigration shares consistently above their population shares are Ontario and British

TABLE 1-11
THE DISTRIBUTION OF EMIGRATION
BY PROVINCE OF ORIGIN, 1961-1979[a]
(%)

Period	Nfld	PEI	NS	NB	PQ	Ont	Man	Sask	Alta	BC	Yukon/ NWT
1961-66	2.5	0.6	4.0	3.2	28.9	34.2	5.0	5.0	7.4	9.0	0.2
1966-71	2.9	0.5	3.7	4.3	30.5	38.2	3.2	3.3	5.0	8.1	0.2
1971-76	1.0	0.1	1.4	1.0	23.0	45.7	3.5	2.5	7.4	14.5	—[b]
1976-79	1.2	0.3	1.8	1.5	27.2	44.2	2.4	2.1	4.7	14.4	0.2

Notes: [a] Row totals may not equal 100.0 due to rounding.
[b] Not available.

Source: Calculated by the author from Statistics Canada, *International and Interprovincial Migration in Canada, 1978-79* (Catalogue No. 91-208), Table 5.

29

Columbia. A substantially higher percentage of emigrants compared to immigrants come from Quebec and, to a lesser extent, from the Atlantic provinces, while the opposite is true for the Prairie provinces (although only recently for Saskatchewan). Ontario and British Columbia experience a slightly higher percentage of immigrants compared to emigrants.

These comparisons, however, do not show the gainers and losers in terms of net international migration *numbers*. These data are summarized in Table 1-12, where it is apparent that in recent years the Atlantic provinces generally have been net losers and Ontario, the Prairie provinces and British Columbia net gainers from international migration. From these data Quebec appears to be a net gainer in high immigration periods (1966-76) and a net loser in the low immigration periods (1961-66 and 1976-79). Not surprisingly, these numbers reflect the recent westward orientation of immigration, although the large gains to the Ontario population during the high immigration period of 1966-76 are readily apparent. Also apparent is a major change in the latter half of the 1970s: proportionally more "net migrants" went to Alberta at the expense of Quebec, Ontario and British Columbia. The trend will be considered further in regard to the population projections presented later in this study.

The remaining component of provincial population growth is the net gain or loss that occurs as a result of the mobility of persons *within* the country. However, all movers are not interprovincial migrants, since by far the majority of movers do not cross provincial boundaries.[25] Nonetheless, as will become clear, interprovincial migration provides a quantitatively more important source of provincial population change than does international migration. (Note that an out-migrant from one province is an in-migrant to another province, so the total net effect for the country is by definition zero.)

No data on interprovincial migration have been collected in Canada over a long period of time. To obtain an insight into interprovincial migration patterns during the first half of the century, it is necessary to examine census data on the number of persons residing outside the province of their birth. In this source a person is defined as a migrant if he or she is enumerated in a province other than the province of birth. These data, of course, have numerous limitations as a measure of interprovincial migration, since they only measure interprovincial migration among Canadian-born residents, do not include Canadians who returned to their provinces of birth within the intercensal period, and do not measure the intercensal flow migration. They are not

TABLE 1-12
NET INTERNATIONAL MIGRATION
FOR CANADA AND THE PROVINCES, 1961-1979
(000's)

Period	Can	Nfld	PEI	NS	NB	PQ	Ont	Man	Sask	Alta	BC	Yukon	NWT
1961-66	106.5	-8.7	-1.9	-11.0	-9.5	-2.0	139.2	-6.2	-12.4	-2.6	21.9	-0.1	-0.3
1966-71	417.9	-9.5	-1.6	-6.7	-14.5	22.6	294.3	20.6	-1.4	36.2	77.9	0.0	-0.1
1971-76	483.8[a]	1.1	0.8	5.9	5.2	45.4	288.1	19.3	1.1	35.4	79.9	0.5[a]	0.9[a]
1976-79	104.8	-1.2	-0.0	0.3	-0.0	-2.0	61.0	8.0	1.2	24.8	12.6	-0.1	0.1

Note: [a] Emigration Statistics for the Yukon and Northwest Territories are not available.

Sources: Calculated from Tables 1-10 and 1-11. See also Statistics Canada, *International and Interprovincial Migration In Canada, 1978-79* (Catalogue No. 91-208), Tables 1 and 5.

time-specific as they relate to surviving lifetime migrants (those who resettle permanently) and, as such, have a cumulative effect, since they are repeated at each census. They can, however, provide some indication of intercensal interprovincial migrant flows by aiding in an examination of the differences in lifetime net migration between censuses.[26] These data mirror the trends discussed above: namely, the heavy westward movement at the beginning of the century (except to Manitoba), with approximately two-thirds of the movers coming from Ontario; the subsequent decline in the Prairie provinces, largely to the benefit of Quebec (over 1921-41) and Ontario; the continued net gain in British Columbia and net loss in the Maritime provinces throughout the entire period; and the recent upward trend in interprovincial migration to Alberta. It is also apparent from these data that interprovincial migration was high during the 1901-11 intercensal period, low during the years of the First World War and relatively low during the 1920s. It picked up in the 1930s[27] and has been at relatively high levels ever since.

The above discussions are based on changes in the place-of-birth-based lifetime migration estimates by province, which indicate only the cumulative effect of migration at each census, without reference to any time period. This is an indirect procedure of measurement. The first census year in Canada that interprovincial migration data were collected directly was 1941. Information was requested on previous place of residence and duration of continuous residence at the place of enumeration. Further information (including sex, age and type of residence) was obtained in the 1961 and 1971 censuses. More recently Canada has made use of an administrative data base—the family allowance files—to assess the extent of interprovincial migration. To receive a family allowance cheque at its new address, a family that moves must notify the regional office of the federal Department of Health and Welfare of its change of address. Of course, these data also have limitations as an indication of *total* interprovincial migration, as they are based only on migrant families with children eligible for family allowances.

Estimates of interprovincial migration (presented in Table 1-13) are available since 1961 and, for the 1961-76 period, have been made consistent with the quinquennial census results. Post-censal estimates beyond 1976 are available, based on the above-mentioned family allowance data base, but the possible biases of the data base should be kept in mind when using these data. For the 1961-71 period they show that over the 1960s all provinces except Ontario, Alberta and British

TABLE 1-13
INTERPROVINCIAL MIGRATION BY PROVINCE, 1961-1979
(000's)

Period	Can	Nfld	PEI	NS	NB	PQ	Ont	Man	Sask	Alta	BC	Yukon/ NWT
IN-MIGRATION												
1961-66	1,688.3	32.8	18.2	104.9	88.6	218.5	468.2	132.6	113.7	230.1	262.3	18.4
1966-71	1,971.9	43.6	18.8	115.9	95.8	195.1	574.2	141.3	114.6	289.5	356.9	26.3
1971-76	2,016.0	61.4	23.2	125.4	109.9	185.9	476.1	145.2	126.7	352.1	377.2	33.0
1976-79	1,198.5	30.7	13.9	70.4	60.7	82.9	293.6	76.9	84.6	265.5	200.7	18.5
OUT-MIGRATION												
1961-66	1,688.3	48.0	21.2	132.0	114.3	238.4	382.8	156.1	155.8	232.0	184.6	23.1
1966-71	1,971.9	62.9	21.5	132.3	115.4	317.9	423.5	182.0	195.9	257.4	241.9	21.1
1971-76	2,016.0	63.2	19.5	114.0	93.1	263.5	514.6	172.0	167.4	293.5	284.9	30.1
1976-79	1,198.5	36.6	12.0	68.2	55.1	185.0	299.6	99.1	74.1	184.0	162.9	22.2
NET MIGRATION												
1961-66	163.1[a]	-15.2	-3.0	-27.1	-25.7	-19.9	85.4	-23.5	-42.1	-2.0	77.7	-4.7
1966-71	302.9[a]	-19.3	-2.8	-16.4	-19.6	-122.7	150.7	-40.7	-81.4	32.0	115.0	5.2
1971-76	185.7[a]	-1.9	3.8	11.3	16.8	-77.6	-38.6	-26.8	-40.8	58.6	92.3	2.9
1976-79	139.6[a]	-5.9	1.9	2.2	5.6	-102.0	-6.0	-22.3	10.5	81.5	37.9	-3.4

Note: [a] Sum of net gain (+) or net loss (−).

Source: Statistics Canada, *International and Interprovincial Migration in Canada* (Catalogue No. 91-208), various issues.

Columbia experienced net losses due to interprovincial migration. However, the decade of the 1970s has seen a reversal of many of these historical trends. Most notable are the establishment of the Maritime provinces as net gainers (Newfoundland's outflow has been reduced, but it is still a net loser), and Ontario as a net loser for the first time since the early part of this century. In addition, previous trends have intensified, especially in Quebec (a net loser) and Alberta (a net gainer). For the post-1976 period these data show that Saskatchewan has become a net gainer and British Columbia, always a net gainer, has received a reduced share of the net inflows.

Review of Recent Trends

By way of a review of these recent trends and of the relative importance of the components of population growth in their determination, Tables 1-14 and 1-15 summarize the relevant data for the intercensal periods since 1961.[28] They show very clearly that the most important component of population growth was the natural increase. For Canada as a whole, the natural increase accounted for 84 per cent of population growth in the 1960s and for 72 per cent in the 1970s (see Table 1-15). This suggests a greater reliance on net immigration in the latter decade. However, when broken down into quinquennial periods, it is apparent that net immigration was much more important over the 1966-76 period than during the earlier and later periods.[29]

In all of the provinces, the natural increase has made an important positive contribution to population growth. Only in less than 10 per cent of the disaggregations presented in Table 1-14 did net international or interprovincial migration account for a greater proportion of the population change than the natural increase.[30] Net interprovincial migration is clearly a more important component of provincial population growth than net international migration. Only in the provinces of Ontario and Alberta (in the 1960s) has net international migration been a more important determinant of population change than net interprovincial migration over this period. These two components were either both positive or both negative determinants of a province's growth in about three-quarters of the disaggregations presented in Table 1-14.[31] Obviously, these are the conditions most conducive to provincial population growth. The most significant contrasts (that is, one positive, the other negative) were in Quebec (1966-76), Ontario (1971-79) and Manitoba (1966-79), where population growth was enhanced by net international migration but

34

TABLE 1-14

COMPONENTS OF POPULATION GROWTH FOR CANADA AND THE PROVINCES, 1961-1979

(000's)

Period and Component	Can	Nfld	PEI	NS	NB	PQ	Ont	Man	Sask	Alta	BC	Yukon/NWT
1961-66												
Natural Increase	1,670.2	59.4	8.8	57.1	54.1	543.5	500.2	71.1	84.7	135.9	145.0	10.6
Net Internat. Mig.	106.5	-8.7	-1.9	-11.0	-9.5	-2.0	139.2	-6.2	-12.4	-2.6	21.9	-0.4
Net Interprov. Mig.	(163.1)[b]	-15.2	-3.0	-27.1	-25.7	-19.9	85.4	-23.5	-42.1	-2.0	77.7	-4.7
Total	1,776.7	35.5	3.9	19.0	18.9	521.6	724.8	41.4	30.2	131.3	244.6	5.5
1966-71												
Natural Increase	1,135.5	57.5	7.5	56.1	51.9	347.1	297.2	45.2	53.6	96.5	118.0	5.0
Net Internat. Mig.	417.9	-9.5	-1.6	-6.7	-14.5	22.6	294.3	20.6	-1.4	36.2	77.9	-0.1
Net Interprov. Mig.	(302.9)[b]	-19.3	-2.8	-16.4	-19.6	-122.7	150.7	-40.7	-81.4	32.0	115.0	5.2[a]
Total	1,553.4	28.7	3.1	33.0	17.8	247.0	742.2	-25.1	29.2	164.7	310.9	10.1
1971-76												
Natural Increase	940.6	36.4	2.0	22.4	20.6	238.8	311.9	40.8	34.8	116.1	109.8	6.9
Net Internat. Mig.	483.8	1.1	0.8	5.9	5.2	45.4	288.1	19.3	1.1	35.4	79.9	1.4
Net Interprov. Mig.	(185.7)[b]	-1.9	3.8	11.3	16.8	-77.6	-38.6	-26.8	-40.8	58.6	92.3	2.9
Total	1,424.3	35.6	6.6	39.6	42.6	206.6	561.4	33.3	-4.9	210.1	282.0	11.2
1976-79												
Natural Increase	573.3	23.1	2.9	16.6	18.1	153.3	183.8	24.8	25.9	68.2	52.8	4.0
Net Internat. Mig.	104.8	-1.2	-0.0	0.3	-0.0	-2.0	61.0	8.0	1.2	24.8	12.6	0.0
Net Interprov. Mig.	(139.6)[b]	-5.9	1.9	2.2	5.6	-102.0	-6.0	-22.3	10.5	81.5	37.9	-3.4
Total	678.1	16.0	4.8	19.1	23.7	49.3	238.8	10.5	37.6	174.5	103.3	0.6

Notes: [a] Emigration for the Yukon and Northwest Territories are not available.   [b] Sum of net gain (+) or net loss (−).

Sources: Statistics Canada, *Estimates of Population by Sex and Age for Canada and the Provinces* (Catalogue No. 91-202), various issues; and Tables 1-12 and 1-13. (See also Table 1-9.)

35

TABLE 1-15

COMPONENT DISTRIBUTION AND RATES OF POPULATION GROWTH FOR CANADA AND THE PROVINCES, 1961-1979

Period and Component	Can	Nfld	PEI	NS	NB	PQ	Ont	Man	Sask	Alta	BC	Yukon/NWT
					DISTRIBUTION (%)[a]							
1961-71												
Natural Increase	84.3	182.1	232.9	217.7	288.8	115.9	54.4	174.9	. . .[b]	78.5	47.3	100.0
Net Internat. Mig.	15.7	−28.3	−50.0	−34.0	−65.4	2.7	29.5	21.7	. . .[b]	11.4	18.0	−3.2
Net Interprov. Mig.	0.0	−53.7	−82.9	−83.7	−123.4	−18.6	16.1	−96.5	. . .[b]	10.1	34.7	3.2
1971-79												
Natural Increase	72.0	115.3	43.0	66.4	58.4	153.2	61.9	149.8	185.6	47.9	42.2	92.4
Net Internat. Mig.	28.0	−0.2	7.0	10.6	7.8	17.0	43.6	62.3	7.0	15.7	24.0	11.9
Net Interprov. Mig.	0.0	−15.1	50.0	23.0	33.8	−70.2	−5.6	−112.1	−92.7	36.4	33.8	−4.2
					RATE (Per 1,000 Population)							
1961-79												
Natural Increase	141	237	150	149	172	156	115	167	147	157	140	355
Net Internat. Mig.	26	−37	−32	−23	−39	4	62	15	−15	23	53	−11
Net Interprov. Mig.	0	−70	−53	−57	−73	−25	34	−67	−131	20	102	11[c]
Total[d]	167	130	65	68	59	135	211	96	1	200	295	355
1971-79												
Natural Increase	67	108	42	48	58	64	61	65	66	103	68	178
Net Internat. Mig.	26	0	7	8	8	7	43	27	2	33	39	23
Net Interprov. Mig.	0	−14	49	16	34	−29	−5	−48	−33	78	54	−8
Total[d]	93	94	97	72	99	41	98	43	35	214	161	193

Notes: [a] Column totals may not equal 100.0 due to rounding. [c] Emigration not available. [d] Column totals may not add due to rounding. [b] Calculation not meaningful.

Sources: Statistics Canada, *Estimates of Population by Sex and Age for Canada and the Provinces* (Catalogue No. 91-202), various issues; and Table

retarded by net interprovincial migration. Interestingly, no significant example of the opposite case is recorded in the data in Table 1-14.[32]

Some notable interprovincial and intertemporal variations in the relative importance of the three components of growth can be found in these data (see Table 1-15). In Ontario, net international migration has been a more important component of population growth than net interprovincial migration. In contrast, in British Columbia, also an above-average growth province, net interprovincial migration has been the more important migration component, accounting for one-third of the population growth over this period. In Alberta, international and interprovincial migration accounted for approximately equal increases in the 1960s (around 10 per cent each). In the 1970s, however, although both increased in relative importance, interprovincial migration became twice as important as international migration in accounting for the increase in population in that province. The increasing reliance on this source of growth in Alberta is apparent from the 1976-79 data: net interprovincial migration actually exceeded the natural increase as a component of growth.

Of particular general interest is the turnaround in interprovincial migration patterns in the 1970s. The Maritime provinces moved from being substantial losers to being substantial gainers on this account, as did Saskatchewan in the 1976-79 period. Ontario, on the other hand, moved from being a moderate gainer to being a slight loser, and Quebec, from a slight loser to a substantial loser. These two latter provinces, along with Manitoba, now provide the net source of interprovincial migrants.

Generally, in the 1970s net international migration contributed *positively* to population growth in all provinces, unlike the 1960s when it provided a substantial drain on the populations of the Atlantic provinces and Saskatchewan. This was certainly true of the high immigration period (1971-76), but, surprisingly, also applies to the later period (1976-79) when net international migration in the Atlantic provinces was negative but very small. This suggests that even though Ontario continues to receive a majority of "net immigrants," there has been a redistribution primarily in favour of the Atlantic provinces in recent years.

Finally, the rate data (see the bottom half of Table 1-15) show that there was a general reduction in the rates of provincial population change in the 1970s, especially in the natural and interprovincial components. Almost all of the rate numbers for the 1970s are below the corresponding numbers for the 1960s, the only exceptions being in

Quebec (where there are only slight increases) and in Alberta. This suggests that only in these two provinces was population change relatively greater in the 1970s than in the 1960s. In all of the remaining provinces there was a general reduction in all of the components of population change.

Summary

The population of Canada is measured by a decennial census that was first used in the provinces in 1851 and has been conducted nationally since 1871. Total population has grown approximately tenfold from the 2.4 million persons recorded in 1851. Throughout this period average annual population growth between the censuses has never been below 1 per cent, and in three periods it has exceeded 2.5 per cent. These rapid-growth periods—the 1850s, 1900s and 1950s—were all characterized by increases in the number of births, although the strong growth of the 1900s was also augmented by considerable increases in net international migration. Over the 130 years since the first census, approximately four-fifths of the population increase can be attributed to natural causes and the remaining one-fifth to international migration.

In terms of population numbers, Canada has always had a slightly male-dominant population, but the 1981 census is expected to show a higher proportion of females for the first time in Canadian history. Since male mortality tends to be higher at all ages, declining male dominance reflects a population of increasing average age. However, population aging in Canada is *not* a new phenomenon—it has been occurring since the first census. By all measures, two periods can be identified as periods of especially rapid aging in Canada—the latter two thirds of the 1930s and the decade of the 1970s. In many respects the 1970s was a unique period in Canadian history. The percentage of the young was never so low, the percentage of the old was never so high, and more than two in three Canadians were of working age—a historically high figure.

Ontario and Quebec have always accounted for more than 60 per cent of the nation's population. However, throughout Canadian history there has been a continuous, if uneven, westward drift of the population, with Maritime provinces losing their relative shares to the Prairie provinces and British Columbia. Since the Depression, the western drift has been concentrated in Alberta and British Columbia. This geographical redistribution of the population is influenced not only by different rates of natural increase and different intakes of international migration among the provinces, but also by interprovincial migration flows.

Of these three components of provincial population change, the quantitatively most important has been the natural increase, which has always contributed positively to growth in all provinces. Due to a gradual decline in the death rate in all provinces, the rate of natural increase has been dominated by fertility rates. These were declining up to the mid-1930s and thereafter increased to create the Baby Boom of the 1950s. Since then, all three measures—the birth rate, death rate and the rate of natural increase—have reached historically low levels. Currently Newfoundland has the highest rate of natural increase among the provinces, and British Columbia the lowest. The provincial distribution of natural rates is uncorrelated with provincial sex ratios but, not surprisingly, is highly correlated with provincial age distributions. Newfoundland is the youngest province and British Columbia the oldest by most criteria. Population aging has been taking place in all provinces (but not in the territories).

Of the remaining two components of population growth, international migration has been less important quantitatively than interprovincial migration, with the exception of the first decade of the twentieth century. Ontario is the only province to which *net* international migration has made a substantial contribution to population growth, and British Columbia the only other province to have consistently received an above-average share of immigrants. In general, the Atlantic provinces have been net losers and the Prairie provinces net gainers from international migration. There was a westward drift in immigrant destinations in the 1970s, particularly to Alberta at the expense of Quebec, Ontario and British Columbia. However, the real losers from this component of population change are the Atlantic provinces and Quebec, since Ontario continues to receive well above its population share of "net" immigrants.

Although the vast majority of Canadian movers do not cross provincial boundaries, interprovincial migration has been an important component of provincial population growth, especially in the opening decade of this century and since the 1940s. After a substantial western movement at the beginning of the century (largely at the expense of Ontario), the subsequent decline of the Prairie provinces benefitted Quebec (in the 1920s and 1930s), Ontario and British Columbia. Moreover, the Maritime provinces had been consistent net losers from interprovincial migration until the 1970s, when many of these historical trends were reversed.

Movements in the natural increase and in the net effect of international and interprovincial migration on provincial population growth only appear to coincide about half of the time, while the net effects of international and interprovincial migration coincide (either positively or negatively) about three-quarters of the time.

Of particular importance to this study are the "unique" features of provincial population growth in the 1970s, including the universal reductions in the rates of growth for all components, the changing destinations of net international migrants, and, especially, the reversal of historical trends in interprovincial migration patterns. The next chapter is devoted specifically to this decade in preparation for the projections of future populations presented in chapter 3.

The "Unique" Decade of the 1970s

2

Overview

The population of Canada is aging, but this is not a new phenomenon. However, the 1970s, somewhat like the 1930s, was a period of particularly rapid aging. This has resulted in a number of associated developments that can be termed unique in Canadian demographic history. As has been noted in the previous chapter, there were never so few young, or so many old persons, proportionately, as in the 1970s, and two out of three Canadians were of working age—an all-time high. Moreover, Canada gradually shifted from a male-dominant to a female-dominant population during the 1970s. Further, international and, especially, interprovincial migration patterns, although continuing the uneven historical westward drift of Canada's population, have recently displayed dramatic reversals from many of the traditional trends.

Whether the unique characteristics of this decade can be expected to be ongoing must be established if appropriate economic policy is to be developed for the 1980s and beyond. An examination of selected data from the 1970s can help to ascertain whether these recent demographic patterns are transitory or are firmly established. Some answers may already be apparent from the previous chapter, which presented a long-run historical perspective. This chapter is devoted to a brief review of selected demographic developments in Canada during the 1970s and has two main purposes: first, to establish the solidity of the foundation of the current trends; and second, to provide a basis (with some historical perspective) for the assumptions incorporated into the projections of future populations, which are presented in the following chapter.

By way of an overview, Table 2-1 presents the estimated annual population and rates of growth for Canada and the provinces over the 1970s. Although annual population growth in Canada averaged 1.2 per

TABLE 2-1
POPULATION ESTIMATES AND GROWTH FOR CANADA AND THE PROVINCES, 1970-1979

Year[a]	Can	Nfld	PEI	NS	NB	PQ	Ont	Man	Sask	Alta	BC	Yukon	NWT
						POPULATION (000's)							
1970	21,297.0	517.0	110.0	782.0	627.0	6,013.0	7,551.0	983.0	941.0	1,595.0	2,128.0	17.0	33.0
1971[b]	21,568.3	522.1	111.6	789.0	634.6	6,027.8	7,703.1	988.2	926.2	1,627.9	2,184.6	18.4	34.8
1972	21,801.3	530.0	112.6	794.6	640.1	6,053.6	7,809.9	991.2	914.0	1,657.3	2,241.4	19.5	37.3
1973	22,043.0	537.2	114.0	804.3	647.1	6,078.9	7,908.8	996.2	904.5	1,689.5	2,302.4	20.5	39.4
1974	22,363.9	541.5	115.2	811.5	653.6	6,122.7	8,054.1	1,007.5	899.7	1,722.4	2,375.7	20.5	39.6
1975	22,697.1	549.1	117.1	819.5	665.2	6,179.0	8,172.2	1,013.6	907.4	1,778.3	2,433.2	21.3	41.2
1976[b]	22,992.6	557.7	118.2	828.6	677.2	6,234.4	8,264.5	1,021.5	921.3	1,838.0	2.466.6	21.8	42.6
1977	23,257.6	564.0	120.2	835.0	687.1	6,275.8	8,355.0	1,029.1	937.0	1,896.4	2,493.7	21.1	43.3
1978	23,475.6	568.8	122.1	841.4	694.8	6,272.8	8,444.3	1,033.5	948.4	1,954.2	2,530.1	21.7	43.7
1979[c]	23,670.7	573.7	123.0	847.7	700.9	6,283.7	8,503.3	1,032.0	958.9	2,012.5	2,569.9	21.6	43.4

Period	Can	Nfld	PEI	NS	NB	PQ	Ont	Man	Sask	Alta	BC	Yukon	NWT
						GROWTH (%)							
1970-71	1.3	1.0	1.5	0.9	1.2	0.2	2.0	0.5	−1.6	2.1	2.7	8.2	5.5
1971-72	1.1	1.5	0.9	0.7	0.9	0.4	1.4	0.3	−1.3	1.8	2.6	6.0	7.2
1972-73	1.1	1.4	1.2	1.2	1.1	0.4	1.3	0.5	−1.0	1.9	2.7	5.1	5.6
1973-74	1.5	0.8	1.1	0.9	1.0	0.7	1.8	1.1	−0.5	1.9	3.2	0.0	0.5
1974-75	1.5	1.4	1.6	1.0	1.8	0.9	1.5	0.6	0.9	3.2	2.4	3.9	4.0
1975-76	1.3	1.6	0.9	1.1	1.8	0.9	1.1	0.8	1.5	3.4	1.4	2.3	3.4
1976-77	1.2	1.0	1.7	0.8	1.5	0.7	1.1	0.7	1.7	3.2	1.1	−3.2	1.6
1977-78	0.9	0.9	1.6	0.8	1.1	−0.0	1.1	0.4	1.2	3.0	1.5	2.8	0.9
1978-79	0.8	0.9	0.7	0.7	0.9	0.2	0.7	−0.1	1.1	3.0	1.6	−0.5	−0.7
Average[d]	1.2	1.1	1.0	0.9	1.1	0.5	1.4	0.5	0.0	2.6	2.2	3.0	3.4

Notes: [a] As at June 1.   [c] Preliminary.
         [b] Census data.   [d] Annual average, 1970-1979.

Sources: Statistics Canada, Population: Revised Annual Estimates of Population by Sex and Age for Canada and the Provinces, 1971-76 (Catalogue No. 91-518), and Estimates of Population by Sex and Age for Canada and the Provinces (Catalogue No. 91-202), various issues.

cent over the decade, it was relatively stronger during the middle of the decade and relatively weaker towards the end. This pattern is primarily attributable to the variation in net international migration, which accounted for over 40 per cent of the Canadian population growth during 1973-74 and 1974-75; its contribution declined to only 2.2 per cent of population growth by 1978-79. The natural increase (and both of its components) has remained remarkably constant since 1973-74 at around 190,000 persons annually. Consequently, the annual *level* of growth is primarily attributable to natural increases, but the variation in growth can be almost entirely accounted for by the variation in international migration.

Similar conclusions apply to provincial population growth. Over the 1970s the lowest growth rates were in Saskatchewan, Quebec and Manitoba, and the highest growth rates were in Alberta and British Columbia. The Atlantic provinces generally experienced slightly below-average growth, and Ontario slightly above-average growth, over the decade. The reasons for these differing growth rates have been summarized previously (see Table 1-14). These results show that natural increases were the dominant source of growth in Newfoundland, Quebec, Manitoba and Saskatchewan and accounted for over half the increases in Nova Scotia, New Brunswick and Ontario. Net international migration primarily benefitted Ontario and Manitoba, and to a lesser extent British Columbia, in terms of relative importance. Net interprovincial migration benefitted the Maritime provinces, Alberta and British Columbia at the expense of all of the remaining provinces, but especially Quebec, Manitoba and, in the early 1970s, Saskatchewan.

In summary, the slightly below-average growth of the Atlantic provinces is attributable primarily to unfavourable net international migration movements. Ontario's maintenance of above-average growth over the first half of the decade was due to favourable net international migration, which was almost as important quantitatively as the net natural increase. Ontario's subsequent decline to approximately average growth can be attributed to the reduced number of immigrants. Alberta and British Columbia benefitted from all three components of growth, with net natural increases being the most important, closely followed by net interprovincial migration, and then international migration. The latter was relatively more important in British Columbia than in Alberta.

It is interesting to note that throughout the decade net increases from natural causes were always positive in all provinces, and the net

44

migration components worked in *opposite* directions nearly half of the time (see Table 1-15). This latter result, which is somewhat surprising, is contrary to the evidence of the 1960s, when the direction of both components was coincident almost all of the time.[1]

Generally, during the 1970s population growth was gradually slowing, certainly in all provinces east of Saskatchewan. In Saskatchewan the new-found growth of the 1970s was waning. In British Columbia the above-average growth of the late 1970s was below the decadal average for the province. Only in Alberta did the population growth appear to be continuing unabated. Of course, this overall declining growth is largely a reflection of the substantial decline in immigration over the latter half of the 1970s, but it would be evident even in the absence of this component.[2]

One of the main purposes of the subsequent projections will be to ascertain whether or not there will be a continuation of the decline in population growth in Canada that has been taking place since the 1950s (see Table 1-1). The following surveys of each of the components of provincial population growth examine the main determinants of these recent patterns and concentrate on the measures required for the subsequent projection exercises.

Births and Deaths

The excess of births over deaths throughout Canadian history (see Figure 1-1) has meant that natural increase has continued to be the dominant source of population growth. However, this difference relative to the population is currently at an all-time low, with birth rates having declined much faster than death rates over the 1960s and 1970s.[3] Moreover, the provincial differences tended to narrow slightly over the same period. As was noted previously, the rates of natural increase are influenced by, and in turn influence, the age structures of the provincial populations. It follows that Newfoundland, being the youngest province, has the highest rate of natural increase, and British Columbia, being the oldest province, has the lowest rate of natural increase. In order that the differences between provinces be fully understood, it is necessary to eliminate the impact of differences in provincial age composition (see, for example, Tables 1-7 and 1-8) on these measures. This is known as the *standardization* of birth and death rates.[4]

There are a number of basic measures of fertility,[5] but the most common standardized measure is the total fertility rate. This is calculated as a sum of the age-specific fertility rates, which express the

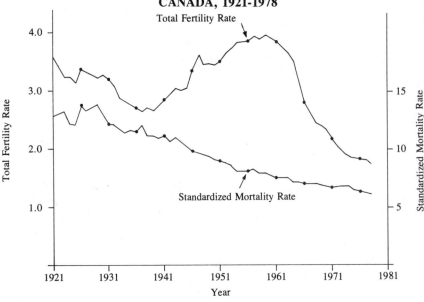

FIGURE 2-1
STANDARDIZED BIRTH AND MORTALITY RATES,
CANADA, 1921-1978

Note: Dots represent the data reported in tables.

Source: Statistics Canada, *Vital Statistics*, vols. I and III, various issues.

average number of births per year to a woman (or 1,000 women) of a particular age or age group. In Canada the reproductive age-span of a woman is taken to be 15 to 49 years. This span is broken down into seven five-year age groups.[6] Obviously, this measure could also be calculated for finer age intervals (for example, one-year groups) and finer time intervals (for example, a month). The chosen calculation, however, provides sufficient information without cumbersome detail. The advantage of this as a measure of fertility is that it standardizes for the effect of variations in the age compositions of women in the childbearing age groups (both over time and between provinces). It reveals the average number of children a women would bear if she could live her childbearing lifetime instantaneously; that is, if she could experience the observed age-specific fertility rate at each age in her reproductive life span.

Table 2-2 summarizes the total fertility rates for Canada and the provinces over the period 1921-78. Figure 2-1 shows the time profiles of the fertility rates for Canada. Not surprisingly, the time profile of

46

TABLE 2-2
TOTAL FERTILITY RATES FOR CANADA AND THE PROVINCES, 1921-1978
(Children per Woman)

Year	Can	Nfld	PEI	NS	NB	PQ	Ont	Man	Sask	Alta	BC	Yukon	NWT
1921	3.54	—	3.78	3.59	4.27	—[a]	3.22	4.05	4.32	3.97	2.79	—[a]	—[a]
1926	3.36	—	3.20	3.20	3.84	4.31	2.73	3.17	3.88	3.53	2.30	—[a]	—[a]
1931	3.20	—	3.52	3.40	3.99	4.00	2.65	2.82	3.48	3.38	2.17	—[a]	—[a]
1936	2.70	—	3.18	3.00	3.49	3.36	2.22	2.34	2.95	2.82	1.87	—[a]	—[a]
1941	2.83	—	3.23	3.10	3.69	3.39	2.40	2.51	2.81	2.83	2.31	—[a]	—[a]
1946	3.37	—	4.36	3.75	4.57	3.83	2.97	3.17	3.44	3.51	2.68	—[a]	—[a]
1951	3.50	—[a]	4.19	3.68	4.38	3.78	3.22	3.30	3.59	3.72	3.20	5.02	6.16
1956	3.86	—[a]	4.54	4.09	4.58	3.90	3.66	3.68	4.08	4.28	3.90	4.76	6.32
1961	3.84	—[a]	4.88	4.16	4.54	3.70	3.74	3.94	4.22	4.27	3.79	5.38	7.19
1966	2.81	4.58[b]	3.58	3.15	3.31	2.65	2.79	2.94	3.28	3.07	2.66	3.63	6.15
1971	2.19	3.40[b]	2.91	2.50	2.67	1.88	2.22	2.54	2.69	2.43	2.14	3.23	4.76
1972	2.02	—[a]	2.61	2.30	2.46	1.73	2.05	2.38	2.55	2.24	2.00	2.78	4.36
1973	1.93	—[a]	2.27	2.15	2.24	1.68	1.96	2.24	2.39	2.15	1.87	2.52	3.99
1974	1.88	—[a]	2.22	2.00	2.14	1.66	1.88	2.18	2.39	2.11	1.82	3.11	3.47
1975	1.85	—[a]	2.05	1.95	2.06	1.75	1.84	2.09	2.22	2.11	1.78	2.20	3.90
1976	1.83	—[a]	2.14	1.88	2.07	1.77	1.77	2.02	2.30	2.04	1.72	2.02	3.18
1977	1.81	—[a]	2.08	1.77	1.96	1.76	1.73	1.97	2.27	2.01	1.74	1.97	3.04
1978	1.76	—[a]	2.04	1.77	1.78	1.69	1.68	1.91	2.20	1.98	1.72	2.03	3.04

Notes: [a] Not available.

[b] Estimated from hospital statistics (see note 10).

Sources: Statistics Canada, *Vital Statistics*, vol. 1 (Catalogue No. 84-204), various issues; and Y. Lovie, "Fertility Projections for Canada and the Provinces, 1976-1991," mimeo. (Ottawa: Statistics Canada, 1979), p. 29.

47

the total fertility rates closely follows that of the crude birth rate (see Figure 1-1), although the Baby Boom of the 1950s is even more apparent when the birth data are standardized for age composition. At the provincial level, the Maritime and Prairie provinces generally have been above average, and Ontario and British Columbia below average. As noted previously, Quebec moved from a pre-Baby Boom above-average fertility rate to a post-Baby Boom below-average rate. By the late 1970s Quebec, Ontario and British Columbia were below-average fertility provinces, while the highest fertility rates were observed in the territories and the provinces of Newfoundland and Saskatchewan. These latter regions were the only ones with fertility rates above or near replacement levels[7]—all other provinces had fertility rates well below replacement levels.

For future reference it is also useful to present the age-specific fertility rates on which the total fertility rate is based. The Canada-wide figures are presented in Table 2-3. From these data it is apparent that the average age of childbearing has been falling since the 1930s. In

TABLE 2-3
AGE-SPECIFIC FERTILITY RATES FOR CANADA, 1921-1978
(Children per Woman)

Year	*Age Groups (Years)*						
	15-19	*20-24*	*25-29*	*30-34*	*35-39*	*40-44*	*45-49*
1921	0.38	1.65	1.86	1.55	1.10	0.47	0.07
1931	0.30	1.37	1.75	1.45	1.03	0.44	0.06
1941	0.31	1.38	1.60	1.22	0.80	0.32	0.04
1951	0.48	1.89	1.99	1.45	0.87	0.31	0.03
1961	0.58	2.34	2.19	1.45	0.81	0.29	0.02
1971	0.40	1.34	1.42	0.77	0.34	0.09	0.01
1972	0.39	1.20	1.37	0.72	0.29	0.08	0.01
1973	0.37	1.18	1.32	0.67	0.26	0.06	0.00
1974	0.35	1.13	1.31	0.67	0.23	0.06	0.00
1975	0.35	1.13	1.31	0.64	0.22	0.05	0.00
1976	0.33	1.10	1.30	0.66	0.21	0.04	0.00
1977	0.32	1.08	1.30	0.67	0.21	0.04	0.00
1978	0.30	1.03	1.28	0.67	0.20	0.04	0.00

Source: Statistics Canada, *Vital Statistics,* vol. 1 (Catalogue No. 84-204), various issues.

1931, for example, mothers under 20 years of age accounted for less than 5 per cent of total fertility, whereas by the mid-1970s this figure had doubled. Mothers in their twenties accounted for almost half the total fertility in 1931; by 1971 the figure was over 60 per cent. At the other end of the age spectrum, there has been a substantial decline in the contribution of mothers aged 40 years and over, from 7.8 per cent in 1931 to 2.2 per cent in 1971.[8]

The decade of the 1970s produced some apparent turnarounds in these long-term trends. The contribution to total fertility of young mothers (aged 15 to 19 years) has been *declining* since the mid-1970s, a trend that also appears to be entering the early twenties age group. However, by 1971 the preference for motherhood had clearly moved from the early twenties age group into the late twenties age group, and the upward trend in the contribution of this latter group continued through the 1970s even though its fertility rate *continued* to decline. Thus, these data support the popular perceptions that, in contrast to previous history, women in Canada in the 1970s generally were postponing their childbearing and (perhaps consequently) having fewer children. In fact, the only age group for which fertility actually appeared to increase in the 1970s was the early thirties age group. Consequently, the relative importance of this age group in childbearing has almost returned to its role of the early 1950s. The relative importance of the older ages (35 to 40 years) continued to decline in the 1970s. In summary, there was a slight but noticeable turnaround in the fertility patterns of the late 1970s, with Canadian women not only continuing to have fewer children, but also postponing childbearing.

It is important to recall that even though there has been increased fertility in the 30-to-34-year-old age group, this group still contributes less than 20 per cent to the total fertility rate, and its pattern has been more than offset by the patterns in the other age groups. To illustrate the point, a *doubling* of the fertility rate of this age group (from 0.67 to 1.34, which would almost take it back to the Baby Boom levels of the 1950s) would increase the total fertility rate in Canada in 1978 by 19 per cent.[9] The relatively small magnitude of this sensitivity places discussion of a turnaround in total fertility based on this group in a somewhat better perspective than the casual conclusions so often inferred from popular perceptions.

The same general patterns are recorded in all provinces (see Table 2-4) with few exceptions.[10] The substantial decline in the relative importance of the oldest age group has occurred without exception, with the territories and Prince Edward Island having the highest

TABLE 2-4

THE AGE DISTRIBUTION OF AGE-SPECIFIC FERTILITY RATES FOR CANADA AND THE PROVINCES, SELECTED AGE GROUPS AND YEARS

(%)

Year	Can	Nfld	PEI	NS	NB	PQ	Ont	Man	Sask	Alta	BC	Yukon	NWT
15 TO 24 YEARS													
1921	28.8	—[a]	21.0	26.3	26.2	20.5[b]	28.8	27.9	29.7	31.3	29.9	—[a]	—[a]
1941	29.9	—[a]	27.6	34.5	29.4	23.5	35.4	30.4	27.7	32.1	36.1	—[a]	—[a]
1961	38.0	—[a]	33.4	39.9	37.1	31.1	41.3	38.8	39.3	42.5	43.3	43.8	36.0
1978	37.8	—[a]	39.9	43.5	45.2	32.9	37.1	40.0	46.0	41.8	39.2	42.8	44.1
25 TO 34 YEARS													
1921	48.2	—[a]	50.1	49.1	48.5	48.3[b]	49.1	47.1	45.8	44.8	49.7	—[a]	—[a]
1941	49.8	—[a]	48.2	46.7	47.6	51.2	48.6	50.2	49.9	48.9	49.9	—[a]	—[a]
1961	47.4	—[a]	47.6	45.3	46.7	50.4	46.2	47.5	46.2	44.5	45.3	40.6	41.5
1978	55.5	—[a]	52.1	50.5	49.7	60.1	56.2	52.8	48.2	52.2	54.5	49.6	44.4
35 TO 49 YEARS													
1921	23.1	—[a]	28.9	24.6	25.3	31.2[b]	22.1	25.0	24.5	23.8	20.4	—[a]	—[a]
1941	20.4	—[a]	24.2	18.8	23.0	25.3	16.0	19.4	22.5	18.9	14.0	—[a]	—[a]
1961	14.6	—[a]	18.9	14.8	16.2	18.5	12.5	13.6	14.6	13.0	11.4	15.6	22.5
1978	6.7	—[a]	8.0	5.9	5.1	6.9	6.7	7.1	5.8	6.0	6.3	7.6	11.5

Notes: [a] Not available (see note 10).
[b] 1926 data (1921 data not available).

Sources: Statistics Canada, *Vital Statistics*, vol. I (Catalogue No. 84-204), various issues.

proportions and New Brunswick the lowest. The turnaround in the relative importance of the 25-to-34-year age group is also readily apparent in all provinces, although it clearly has been greater in Quebec, Ontario and, to a lesser degree, in Alberta and British Columbia than in the remaining provinces. It is interesting to note that for some time Quebec has had a larger proportion of its mothers in this age group than have the other provinces. The relative reduction in the importance of the youngest age group is only apparent (from these data) in Ontario, Alberta and British Columbia. However, as noted above (in Table 2-3), there was a trough in these data between 1961 and 1978, and a comparison of recent data shows the turnaround in all provinces except perhaps Prince Edward Island. In summary, the increasing concentration of mothers in the 25-to-34-year-old age group in the late 1970s is a phenomenon that appears to be country-wide. In most provinces over half of all mothers are in this age group.[11]

Like fertility rates, mortality rates also need to be standardized for the impact of variations in age distributions. Perhaps the most common standardized mortality measure is the age-specific death rate, which is usually calculated separately for each sex by taking, over some time period, the ratio of deaths to the relevant population, usually measured at the mid-point of the period. Since mortality is relatively high among the very young, subsequently decreases and then increases sharply with age after the mid-fifties, the resulting distribution of age-specific death rates is U-shaped, with male mortality rates generally being higher than female rates (see Figure 2-2).[12] Unlike the fertility measure, however, no comparable mortality measure of the total death rate is generally calculated.[13] Rather a standardized death rate is calculated by applying the observed rates to a ''standard population.'' Since the age-sex distribution of the standard population is, by definition, unchanging, this effect is removed from the resulting numbers.

A standardized death rate for Canada and the provinces based on the 1956 Canadian census population is presented in Table 2-5 and included in Figure 2-1 (for Canada only). A secularly declining trend is apparent throughout, with Quebec continuing to maintain the highest provincial standardized mortality rate. Since the Canadian population has been gradually aging over this period, the standardized death rate has not declined as fast as the crude death rate, although a decrease in mortality over the period is still noticeable.

A more common approach to a unified mortality index that can be compared across populations is given by life expectancy data. These

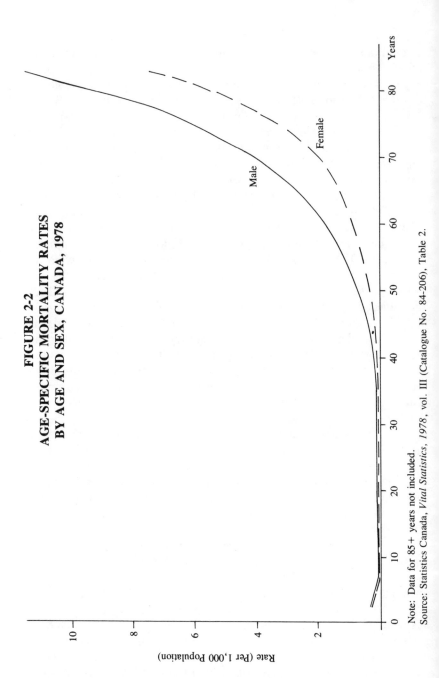

FIGURE 2-2

AGE-SPECIFIC MORTALITY RATES

BY AGE AND SEX, CANADA, 1978

Male

Female

Years

Rate (Per 1,000 Population)

Note: Data for 85+ years not included.
Source: Statistics Canada, *Vital Statistics, 1978*, vol. III (Catalogue No. 84-206), Table 2.

52

TABLE 2-5
STANDARDIZED[a] MORTALITY RATE FOR CANADA AND THE PROVINCES, 1921-1978

Year	Can	Nfld	PEI	NS	NB	PQ	Ont	Man	Sask	Alta	BC	Yukon	NWT
1921	12.9	—	12.7	12.5	15.1	—	13.6	12.0	10.4	12.1	10.9	—	—
1926	13.9	—	9.4	12.3	13.9	16.8	13.0	11.8	11.0	12.8	11.9	—	—
1931	12.2	—	9.3	11.6	12.4	14.6	11.7	10.4	10.0	10.6	10.5	—	—
1936	11.5	—	9.9	10.9	12.2	12.6	11.2	11.1	9.5	10.8	10.8	—	—
1941	11.2	—	10.7	11.9	12.1	12.9	10.4	10.3	9.2	10.2	10.2	—	—
1946	9.9	—	7.9	9.5	10.5	11.2	9.3	9.5	8.8	9.5	9.5	—	—
1951	9.0	8.9	7.4	8.3	9.3	10.2	8.7	8.4	7.8	8.4	8.4	10.3	18.6
1956	8.2	8.3	7.3	7.5	8.1	9.1	8.1	7.6	7.1	7.4	7.9	8.0	18.1
1961	7.6	7.6	7.1	7.4	7.5	8.4	7.6	7.0	6.7	7.0	7.1	8.5	14.6
1966	7.2	7.2	7.1	7.3	7.1	7.8	7.2	6.8	6.4	6.7	6.9	7.1	10.0
1971	6.7	6.9	6.4	7.0	6.8	7.2	6.6	6.4	5.9	6.3	6.5	8.5	11.6
1972	6.8	7.1	6.8	7.1	6.8	7.4	6.7	6.5	6.1	6.3	6.4	6.2	10.1
1973	6.8	7.1	6.4	7.1	6.9	7.4	6.8	6.4	5.9	6.1	6.3	7.4	10.8
1974	6.8	6.7	6.6	7.0	6.9	7.3	6.7	6.5	6.1	6.2	6.5	5.9	7.7
1975	6.5	6.5	6.2	6.7	6.6	7.0	6.4	6.2	5.9	6.1	6.2	7.2	8.1
1976	6.4	6.5	6.5	6.7	6.6	7.0	6.4	6.1	5.9	6.1	6.0	8.7	7.9
1977	6.3	6.1	6.3	6.6	6.5	6.9	6.3	6.1	5.7	5.8	5.8	5.5	6.0
1978	6.2	5.8	5.6	6.4	6.3	6.7	6.1	5.9	5.7	5.9	5.8	4.7	5.9

Note: [a] Standardized to the Canada 1956 census population.

Source: Statistics Canada, *Vital Statistics*, vol. III (Catalogue No. 84-206), various issues.

are calculated from a life table (or mortality table), which is a convenient summary of the age-specific mortality rates of a population.[14] Usually these tables are produced by starting in a particular period (year) with a cohort of 100,000 persons of age zero (this cohort is called the "radix" of the life table). The age-specific mortality rates prevailing during that period are then applied to the radix to determine the number of deaths and survivors by the end of this period. This process is then repeated with the survivors (who have aged over the period) and continues until all members of the radix have died. Thus, a set of age-specific mortality rates are applied instantaneously to a "lifetime" period of a hypothetical cohort. The interpretation is analogous to the total fertility measure. For a person who leads his or her entire life under the given set of age-specific mortality rates, it is possible to calculate the average remaining years of life at each age (including at birth) by dividing by the number of survivors the total number of person-years to be lived by the surviving cohort before the last one dies. At age zero (or birth) this is referred to as "life expectancy at birth," and this is probably the most commonly used summary measure of mortality conditions in a population. Since it is based on age-specific mortality rates, it is unaffected by the age composition of the population.

Life tables are available in Canada for periods centred on census years since 1931.[15] Separate tables are constructed for males and females because of the differences in age-specific mortality rates between the two sexes (see Table 2-6). In Canada life expectancy has increased continuously for both sexes throughout the period (1931-76), with an additional 10 years being added to the male age and 15 years to the female age. Female life expectancy has always exceeded male life expectancy, and the historical trend has been a widening of the gap between the two sexes. By 1976 the difference was 7.3 years. Perhaps of even more interest is the apparent increase in the rate of mortality improvement during the 1970s, especially for males. During the first half of the 1970s, almost a full year was added to male life expectancy in Canada, an amount equal to the improvement gained in the *entire* decade of the 1960s. This is certainly in contradiction to the long-term trend of increasing life expectancy at a decreasing rate and to the often-stated observation, based on international comparisons and medical data, that "any further reductions in mortality from the current low level are likely to be small."[16] This is, then, another unique feature of Canadian demographic developments in the 1970s.

All provinces have shared equally in these trends, and there is very

TABLE 2-6
LIFE EXPECTANCY AT BIRTH BY SEX FOR CANADA AND THE PROVINCES, 1931-1976
(Years)

Period[a]	Can	Nfld	PEI	NS	NB	PQ	Ont	Man	Sask	Alta	BC
MALES											
1930-32	60.0	↓	— 60.2	↑	↑	56.2	61.3	↓	— 63.5	↑	62.2
1940-42	63.0	↓	— 61.7	↑	↑	60.2	64.6	↓	— 65.4	↑	63.7
1950-52	66.3	↓	— 66.6	↑	↑	64.4	66.9	↓	— 68.4	↑	66.7
1955-57	67.6	↓	— 67.9	↑	↑	66.1	67.8	↓	— 69.3	↑	68.1
1960-62	68.4	↓	— 68.6	↑	↑	67.3	68.3	↓	— 69.8	↑	68.9
1965-67	68.8	68.9	68.3	68.3	68.5	67.9	68.7	69.8	70.5	70.1	69.2
1970-72	69.3	69.3	69.3	68.7	69.1	68.3	69.6	70.2	71.1	70.4	69.9
1975-77	70.2	70.6	69.2	69.5	69.7	69.1	70.6	70.7	71.1	71.1	71.0
FEMALES											
1930-32	62.1	↓	— 61.9	↑	↑	57.8	63.9	↓	— 65.5	↑	65.3
1940-42	66.3	↓	— 64.6	↑	↑	63.1	68.4	↓	— 68.2	↑	69.0
1950-52	70.8	↓	— 70.5	↑	↑	68.6	71.9	↓	— 72.3	↑	72.4
1955-57	72.9	↓	— 72.9	↑	↑	71.0	73.6	↓	— 74.2	↑	73.9
1960-62	74.2	↓	— 73.9	↑	↑	72.8	74.4	↓	— 75.7	↑	75.4
1965-67	75.2	74.4	75.5	74.8	75.3	73.9	75.5	76.1	76.5	76.2	75.8
1970-72	76.4	75.7	77.4	76.0	76.4	75.3	76.8	76.9	77.6	77.3	76.7
1975-77	77.5	77.4	78.2	77.8	77.7	76.5	77.7	77.9	78.6	77.9	78.4

Note: [a] Centred on census years.

Source: Statistics Canada, *Vital Statistics*, vol. III (Catalogue No. 84-206), various issues.

little variation in life expectancy across the provinces (see Table 2-6). Generally, life expectancy at birth is lowest in Quebec and highest in Saskatchewan, although for both males and females only two years separate these extreme values. There appear to be no special geographical characteristics to the observed patterns; for example, the Maritime provinces currently have slightly below-average life expectancy for males and slightly above-average life expectancy for females. The greatest gains in life expectancy in the 1970s appear to be on the coasts—in Newfoundland and British Columbia.

A more detailed analysis by age groups (not presented here)[17] shows that the recent life expectancy improvement occurred in most post-teen male ages under 75 years and most post-teen female ages under 55 years—that is, in the middle age groups. It was no longer concentrated in the very young or in the very old. Moreover, there appears to be little or no historical relationship between the sexes in life expectancy improvements. Until recently, there were substantial improvements in the life expectancy rates for females aged 60 years and over that were not reflected in the male rates. These trends are somewhat confusing, but if nothing else, they emphasize the importance of including recent data in any projection of population futures.

Immigration and Emigration

As noted previously, much of the differences in the annual growth rates over the decade of the 1970s can be explained by large variations in net international migration, especially immigration. The provincial distribution of these immigrant flows over the 1970s is summarized in Table 2-7 (see also Table 1-10), together with the average of the 1950s and 1960s. Even though immigrant *levels* varied considerably in the 1970s, there was little variation in their patterns of destination, with the possible exception of Quebec, whose share dropped by four percentage points in 1977-78, only to increase in 1978-79. It is clear that Ontario's share slipped slightly in the late 1970s and that Alberta's share rose. Saskatchewan's share also increased slightly but exhibited no dramatic changes over the 1970s. Compared to the 1960s, Quebec and Ontario have suffered to the relative benefit of Alberta and British Columbia.

Although the *composition* of immigrant flows in any one year has a very minor impact on the composition of the Canadian population, the cumulative effects of immigrant flows that are not reflective of the composition of the receiving population can be substantial. This effect has already been noted with respect to the high proportion of males in

TABLE 2-7
THE DISTRIBUTION OF IMMIGRANTS BY PROVINCE OF INTENDED DESTINATION, 1951-1979
$(\%)^a$

Period	Nfld	PEI	NS	NB	PQ	Ont	Man	Sask	Alta	BC	Yukon/NWT
1951-61	0.2	0.1	1.3	0.6	21.0	53.0	4.4	2.0	7.4	10.0	0.1
1961-71	0.5	0.1	1.2	0.7	20.3	53.3	3.6	1.6	6.2	12.4	0.1
1971-72	0.6	0.2	1.5	0.9	15.2	53.3	4.3	1.2	7.0	15.7	0.2
1972-73	0.6	0.1	1.4	1.1	14.4	53.1	4.1	1.2	6.9	16.8	0.3
1973-74	0.5	0.2	1.4	1.0	15.1	55.9	3.5	1.0	6.2	15.0	0.1
1974-75	0.5	0.1	1.2	1.0	14.9	54.4	3.5	1.1	7.2	16.0	0.1
1975-76	0.6	0.1	1.1	1.2	16.1	50.6	3.9	1.6	9.4	15.2	0.2
1976-77	0.5	0.2	1.5	1.2	19.8	48.0	3.8	1.7	10.2	13.0	0.2
1977-78	0.5	0.2	1.3	0.8	15.9	49.5	4.4	1.9	11.5	13.9	0.2
1978-79	0.4	0.2	1.1	0.8	17.5	48.5	4.0	2.0	10.8	14.6	0.2

Note: ^{a} Row totals may not equal 100.0 due to rounding.

Source: Calculations by the author using Statistics Canada, *International and Interprovincial Migration in Canada* (Catalogue No. 91-208), various issues.

the Canadian population in the early part of this century (see Table 1-2), which was a direct result of the male-dominant immigration of the pre-First World War period, a group that had been attracted by the opening up of the Canadian West. Immigration data on the sex and age of the immigrant flows are available from 1933. These data are summarized in Table 2-8. This table shows that the immigration of the 1930s and 1940s was largely female-dominant and that of the 1950s was largely male-dominant. The 1960s were balanced, and the 1970s returned to a slightly female-dominant inflow.[18] In general, however, the decades of the 1960s and 1970s were characterized by sexually balanced immigration flows, unlike the decades that preceded them. It should be remembered that over this period the domestic population was also gradually becoming female-dominant (see Table 1-2).

TABLE 2-8
THE SEX AND AGE COMPOSITION OF IMMIGRANTS TO CANADA
1933-1979
(%)

Period[a]	Male				Female				Sex Ratio[b]
	0-14 Years	15-64 Years	65+ Years	Total Male	0-14 Years	15-64 Years	65+ Years	Total Female	
1933-40	14.8	←28.3→		43.1	14.0	←42.9→		56.9	0.75
1941-50	10.9	←37.3→		48.2	10.2	←41.6→		51.8	0.93
1951-60	11.6	←42.4→		54.0	10.7	←35.3→		46.0	1.17
1961-70	11.9	37.1	1.1	50.1	11.2	37.1	1.6	49.9	1.00
1971	11.3	37.1	1.2	49.6	10.5	37.9	2.0	50.4	0.98
1972	11.5	36.5	1.2	49.2	11.1	37.6	2.1	50.8	0.97
1973	10.9	39.5	1.0	51.4	10.3	36.5	1.8	48.6	1.06
1974	12.8	37.0	1.1	50.9	12.0	35.6	1.6	49.1	1.04
1975	13.9	33.9	1.5	49.3	13.3	35.3	2.1	50.7	0.97
1976	13.2	33.4	2.0	48.6	12.3	36.3	2.8	51.4	0.95
1977	12.1	33.3	2.3	47.7	11.6	37.4	3.3	52.3	0.91
1978	10.7	33.0	2.7	46.4	10.4	39.3	3.9	53.6	0.87
1979	11.5	35.3	2.1	48.9	10.7	37.3	3.1	51.1	0.96

Notes: [a] Calendar year data.
        [b] Ratio of males to females.

Sources: M. C. Urquhart, *Historical Statistics of Canada* (Toronto: Macmillan, 1965), p. 26; a Employment and Immigration Canada, *Immigration Statistics*, various issues.

Since the 1940s, the percentage of pre-working-age immigrants has been very gradually increasing: from 21.1 per cent of the total inflow in the 1940s, to 22.3 per cent in the 1950s, to 23.1 per cent in the 1960s, and to 23.7 per cent over the 1971-79 period. This group has been slightly male-dominant since the 1950s.[19] At the other end of the age spectrum, the percentage of the elderly among the immigrants also has been rising, especially since the mid-1970s. In the 1960s those aged 65 years and over averaged 2.7 per cent of the total; for the 1971-74 period the average was 2.9 per cent; and in the 1975-79 period it rose to 4.9 per cent. In 1978 it was 6.6 per cent (but note that this is still below the Canadian percentage for this age group [see Table 1-2]). Presumably, this trend is a result of recent changes in the Immigration Act[20] that tied immigration more closely to the (generally over-supplied) job market and to reuniting families. Note that this group is extremely female-dominant.[21] With the percentages of both immigrant non-working-age groups rising, the percentage of the remaining group of immigrants of working age must be falling. In fact, this latter group accounted for over three-quarters of the total inflow in the 1940s and 1950s, for 74.2 per cent in the 1960s, and for 72.4 per cent in the 1970s. This is also a female-dominant group.[22] Although still above the Canadian working-age percentage,[23] the data of the 1970s suggest increasing female dominance and "dependence" in Canadian immigration inflows.

These conclusions are confirmed by the provincial data presented in Table 2-9. Few consistent trends emerge from the sex ratio, although Quebec generally appears to have received more immigrant males than females, while the reverse applies to Ontario over the 1970s. Even the territories have not always received more males than females, as might be expected.[24]

The distribution of immigrants by age by province is also included in Table 2-9, where it is apparent that there has been relatively little variation in the age distribution between provinces. Prince Edward Island (which has very small numbers) had an unusually high percentage of older immigrants in 1961, 1966 and 1971 but obtained a relatively average percentage in 1976. New Brunswick is the "odd" province in 1976 with an uncharacteristically high percentage of younger immigrants. However, the remaining provinces remain remarkably similar, all approximately following the national trends in immigrant age distributions (see Table 2-8).

Emigration, like immigration, was somewhat volatile over the 1970s. All provinces except Quebec and British Columbia experienced

TABLE 2-9
SEX RATIO AND AGE COMPOSITION OF IMMIGRANTS
FOR CANADA AND THE PROVINCES, SELECTED YEARS, 1961-1979
(%)

Age Group (Years)	Can	Nfld	PEI	NS	NB	PQ	Ont	Man	Sask	Alta	BC	Yukon/ NWT
						1961						
Ratio[a]	0.81	1.02	1.16	0.90	1.17	0.83	0.78	0.93	0.81	0.88	0.79	0.80
0-14	21.9	30.7	31.9	18.7	23.6	20.7	21.8	24.3	22.7	25.2	21.7	27.7
15-64	74.9	66.3	52.2	69.7	69.6	76.9	75.1	72.5	74.4	72.5	73.7	70.8
65+	3.2	3.0	15.9	11.5	6.8	2.4	3.1	3.2	2.9	2.3	4.6	1.5
						1966						
Ratio[a]	1.06	1.10	1.07	1.25	1.09	1.14	1.05	1.03	0.89	1.03	1.01	1.11
0-14	25.4	26.0	19.1	24.6	21.8	22.2	26.4	26.1	27.5	27.6	25.0	21.4
15-64	72.6	72.6	57.5	68.7	72.0	75.8	71.8	71.9	70.8	70.7	72.8	78.5
65+	2.0	1.4	23.4	6.7	6.2	2.0	1.8	2.0	1.7	1.7	2.2	0.5
						1971						
Ratio[a]	0.98	1.12	0.89	0.97	1.00	1.02	0.96	0.93	0.96	0.99	1.03	1.13
0-14	21.8	26.5	18.0	20.8	20.7	19.1	21.6	24.1	24.3	24.5	23.0	16.9
15-64	75.1	71.1	57.0	70.6	70.9	77.7	75.5	74.0	72.4	73.0	73.6	82.0
65+	3.1	2.4	25.0	8.6	8.4	3.2	2.9	1.9	3.3	2.5	3.4	1.1

Age Group (Years)	Can	Nfld	PEI	NS	NB	PQ	Ont	Man	Sask	Alta	BC	Yukon/NWT
						1976						
Ratio[a]	0.95	0.95	1.18	1.04	1.02	1.04	0.90	0.99	1.01	1.05	0.86	1.05
0-14	25.5	24.7	26.8	26.0	40.4	24.3	26.0	26.6	27.2	26.0	23.2	30.0
15-64	69.7	69.5	67.8	68.8	56.8	71.5	68.8	70.2	70.3	70.8	70.7	66.8
65+	4.8	5.8	6.4	5.2	2.8	4.2	5.2	3.2	2.5	3.2	6.1	3.2
						1979						
Ratio[a]	0.96	1.22	0.99	1.06	0.95	1.02	0.93	0.96	1.14	1.01	0.89	1.27
0-14	22.2	23.8	25.5	23.0	24.3	23.6	21.8	22.6	25.9	22.6	20.3	27.8
15-64	72.5	70.4	65.5	69.0	70.9	71.7	72.7	73.5	71.2	73.6	72.8	70.8
65+	5.3	5.8	9.0	8.0	4.8	4.7	5.5	3.9	2.9	3.8	6.9	1.4

Note: [a] Ratio of males to females, all age groups combined.

Source: Employment and Immigration Canada, *Immigration Statistics*, various issues.

reduced shares of emigrants compared to the 1960s (see Table 1-11). Because these data are not based on any primary data source, the provincial allocation is based on longer-run census data, and hence the estimated provincial shares are almost constant over the quinquennial periods. Consequently, the annual data are not reproduced here.

The sex and age composition of emigrants is based on the very incomplete data for emigrants to the United States, a destination of decreasing importance in emigrant flows.[25] According to Statistics Canada, "fragmentary data suggest that there has not been any dramatic change in this distribution over time, although there has been an aging of the distribution reflecting similar changes in the structure of the Canadian population."[26] Consequently, once again there is little reason to examine the annual data of the 1970s for changing patterns in emigrant flows.

Interprovincial Migration

As previously noted (see Table 1-13), the 1970s produced dramatic reversals of traditional trends in interprovincial migration patterns. The annual data for the 1970s are presented in Tables 2-10 (in- and out-migration) and 2-11 (net interprovincial migration). A cursory review of these data shows that the turning point for many of these new trends occurred in the middle of the decade. However, earlier turning points occurred in the Maritime provinces (Prince Edward Island, Nova Scotia and New Brunswick), which reversed their traditional roles as net losers in interprovincial population movements. This was followed by reversals in Ontario, which became a net loser in 1973-74, and in Saskatchewan, which became a net gainer a year later. The substantial increase in the net gain to Alberta also occurred in 1974-75, while the increase in the net losses from Quebec returned to the levels of the early 1970s in 1976-77.[27] In almost all cases these trends can be attributed to complementary changes in both in-migration and out-migration patterns. For example, the changes in Quebec resulted both from reduced in-migration and increased out-migration. An exception might be the increases in Alberta, which are primarily attributable to increased in-migration. British Columbia provides an interesting case. Net migration was exactly the same in 1978-79 as it was in 1970-71, but in the intervening period it had followed a very volatile pattern, having increased in the early 1970s, become a net *loser* by 1975-76, and then having returned to previous levels by the end of the decade. This is perhaps the only province where averaged data (see Table 1-13) may not be indicative of current trends.

62

INTERPROVINCIAL IN- AND OUT-MIGRATION BY PROVINCE BY YEAR, 1970-1979

(000's)

Period	Can[a]	Nfld	PEI	NS	NB	PQ	Ont	Man	Sask	Alta	BC	Yukon	NWT
						IN-MIGRATION							
1970-71	404.4	9.3	4.0	21.7	20.5	34.6	128.5	28.1	20.1	59.5	71.1	←7.0→	
1971-72	398.6	12.6	4.3	23.1	20.6	38.8	109.2	26.6	20.0	61.2	75.2	←7.0→	
1972-73	389.6	11.5	4.3	24.3	20.4	35.6	96.0	28.9	20.8	62.7	77.9	←7.3→	
1973-74	436.4	12.9	4.8	26.3	21.5	40.8	104.7	33.0	27.1	72.1	88.1	←5.2→	
1974-75	416.9	12.3	5.4	26.9	24.1	37.8	85.0	30.2	30.3	79.9	77.7	←7.3→	
1975-76	374.5	12.1	4.4	24.8	23.4	32.9	81.1	26.6	28.5	76.2	58.3	←6.2→	
1976-77	397.8	10.5	5.0	23.9	21.3	31.6	92.6	28.3	30.8	84.8	62.8	2.4	4.0
1977-78	404.9	10.0	4.7	23.4	20.1	25.2	107.1	24.9	27.5	88.6	67.3	2.4	3.7
1978-79	395.7	10.2	4.3	23.2	19.4	26.2	93.9	23.6	26.3	92.0	70.7	2.3	3.6
						OUT-MIGRATION							
1970-71	404.4	13.0	3.8	25.5	20.9	72.6	81.2	35.4	44.2	52.6	51.0	←4.0→	
1971-72	398.6	11.7	4.0	23.4	20.0	59.3	95.1	34.9	39.2	57.6	48.2	←5.2→	
1972-73	389.6	12.0	3.4	20.0	18.3	55.7	95.0	34.6	37.0	57.2	50.5	←5.9→	
1973-74	436.4	16.2	4.3	25.0	20.0	55.9	107.6	34.6	38.7	69.8	57.6	←6.6→	
1974-75	416.9	11.8	4.0	24.6	18.0	47.1	114.5	37.1	29.9	57.3	65.9	←6.6→	
1975-76	374.5	11.5	3.7	21.0	16.8	45.6	102.3	30.8	22.6	51.6	62.7	←5.9→	
1976-77	397.8	11.9	3.9	23.7	18.7	54.6	100.6	32.5	24.0	59.5	60.7	3.4	4.4
1977-78	404.9	12.6	3.7	22.7	18.2	72.1	97.0	32.1	25.5	62.9	51.6	2.1	4.4
1978-79	395.7	12.1	4.4	21.8	18.2	58.3	102.0	34.6	24.6	61.7	50.6	2.7	4.9

Note: [a] Total out-migration equals total in-migration.

Source: Statistics Canada, *International and Interprovincial Migration in Canada* (Catalogue No. 91-208), various issues.

TABLE 2-11
NET INTERPROVINCIAL MIGRATION BY PROVINCE BY YEAR, 1970-1979
(000's)

Period	Can[a]	Nfld	PEI	NS	NB	PQ	Ont	Man	Sask	Alta	BC	Yukon	NWT
1970-71	202.2	-3.7	0.2	-3.8	-0.4	-38.0	47.3	-7.4	-24.2	6.9	20.1	← 2.9 →	
1971-72	199.3	0.9	0.3	-0.4	0.6	-20.5	14.1	-8.3	-19.2	3.6	27.0	← 1.8 →	
1972-73	199.8	-0.5	0.9	4.3	2.1	-20.1	1.0	-5.8	-16.2	5.6	27.3	← 1.4 →	
1973-74	218.2	-3.3	0.5	1.3	1.4	-15.1	-2.9	-1.6	-11.6	2.2	30.5	← -1.4 →	
1974-75	208.4	0.5	1.4	2.2	6.1	-9.3	-29.5	-6.9	0.4	22.6	11.8	← 0.7 →	
1975-76	187.2	0.6	0.6	3.9	6.6	-12.6	-21.2	-4.2	5.8	24.6	-4.4	← 0.3 →	
1976-77	198.9	-1.4	1.0	0.2	2.6	-23.0	-8.0	-4.2	6.8	25.3	2.1	-1.0	-0.4
1977-78	202.5	-2.6	1.0	0.7	1.9	-46.9	10.1	-7.2	2.0	25.8	15.7	0.3	-0.7
1978-79	197.9	-1.9	-0.1	1.4	1.1	-32.1	-8.1	-10.9	1.7	30.4	20.1	-0.4	-1.3

Note: [a] Sum of net gain (+) or net loss (−).

Source: Table 2-10.

A comparison of the out-migration data with the source population permits a more accurate assessment of the comparative mobility of provincial populations. Table 2-12 presents the out-migration rates (per 100 of population) for the 1970s. It is apparent from these data that Quebecers are the least mobile, probably for linguistic and cultural reasons, and the frontier populations of the territories are the most mobile. Of the provinces, the populations of the Prairie provinces appear to be more mobile then those of the Atlantic provinces (except, perhaps, for Prince Edward Island), and all are more mobile than British Columbians and much more mobile than Ontarians. No clear temporal pattern emerges from these rates over the decade, with the possible exception of Saskatchewan's population, which clearly became less mobile in the latter half of the 1970s.

The provincial populations can be conceived of as the sources of interprovincial migrants, whose probability of movement is determined by the above rates. These migrants then settle in other provinces (or destinations). It is possible to examine the *rate* of interprovincial migrant *inflow* to these destinations by dividing the inflow by the relevant destination population. However, the rates of inflow are determined by the rates of outflow in any period. Therefore, it is probably more useful to examine the allocation of the "pool" of interprovincial migrants over the receiving provinces.[28] These data for the 1970s are presented in Table 2-13. From these data, it is clear that Ontario was the most preferred destination, followed by Alberta and British Columbia. Over the decade, Alberta replaced British Columbia as the second most preferred destination. The province of Quebec received less than 10 per cent of interprovincial migrants, again probably for linguistic and cultural reasons. With the exception of the increase in Alberta and perhaps a recently reduced share for Quebec, no clear trends upward or downward emerge from these data over the decade. Compared to the 1960s, the Atlantic provinces received a slightly higher share of interprovincial migrants, Quebec and Ontario somewhat reduced shares, Manitoba a slightly reduced share, and the remaining provinces somewhat increased shares (see Table 1-11).

It should be noted, of course, that these data on out-migration rates and in-migration percentages are a summary of a wealth of information on origin-destination flows for Canada that has been published since 1961. With the use of these data, it would be possible to calculate origin-destination-specific migration rates, thus avoiding a separate analysis of out- and in-migration patterns. However attractive, this method involves cumbersome detail.[29]

TABLE 2-12

OUT-MIGRATION RATES BY PROVINCE BY YEAR, 1969-1979

(%)[a]

Period	Nfld	PEI	NS	NB	PQ	Ont	Man	Sask	Alta	BC	Yukon	NWT
1969-70	2.96	4.33	3.42	4.04	1.20	1.08	3.80	4.80	3.48	2.38	← 8.22→	
1970-71	2.52	3.46	3.26	3.34	1.21	1.08	3.60	4.70	3.30	2.40	← 8.03→	
1971-72	2.23	3.59	2.97	3.15	0.98	1.24	3.53	4.23	3.54	2.21	← 9.72→	
1972-73	2.26	3.03	2.52	2.86	0.92	1.22	3.49	4.05	3.45	2.25	←10.30→	
1973-74	3.02	3.73	3.11	3.09	0.92	1.36	3.47	4.28	4.13	2.50	←11.05→	
1974-75	2.19	3.50	3.04	2.75	0.77	1.42	3.68	3.32	3.33	2.77	←10.91→	
1975-76	2.10	3.20	2.56	2.53	0.74	1.25	3.04	2.49	2.90	2.58	← 9.48→	
1976-77	2.13	3.33	2.86	2.75	0.88	1.22	3.18	2.61	3.24	2.46	15.61	10.36
1977-78	2.24	3.10	2.72	2.65	1.15	1.16	3.12	2.72	3.32	2.07	10.02	10.18
1978-79	2.12	3.58	2.59	2.62	0.93	1.21	3.35	2.60	3.16	2.00	12.39	11.25

Note: [a] Per 100 population.

Source: Calculations by the author (see Tables 2-1 and 2-10).

TABLE 2-13
THE DISTRIBUTION OF INTERPROVINCIAL IN-MIGRATION BY PROVINCE BY YEAR, 1969-1979
(%)[a]

Period	Nfld	PEI	NS	NB	PQ	Ont	Man	Sask	Alta	BC	Yukon	NWT
1969-70	1.8	0.8	5.5	4.3	8.8	32.0	6.8	4.9	15.3	18.6	←1.3→	
1970-71	2.3	1.0	5.4	5.1	8.6	31.8	6.9	5.0	14.7	17.6	←1.7→	
1971-72	3.2	1.1	5.8	5.2	9.7	27.4	6.7	5.0	15.4	18.9	←1.8→	
1972-73	2.9	1.1	6.2	5.2	9.1	24.6	7.4	5.4	16.1	20.0	←1.9→	
1973-74	3.0	1.1	6.0	4.9	9.3	24.0	7.6	6.2	16.5	20.2	←1.2→	
1974-75	3.0	1.3	6.5	5.8	9.1	20.4	7.2	7.3	19.2	18.6	←1.2→	
1975-76	3.2	1.2	6.6	6.2	8.8	21.7	7.1	7.6	20.4	15.6	←1.8→	
1976-77	2.6	1.3	6.0	5.4	7.9	23.3	7.1	7.7	21.3	15.8	0.6	1.0
1977-78	2.5	1.2	5.8	5.0	6.2	26.4	6.2	6.8	21.9	16.6	0.6	0.9
1978-79	2.6	1.1	5.9	4.9	6.6	23.7	6.0	6.7	23.3	17.9	0.6	0.9

Note: [a] Row totals may not equal 100.0 due to rounding.

Source: Calculations by the author (see Table 2-10).

Unfortunately, there is a dearth of published information on the age-sex composition of interprovincial migrants. Of course, if the out-migration rates (see Table 2-12) and in-migration percentages (see Table 2-13) were the same for all age-sex groups, then the composition of interprovincial migrants would be a weighted average of the provincial populations. Since age-sex compositions of the provinces differ (see Tables 1-6 to 1-8), even this assumption would inevitably lead one to expect changes in the age-sex composition of provincial populations from interprovincial migration. The point to note, however, is that the concept of out-migration *rates* explicitly links the composition of interprovincial migrants to the compositions of the source (that is, provincial) populations.[30]

The only source of compositional information on interprovincial migrants in Canada is the population census. The limitations of these data, already noted, are that they cover movements over five-year periods and provide no information (until the results of the 1981 census are available) on the post-1976 period. Analyses of the five-year migration patterns since the 1961 census show that the young, especially persons in their twenties and early thirties, are more likely to migrate than other age groups and that there is no significant difference in the patterns between the sexes.[31] They also suggest that interprovincial migration trends have reflected the national trends in age-sex composition. More recently, Statistics Canada has provided an estimated age-sex composition of interprovincial migrants with its annual estimates. These are based on the 1971-76 census movements and are summarized in Figure 2-3. For 1978-79 they suggest that interprovincial migration was somewhat male-dominant (with an overall sex ratio of 1.05), although not in the older age groups, and that young persons, especially those in their twenties, were much more likely to migrate interprovincially than those of other ages.

The associated age distributions for each of the provinces for 1978-79 are presented in Tables 2-14 (out-migration rates) and 2-15 (in-migration percentages). They generally confirm the interprovincial patterns discussed above.

The out-migration rates (which give the probability of migrating to another province) were much lower in Quebec and Ontario than elsewhere in the country and much higher in the territories. The highest provincial rate was in Prince Edward Island. In seven provinces, the maximum rate occurred in the 20-to-24-year-old age group, and in three provinces it occurred in the 25 to 29 age group. The age pattern in

FIGURE 2-3
EX RATIO AND INTERPROVINCIAL MIGRATION RATES BY
AGE AND SEX, CANADA, 1978-1979

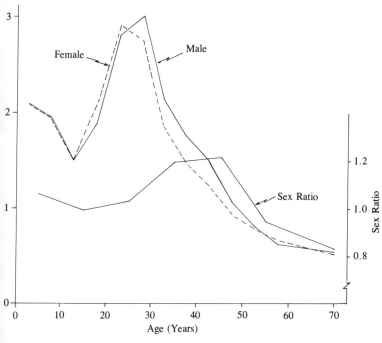

Source: Calculated from Statistics Canada, *International and Interprovincial Migration, 1978-79*, Table 11.

all provinces approximately followed the national pattern (see Figure 2-3).

The provincial allocation of in-migrants shows that Ontario and Alberta both received over 23 per cent of all interprovincial migrants in 1978-79. British Columbia received almost 18 per cent. It is interesting to note that in 1978-79 Saskatchewan is estimated to have received *more* in-migrants than Quebec. The distribution was remarkably stable over age groups,[32] although it is apparent that interprovincial migration to Quebec, Saskatchewan and British Columbia was characterized by a slightly below-average proportion of younger people (especially 15-to-24-year-olds) and a slightly above-average proportion of older

69

TABLE 2-14

SEX RATIO AND OUT-MIGRATION RATES BY AGE AND SEX FOR CANADA AND THE PROVINCES, 1978-1979

(%)[a]

Age Group (Years)	Can	Nfld	PEI	NS	NB	PQ	Ont	Man	Sask	Alta	BC	Yukon	NWT
Sex Ratio[b]	1.05	1.03	0.98	1.05	1.02	1.01	1.08	1.05	0.98	1.03	1.07	1.14	1.22
Less than 5	2.07	1.99	3.81	3.20	3.10	0.98	1.63	3.98	2.84	3.50	2.69	13.85	8.80
6 to 9	1.94	1.55	2.93	2.76	2.66	0.99	1.44	3.95	2.58	3.65	2.46	13.24	10.56
10 to 14	1.50	1.52	2.29	2.14	2.14	0.85	1.03	3.09	2.16	2.95	1.99	11.05	7.19
15 to 19	1.96	4.05	6.46	3.46	3.56	1.11	1.27	3.59	4.00	2.80	2.49	7.74	6.10
20 to 24	2.87	4.53	8.92	5.12	5.06	1.44	2.19	5.84	5.29	4.29	3.40	11.44	14.24
25 to 29	3.20	2.71	6.43	4.67	4.27	1.38	2.35	6.08	4.06	4.93	3.39	22.43	23.58
30 to 34	2.00	2.19	3.47	3.05	2.97	1.06	1.53	4.31	2.86	3.68	2.43	17.24	19.09
35 to 39	1.62	1.94	3.58	2.64	2.70	0.90	1.14	3.50	2.48	3.22	1.94	12.67	13.40
40 to 44	1.37	1.56	3.12	2.24	2.22	0.83	0.90	2.86	2.16	2.89	1.59	12.18	9.91
45 to 49	1.02	1.11	1.67	1.49	1.53	0.70	0.66	2.19	1.56	2.30	1.09	8.00	8.28
50 to 54	0.81	0.81	1.02	0.83	1.01	0.55	0.55	1.64	1.24	2.06	0.82	7.33	8.43
55 to 59	0.66	0.66	0.59	0.56	0.61	0.45	0.44	1.22	1.13	1.88	0.63	6.43	6.36
60 and over	0.54	0.45	0.44	0.48	0.57	0.44	0.31	0.96	0.86	1.47	0.58	8.45	4.32
Total	1.69	2.12	3.58	2.59	2.62	0.93	1.21	3.35	2.60	3.16	2.00	12.39	11.22

Notes: [a] Rate per 100 Population as at June 1, 1978.
          [b] Ratio of males to females.

Source: Statistics Canada, *International and Interprovincial Migration in Canada, 1978-79* (Catalogue No. 91-208), Table 11.

TABLE 2-15

SEX RATIO AND DISTRIBUTION OF IN-MIGRATION BY AGE AND SEX FOR CANADA AND THE PROVINCES, 1978-1979

(%)[a]

Age Group (Years)	Can[b]	Nfld	PEI	NS	NB	PQ	Ont	Man	Sask	Alta	BC	Yukon	NWT
Sex Ratio[c]	1.05	1.06	1.06	1.05	1.05	1.07	1.03	1.05	1.05	1.06	1.05	1.07	1.05
Less than 5	9.14	2.65	1.12	5.95	4.84	6.91	22.41	6.07	6.83	23.57	18.12	0.61	0.92
6 to 9	8.97	2.62	1.09	5.78	4.79	6.74	22.64	6.02	7.01	23.35	18.41	0.62	0.93
10 to 14	8.00	2.51	1.07	5.72	4.81	6.41	24.19	5.94	6.79	23.03	18.02	0.57	0.94
15 to 19	11.83	2.48	1.15	6.27	5.07	6.32	25.38	5.97	5.88	23.75	16.23	0.59	0.91
20 to 24	16.28	2.63	1.15	6.14	5.03	6.75	23.71	6.01	6.32	23.52	17.24	0.58	0.92
25 to 29	14.68	2.74	1.10	5.91	4.96	7.05	22.27	6.00	6.83	23.47	18.10	0.64	0.93
30 to 34	9.19	2.65	1.08	5.78	4.92	6.82	23.18	5.91	6.80	23.31	17.98	0.64	0.93
35 to 39	5.86	2.57	1.09	5.72	4.87	6.54	24.06	5.89	6.82	22.89	18.02	0.59	0.94
40 to 44	4.34	2.52	1.04	5.61	4.86	6.36	24.60	5.89	6.81	22.45	18.30	0.55	1.01
45 to 49	3.25	2.37	0.97	5.42	4.84	6.12	25.42	5.86	6.84	22.08	18.62	0.54	0.92
50 to 54	2.47	2.37	0.90	5.44	4.72	6.26	24.54	5.96	6.97	22.17	19.16	0.56	0.95
55 to 59	1.84	2.35	0.81	5.30	4.53	6.01	24.28	6.14	7.15	22.12	19.88	0.48	0.95
60 and over	4.15	2.12	0.66	5.16	4.43	5.53	26.45	5.90	6.86	22.93	18.82	0.43	0.71
Average[d]	100.0	2.57	1.08	5.86	4.90	6.61	23.73	5.97	6.65	23.26	17.86	0.59	0.92

Notes: [a] Row totals may not equal 100.0 due to rounding.
[b] Percentage distribution of all interprovincial migrants by age.
[c] Ratio of males to females.
[d] Weighted average.

Source: Statistics Canada, *International and Interprovincial Migration in Canada, 1978-79* (Catalogue No. 91-208), Table 11.

people. The remaining provinces generally experienced the opposite patterns. A preference for retirement in the former provinces would explain this pattern. In general, it is estimated that Ontario and British Columbia had an above-average ratio of male out-migrants, that Prince Edward Island and Saskatchewan actually experienced female-dominant out-migration, and that the in-migration proportions were almost identical across all provinces except for Ontario (with a below-average male ratio) and Quebec (with an above-average male ratio).

Transitory or Permanent?

With these more detailed descriptions of recent trends, it is possible to start to explore the question of whether the demographic developments of the 1970s, many of which appear to be quite unique in Canadian demographic history, are likely to be transitory or permanent. This question becomes crucial when viewing Canada's population futures, the subject of the next chapter. Of course, the examination of past data can only provide a guide as to whether a trend appears to be established or not—it is descriptive rather than explanatory. A more detailed analysis requires the development of empirically verified, theoretical explanations of these trends. This in turn necessitates excursions into numerous relevant disciplines, such as economics, sociology and medicine, all of which can result in specialist studies. With this recognition, almost any discussion of population futures will be deficient in one way or another. Consequently, the methodology adopted in the following chapter is designed to be sufficiently flexible to accommodate different, alternative, views, with the orientation of the analysis towards the *sensitivity* of the results to the various alternative views. However, even this approach requires that the alternatives be bounded within some feasible range, and it is with this in mind that the current brief analysis of the demographic developments of the 1970s is presented.

A number of the unique developments of the 1970s (such as the slowing growth of the population, the historically low percentage of the young, the high percentage of working-age persons and the elderly, and the increasing female dominance of the population) are a direct consequence of population aging. This is not a new phenomenon in Canada and is likely to continue. Besides the natural process of the existing population aging with time, it reflects the rapid decline in the fertility rate, which occurred over the 1960s and 1970s, and a reduction in the levels of international migration. Even a reversal of those patterns would have to be of substantial magnitude *and duration* to moderate the impacts of the aging process. Consequently, there appears to be little doubt that these trends of the 1970s are likely to continue into the 1980s and beyond.

Changes in the Canadian population are dominated by natural causes, namely, births and deaths. The number of births is determined by fertility rates, which over the decade of the 1970s reached historically low levels. Nonetheless, the trend continued downward throughout the decade and showed no signs of reversal. However, what did reverse in the 1970s was the average age of childbearing. The increasing concentration of mothers in the 25-to-34-year-old age group reversed the historical downward trend in the mid-1970s. This can be explained by the desire (and ability) of potential parents to delay the timing of the first child, perhaps until after sufficient income has been accumulated and careers established. Such a delay can not only account for the increasing average age of childbearing, but can also help to explain the historically low fertility rate,[33] since the average number of children in a family tends to decrease with the increase in the age of the mother at the time of the first born. It appears likely that these trends will continue, at least into the near future, although there remains lively debate on the subject in many circles.

The number of deaths is determined by mortality rates, which are also reflected in life expectancy data. In Canada, life expectancy has been steadily increasing, and female life expectancy has always exceeded male life expectancy, with the historical trend being a widening of the gap between the two sexes. Increasing life expectancy primarily reflects medical, hygienic and nutritional advances, but is also influenced by such factors as improved conditions in the workplace and attitudes towards smoking. It is likely that medicine, hygiene and nutrition will continue to contribute to increases in life expectancy, although perhaps at a decreasing rate. However, the experience of the first half of the 1970s, when life expectancy improvements occurred at an *increasing* rate (at least for males), indicates that even the "diminishing marginal returns" hypothesis cannot be taken for granted. In addition, according to recent historical data in Canada, there is no evidence that the gap between the sexes will narrow.

In regard to international migration, it appears certain that there will always be a humanitarian need that will be reflected in Canada's intake. Past responses to international crises suggest that Canada's inflow is likely to remain volatile and, at times, to include a substantial refugee component. Moreover, the reuniting of families of earlier immigrants also ensures a reasonable level of applicants, regardless of international and domestic conditions. These latter do, however, play a role, since the requirements of the domestic labour force are an important component of Canada's immigration program. Labour market surpluses (or high unemployment rates) reduce immigration levels, and labour market shortages increase them. Note, however, that the trends towards increasing dependency and female dominance in immigrant flows observed in the 1970s reflect both the aging in the immigrant source populations and the increasing relative importance of the family class over this period.[34] The former will almost certainly continue, whereas the latter is largely a matter for government policy.

Very little is known about the characteristics, let alone the determinants, of emigration from Canada. Increasing populations tend to have more emigrants, as do populations with large immigrant components. Historically, Canada has experienced waves of immigrants, followed by long periods of attrition, mainly to the United States. The last wave followed the Second World War and continued through the 1950s, with the 1960s and 1970s largely being a period of attrition. The level of emigration may also be influenced by economic opportunities elsewhere in the world (perhaps in relation to opportunities at home) and by barriers to immigrant flows to other countries. Domestically, an aging population can have both a negative and a positive impact on emigration. Since people tend to be more mobile at younger ages, population aging beyond some average age will likely decrease emigrant flows. However, population aging also increases the number of persons of retirement ages, and these persons may seek warmer climates than Canada's for their retirement years. To date, these conjectures have little basis in researched fact; hence the level of emigration from Canada and its determinants remain largely unexplored. About the only conclusion that appears consistent with the observed facts is that, for whatever reasons, the level appears to be gradually increasing.

Historically, the Canadian population has always been moving westward. The trend, although uneven, has been well established. This is further reflected in the gradually changing destinations of immigrant inflows in the 1970s and by the patterns of interprovincial migration. Consequently, these patterns of the 1970s are not new. Of course, as with any population movement, the movements westward must be supported by appropriate relative economic conditions, which, on the basis of the interprovincial migration data, appear to have been in place since the mid-1970s. What is somewhat more surprising from a historical perspective is the reversal of interprovincial migration patterns throughout the 1970s in favour of the eastern Atlantic provinces. This trend appeared to be on the wane by the late 1970s but, nonetheless, represented a reversal of the observed trends of the 1960s. Finally, note that the interprovincial movement of persons may well be influenced by government policies, both federal and provincial. For example, the use of federal monies to establish or maintain industries in economically depressed regions (such as the Atlantic provinces) and the enactment of language legislation in Quebec may have contributed to the patterns of movement observed in the 1970s.

With this more detailed assessment of the recent trends, it is possible to explore which developments of the 1970s appear to represent transitory movements and which are likely to represent established patterns, either traditional or new. Many of the unique demographic developments of the 1970s do *not* appear to be transitory. The task of the next chapter is to use these developments of the 1970s as a base for the development of alternative scenarios regarding the future demographic outlook for Canada and the provinces.

Summary

Are the previously identified unique demographic characteristics of the 1970s transitory or permanent developments? A more detailed analysis of the annual data for the decade shows that population growth is slowing in all provinces except Alberta, and that this would have occurred even without the substantial reduction of international immigration that took place in the latter half of the decade.

The natural increase remains the dominant source of population growth. Detailed comparisons of birth and death rates across populations require the construction of standardized measures that are independent of age composition. The total fertility rate is a standardized measure of fertility constructed from age-specific fertility rates. Over time it has followed the same pattern as the crude birth rate. The age-specific data show that the average age of childbearing had been falling since the 1930s (and perhaps before) and then reversed in the mid-1970s. This increasing concentration of mothers in the 25-to-34-year-old age group appears to be country-wide.

Life tables are constructed from age-specific mortality rates. They permit the calculation of the commonly used summary standardized measure of mortality known as "life expectancy at birth." In Canada, female life expectancy has always exceeded male life expectancy, and the gap between the two sexes has been widening. A further unique, and surprising, development of the 1970s has been an apparent increase in the rate of mortality improvement. The detailed data do not suggest an explanation, but new information cannot be overlooked in developing population futures.

Net immigration was a much more important component of population growth in the first half of the 1970s than in the second half. The trend in Canada is towards increasing dependency in immigrant inflows. Since the 1940s, the proportion of pre-working-age immigrants has been gradually increasing, as has the proportion of the elderly—the former being slightly male-dominant and the latter extremely female-dominant. The sex distribution of immigrants shows no general pattern across the provinces, while the age distribution remains remarkably similar across all provinces. Fragmentary data suggest that there has been no dramatic change in the composition of emigrants over time, although there has been an aging process that reflects similar changes in the structure of the Canadian population.

With a declining rate of population growth due to natural causes and a substantially reduced level of net immigration, interprovincial migration assumed added importance as a component of provincial population growth in the 1970s. The new patterns reported in chapter 1 appear to have emerged in the mid-1970s and can be attributed to complementary changes in both out-migration and in-migration patterns. Quebecers were the least mobile provincial population, closely followed by Ontarians. The most mobile were the populations of the territories. Mobility did not change much over the decade, except perhaps in Saskatchewan, which had a less mobile population in the latter half of the 1970s. Ontario remained the most preferred destination, but Alberta replaced British Columbia as the second most preferred destination. People in their twenties and early thirties were the most likely to move interprovincially, and there was no substantial difference in the age pattern between the sexes in this regard. In general, however, younger migrants tended to be male-dominant and older migrants tended to be female-dominant. There were very insignificant differences between the provinces with respect to the sex ratio and age distribution of in-migrants.

Many of the unique demographic developments of the 1970s do *not* appear to be transitory. In the following chapter, therefore, they are used as a base in the formulation of alternative demographic projections for Canada and the provinces.

Canada's Population Outlook

A Brief Technical Overview

The methodologies employed in developing population calculations, and hence population futures, are briefly reviewed in this section. A discussion of the simple models precedes a summary of the more complicated approach adopted in this study to establish the common antecedents, to demonstrate the proposition of exponential-type population growth that underlined the writings of Malthus and others, and to explain the methodology employed in this study. The results of applying this methodology to Canada's population are then outlined in some detail. The numerical assumptions underlying these alternative population futures are detailed in the Appendix. It should be emphasized, once again, that the methodology employed in this study permits the choice of a wide range and combination of alternative demographic assumptions and, hence, the generation of a number of alternative population futures for Canada and the provinces. This approach not only facilitates an examination of the sensitivity of the results to the assumptions, but also permits the user to assign probabilities or weights to the various alternatives in accordance with his or her own judgement as to the likelihood of the alternatives' realizations in the years ahead (both of which are important aspects of strategic planning and policy analysis).

The common antecedent for all population calculations is the simple identity, introduced in chapter 1, which accounts for the change in the size of a nation's population by the net natural change (defined as births minus deaths) and by net international migration (defined as immigration minus emigration). Mathematically, this can be conveniently expressed with the identity:

$$P(t) - P(t-1) \equiv B(t) - D(t) + I(t) - E(t)$$

or

$$P(t) \equiv P(t-1) + B(t) - D(t) + I(t) - E(t)$$

where, for every time period (t),[1] P denotes population, B denotes births, D denotes deaths, I denotes immigration, and E denotes emigration. Given the population at the commencement of any time period (which is $P(0)$ in the above notation) and a time profile for each of the four components over the calculation horizon, it is possible to derive the total population ($P(t)$) over the complete time horizon by successive substitution into this identity.[2] This calculation horizon may reflect past or future history. It can be used both for inductive analyses, such as determining the hypothetical size of Canada's population under alternative hypothetical historical conditions, and for futures analyses, which is the orientation of this chapter. Both types of analysis could be referred to as population projections, although it is much more common for this terminology to be used for the latter type.[3]

Since these calculations can involve extensive amounts of data, demographers and statisticians have explored ways of reducing the data requirements by parametrizing the above identity. This enables the calculation to be based on a fewer number of important parameters, rather than on the entire time profile for each of the components of population change. This approach can be illustrated and used to demonstrate the concept of exponential-type population growth, which has underlined the works of many authors, by reintroducing some of the definitions presented in previous chapters. The crude birth rate (denoted by β) and the crude death rate (denoted by δ) can be defined for any time period (t) as:

$$\beta(t) = \frac{B(t)}{P(t-1)} \quad \text{and} \quad \delta(t) = \frac{D(t)}{P(t-1)} \quad \text{respectively,}$$

which can be written as:

$$B(t) = \beta(t)P(t-1) \quad \text{and} \quad D(t) = \delta(t)P(t-1) \quad \text{respectively.}$$

Invoking the simplifying assumptions that $\beta(t)$ and $\delta(t)$ are constant over time,[4] reduces the population identity to:

$$P(t) \equiv (1+\beta-\delta)\,P(t-1) + I(t) - E(t)$$

where β and δ are the assumed constant values of $\beta(t)$ and $\delta(t)$ respectively. Now the calculation has been simplified to specifying values for two parameters (β and δ), or rather their net difference $(\beta-\delta)$,[5] and the time profile for only the two migration components of

78

population change (or their net difference). Under the further simplifying assumption that net international migration is approximately constant (and denoted by K),[6] the population identity can be further simplified to:

$$P(t) \equiv (1+\beta-\delta)\, P(t-1) + K.$$

In mathematical terminology, this is a first-order difference equation, and by specifying values for β, δ and K and the size of an initial population, the population $P(t)$ can be calculated over any desired time horizon.[7] Extending the calculations to future time periods results in the simplest of all projections of population futures.

As noted previously, the population identity must be expanded for calculating provincial populations so as to include net interprovincial migration, that is:

$$P(t) \equiv P(t-1) + B(t) - D(t) + I(t) - E(t) + IM(t) - OM(t)$$

where IM and OM denote in-migration and out-migration over time interval $(t - 1)$ to (t) respectively. By applying the previous analysis and noting that an out-migration rate (denoted by $\phi(t)$) can be defined as:

$$\phi(t) = \frac{OM(t)}{P(t-1)} \quad \text{or} \quad OM(t) = \phi(t)\, P(t-1),$$

and that an in-migration rate (denoted by $\iota(t)$) could also be defined analogously as:[8]

$$\iota(t) = \frac{IM(t)}{P(t-1)} \quad \text{or} \quad IM(t) = \iota(t)\, P(t-1),$$

and, again for expository convenience, assuming that these rates are constant over the projection horizon, the provincial population identity can be written as:

$$P(t) \equiv (1+\beta-\delta+\iota-\phi)\, P(t-1) + I(t) - E(t),$$

where ι and ϕ are the constant in- and out-migration rates respectively. If, in addition, net international migration to the province is assumed to be constant (K) the provincial population identity becomes:

$$P(t) \equiv (1+\beta-\delta+\iota-\phi)\, P(t-1) + K.$$

This too is a first-order difference equation, and given values for β, δ, ι, ϕ and K, the calculation of a provincial population could proceed as before.[9] If the values of the parameters are such that $(\beta - \delta + \iota - \phi)$ is greater than zero, an exponential-type growth pattern will be generated.[10]

Consideration of the sex composition of the population introduces little complication to these calculations, since the male and female populations can be considered separately, each with their own relevant set of parameter values.[11] The complications that are introduced by this extension require that all births must be divided by sex, as must the totals of international and interprovincial migrants. Otherwise, the calculations are identical.

However, consideration of the age composition of the population introduces some complexity to the exercise, since the population identity must be applied to each age group separately and since the previous population to be used in the calculation (that is, $P(t-1)$) must be not only from the previous time period but also from the next youngest age group. Moreover, births only enter the calculation for the youngest age group in the population and do not appear in the calculations for all other age groups. Under these conditions the provincial population identity must be rewritten for each sex as follows[12]—for the youngest age group (denoted as group 1), as:

$$P^1(t) \equiv B(t) - D^1(t) + I^1(t) - E^1(t) + IM^1(t) - OM^1(t);$$

and for all other age groups (denoted j, where $1 < j \leqslant N$), as:

$$P^j(t) \equiv P^{j-1}(t-1) - D^j(t) + I^j(t) - E^j(t) + IM^j(t) - OM^j(t).$$

Note that births only affect the youngest age group ($j = 1$), which has no previous population history in its calculation (that is, $P^0(t-1)$ does not exist), whereas the opposite is true for all other age groups (that is, for $1 < j \leqslant N$). Total provincial population is then the simple summation over all age groups and over both sexes.[13]

Once again the parametric-based approaches outlined above can be applied to these equations, only in this case all relevant rates must be *age-sex-specific for each province*. Consequently, births are determined by age-sex-specific fertility rates (see Tables 2-3 and 2-4) or the associated aggregate total fertility rate (see Table 2-2), and deaths by age-sex-specific mortality rates (see Figure 2-2) or the associated aggregate life expectancy (see Table 2-6). The migration rates also must be age-sex-specific. In addition, for the components *not* specified as rates, but rather as levels (such as net international migration in the above illustrations), the magnitudes must be distributed over all the age-sex groups within each province. This is a substantial task and is the approach adopted in this study.[14]

Some General Methodological Observations

The population identities reviewed above can be applied either to past history (that is, *ex post*) or to future time periods (that is, *ex ante*). In either case, they trace out the numerical consequences of the chosen assumptions. If historical data are used for each component of population change, the calculations will reproduce recorded history accurately. However, if parametrizations are used to reduce the data requirements and if average or "representative" parameter values are used, the calculations will only approximate the historical data.[15] However, the gain in simplification may more than offset the slight loss in accuracy.

The main application of these procedures, however, is in developing population projections. Two different types of projections can be identified. The first, and perhaps less commonly used, type is the "what if" or alternative historical scenario—namely, the recalculation of past demographic history under an alternative set of conditions than actually prevailed historically. In this way, for example, it is possible to seek answers to such questions as, "What would have been Canada's demographic history if net immigration had been zero?" or "What would have been Canada's demographic history if the immigration wave of the early 1900s, or if the Baby Boom of the 1950s, or if the changed interprovincial migration patterns of the 1970s had never occurred?" Answers to questions such as these can be useful in understanding historical demographic change.

The second, and more commonly used, type is the projection into future time periods. In this application the time profiles or parameter values of each of the components of population change are assumed for the future time periods (usually based on historical data), and the numerical consequences with regard to future population are developed. Perhaps the most useful application from an economic policy viewpoint is the combination of these two types of projections, through which a series of *alternative* population futures is developed. This enables the sensitivity of the results to the assumptions to be clearly articulated. This study has adopted this approach.

In the construction of any population projection model, one of the crucial issues is the determination of which components of population change are to be specified in rate terms and which are to be specified in level terms.[16] In general, the use of rates relates the component explicitly to the source population, while the use of levels avoids such a relationship, although it always remains implicit. For example, if a provincial population is increasing in size, a constant (level) outflow of interprovincial migrants will imply a decreasing out-migration rate (and vice versa if the population is decreasing). Of course, it is possible for a contrasting rate to be observed for any specific age-sex group, but for all groups in the population the above relationship must hold.

The choice of specification for each component of population change depends on both theoretical and empirical considerations. As a general principle, the composition of the components in question should be related to the population "at risk."[17] The application of this principle would require that for any given (provincial) population:

- births be related to the age composition of the female population;
- deaths be related to the age-sex composition of the entire population;
- immigration be related to the compositions of the populations of all (or, at least, the most important) source countries of immigrants;
- emigration be related to the age-sex composition of the entire population;
- in-migration be related to the age-sex composition of the populations of all (or, at least, the most important) source provinces of in-migrants; and
- out-migration be related to the age-sex composition of the provincial population under consideration.

Under these conditions, empirical considerations might suggest that:

- rates be used for births, deaths, emigration and out-migration;
- levels be used for immigration;[18] and
- in-migration be related to the out-migration of the other provinces.[19]

Note that the requirement for interprovincial migration that total out-migration for the country must equal total in-migration imposes a constraint on the procedures to be adopted for these components. The final choice of specification for any component, however, depends on a combination of theoretical considerations and empirical reality. For example, if a rate has declined or can be expected to decline, then a constant level under a growing population might be an appropriate specification regardless of the above principle.

In developing its population projection models, Statistics Canada has been largely guided by the above considerations. In both its first and second generation of population projections,[20] births and deaths have been related to age-sex-specific rates for each province, and immigration has been specified in level terms. However, in both cases emigration also has been specified in *level* terms, contrary to the above recommendations, on the grounds that although "rates are more useful . . . it was decided [that] their use is not yet justified since so little is known about emigration."[21] Note, then, that a constant level of emigration will imply a declining emigration *rate* in an expanding population (and vice versa in a declining population).

For interprovincial migration, a number of alternative approaches have been investigated. In its first generation of population projections, Statistics Canada chose a levels approach, specifying alternative interprovincial migration patterns based on previous history.[22] As noted above, this has the disadvantage of not explicitly relating interprovincial migration to the source populations of migrants. For this reason a rate approach is preferable. Alternative strategies are possible within this approach. If both out-migration and in-migration rates (or their difference, the net interprovincial migration rate) are used, there is nothing in the procedure to ensure that overall consistency is imposed on the system; that is, that the total number of in-migrants equals the total number of out-migrants (or that net interprovincial migration equals zero) for the nation. Consequently, arbitrary adjustments often become necessary to ensure consistency under this approach.

An alternative approach would be to use origin-destination-specific migration rates (specified as a rate of the source province's population). Since each out-migrant is immediately assigned a destination, there is no problem with consistency, but such an approach has considerable, almost cumbersome, data requirements.[23] The method finally adopted for the second generation of Statistics Canada population projections was to use age-sex-specific out-migration rates for each province to obtain a total number (or pool) of out-migrants in each age-sex group for the country, which was then allocated back to the provinces as in-migrants, using an assumed proportional distribution for each age-sex group.[24] This method imposes national consistency by definition.

In summary, the methodology underlying the Statistics Canada population projection model is based on the standard population identities, which have been parametrized for simplification and modified to include age-sex compositional detail for provincial populations. A rate approach is applied to fertility and mortality, and to interprovincial migration, while a level approach is applied to international migration (both immigration and emigration). It should now be clear that to develop population futures (including alternative scenarios) a number of assumptions regarding these rates and levels are necessary.

Ideally, assumptions about future demographic developments in Canada and elsewhere should be based on a theoretical explanation that is consistent with past observed patterns. The development of appropriate theories and the confrontation of their hypotheses by observed data are cornerstones of scientific methodology in economics and elsewhere. Unfortunately, the *theory* of demographic change, especially the *economic* theory, remains rather fragmentary, with little *systematic* analysis being readily available in Canada and elsewhere. To be sure, much good work has been published, but it has been more descriptive than explanatory. Theories have been confronted by data, especially in analyses of census results, but hypotheses generally have been judged as being *individually* confirmed or not confirmed by the data (simple correlation analysis), rather than being used to develop an overall explanation of the observed data (multiple correlation analysis). This is particularly true of fertility patterns and is also applicable to international and interprovincial migration patterns, where economic variables would appear to be major determinants. The one component of demographic change probably not much influenced by economic considerations is mortality, although even here there might be some contribution of economic conditions to observed mortality patterns.

In the absence of well-developed theories that could provide some guidance to possible future values of the required parameters, demographers and other researchers have resorted to the "alternative scenarios" approach to demographic projections. Under this approach the "what if" type of projection is combined with the futures-type projection to develop a series of alternative possible future population scenarios. From an economic policy point of view, this approach has the advantage of permitting the sensitivity of the results to alternative assumptions to be explicitly explored. It has the disadvantage of providing little or no guidance as to the most likely outcome. Consequently, if the results are relatively insensitive to a variety of assumptions, the user can proceed with considerable confidence, but if the results are sensitive to alternative assumptions, the approach provides little guidance to the user. At the very least, given a range of feasible assumptions, a range of possible outcomes is obtained that can assist in eliminating certain unfeasible outcomes. Moreover, within this methodology it is possible to explore the types of alternative policies (with regard to immigration, for example) that might be able to achieve certain demographic objectives or targets at either the provincial or the national level.

The most common approach to the generation of alternative population futures is to specify a small set of alternative assumptions for each of the components of population change, and then to explore the impacts of alternative combinations of these various assumptions. This is the approach adopted by Statistics Canada, and it will be used in this study. The actual assumptions employed here are briefly summarized in the following section (with the details being presented in the Appendix). The results are outlined in the subsequent section.

A Summary of Assumptions

Table 3-1 presents an overview of the assumptions used in this study. Three alternative fertility patterns are considered—current (1.75 throughout), low (1.55 by 2001) and high (2.25 by 2001). The low fertility assumptions are much lower than anything previously published by Statistics Canada.[25] Two alternative mortality assumptions are considered, reflecting the need to take account of the recent (1975-77) life expectancy data. One (A) combines these data with those used in previous Statistics Canada projections; the other (B) extends the increasing life expectancy even further over the projection horizon. Similar to the Statistics Canada approach, three alternative net international migration assumptions are considered, all reflecting differences in immigration. Annual emigration is assumed to be 75,000 persons throughout; the immigration assumptions are for 140,000, 100,000 and 75,000 persons per year, the latter only being included to generate a hypothetical zero net immigration scenario for study purposes. Finally, three interprovincial migration patterns are considered: the continuation of the 1976-79 patterns; a partial return to the more "traditional" patterns of 1966-75; and a further movement towards western Canadian destinations than has been observed in recent history. Two scenarios are devoted to different combinations of out-migration rates and in-migration proportions to explore the sensitivity of results to the assumptions *within* the interprovincial migration patterns. In addition, the age-sex compositions of immigrants, emigrants and interprovincial migrants are based on data from

85

TABLE 3-1
SUMMARY OF ASSUMPTIONS UNDERLYING THE POPULATION PROJECTIONS FOR CANADA AND THE PROVINCES

Projection Number and Description	Fertility Rate for Canada[a]	Life Expectancy for Canada	Net Int'l. Migration to Canada (000's)	Interprov. Migration Pattern (Period)
1 No change	1.75	A[b]	65	1976-79
2 Increasing life expectancy	1.75	B[c]	65	1976-79
3 Low fertility	1.55	A	65	1976-79
4 High fertility	2.25	A	65	1976-79
5 Low immigration	1.75	A	25	1976-79
6 "Return" interprov. migration	1.75	A	65	1966-75[d]
7 "Westward" interprov. migration	1.75	A	65	C[e]
8 High population	2.25	B	65	1976-79
9 Low population	1.55	A	25	1976-79
10 High population and "westward" migration	2.55	B	65	C
11 Low population and "westward" migration	1.55	A	25	C
12 In-migration sensitivity	1.75	A	65	C/1976-79[f]
13 Out-migration sensitivity	1.75	A	65	1976-79/C[f]
14 Zero net int'l migration	1.75	A	0	1976-79

Notes: [a] Achieved by 2001.

[b] A - Increasing life expectancy based on 1971-76 trends.

[c] B - Further increases in life expectancy beyond those incorporated into A.

[d] A partial reversal to the 1966-75 patterns by 1986-87.

[e] C - Continuation of the 1976-79 patterns with further westward shift.

[f] In-migration pattern/out-migration pattern.

Source: Assumptions by the author — see text and Appendix for a description.

the late 1970s (the most recent available at the time of the research).

Each of these assumptions is implemented at the provincial level, resulting in province-specific assumptions for each of the six components of provincial population change—births, deaths, immigration, emigration, in-migration and out-migration. In the case of births, deaths and interprovincial migration, province-specific values were chosen, with the Canada-wide implications resulting from a summation of the province-specific assumptions. In the case of international migration—immigration and emigration—totals for the country were assumed and then distributed over the provinces. In all cases, a province-specific age-sex composition was developed for projection purposes.

With these assumptions in place, the only remaining decision is when to commence the projections (that is, the starting value for $P(t-1)$ in the population identities). Almost all published projections to date have used the 1976 census population as the starting point. Since this is becoming increasingly obsolete, the estimated 1979 population for Canada and the provinces was used as the starting population for this study. There were 23.7 million people in Canada on 1 June 1979 (see Table 2-1). The associated age-sex compositions are summarized in Figures 3-1 (for Canada in millions of persons) and 3-2 (for each province as a per cent of total provincial population). In most provinces and hence in Canada, the largest single five-year age group is 15 to 19 years, the exceptions being Newfoundland (10 to 14 years) and Alberta (20 to 24 years). Many of the other historical characteristics previously described, such as the rapidly decreased fertility in Quebec, are reflected in these compositions.

In summary, the 1979 estimated age-sex composition of the populations for the Canadian provinces is the starting point for a series of alternative population futures, which are based on various combinations of assumptions concerning the six components of provincial population change. The national results are a simple summation of the provincial results (including the territories). Although adopting the methodology and framework of the Statistics Canada population projections,[26] this study not only takes into consideration the data of the late 1970s, but also includes reports on additional alternative population futures for Canada and the provinces. The results of fourteen scenarios are examined in the following section, the assumptions underlying each having been briefly described above and summarized in Table 3-1. A detailed discussion of the assumptions is presented in the Appendix.

FIGURE 3-1
THE ESTIMATED AGE-SEX COMPOSITION OF
THE CANADIAN POPULATION, 1979
(000,000's)

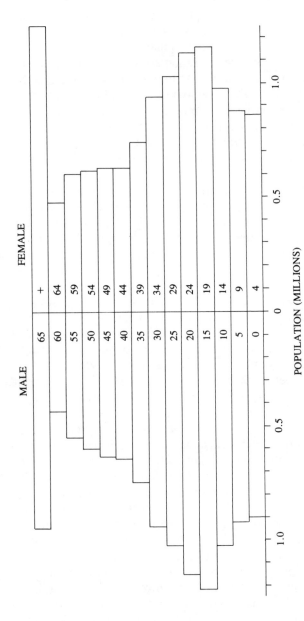

Source: Statistics Canada, *Postcensal Estimates of the Population by Sex and Age Canada and the Provinces*, 1 June 1979.

FIGURE 3-2

THE ESTIMATED AGE-SEX COMPOSITIONS OF THE PROVINCIAL POPULATIONS, 1979

(%)

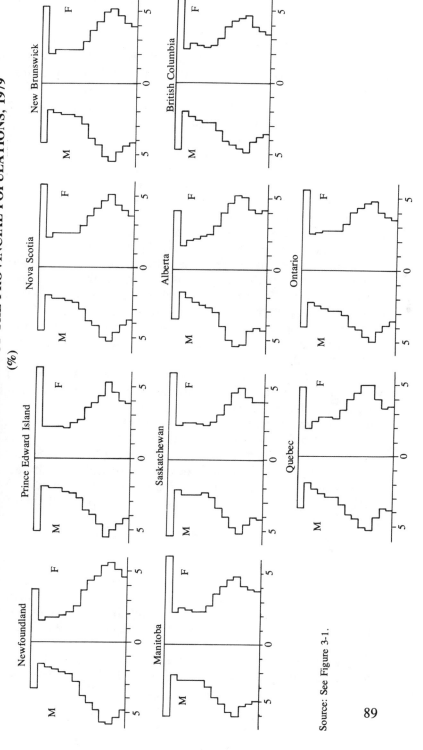

Source: See Figure 3-1.

Canada's Population Futures

The projected populations for Canada in the census years covering the period 1981 to 2051 for each of the fourteen scenarios is presented in Table 3-2. By the turn of the century (2001), these results show a population range between a low of 26.7 million and a high of 29.7 million persons—a range of almost 3 million people in only twenty years! This demonstrates that apparently small differences in assumptions can have substantial cumulative effects. For example, the difference between the low and high fertility scenarios results in a population difference of almost 1.7 million persons, and a difference between 100,000 and 140,000 immigrants a year results in a population difference of over one million persons.[27] The westward movement of interprovincial migrants increases the population slightly, since it is (implicitly) assumed that the migrants will conform to the, on average, higher fertility and lower mortality characteristics of the receiving provinces, such as the Prairie provinces; and the reverse is assumed for the scenario embodying a return to interprovincial migration patterns of the mid-1960s to the mid-1970s. It is interesting to note that even without any net international migration, the Canadian population can be expected to reach 26.8 million people by the year 2001.

The hypothetical maintenance of these patterns for a further fifty years generates some apparently surprising results. In almost all of the scenarios, including the no change scenario, the Canadian population starts to *decrease* after the 2020s. In cases that combine a low fertility (1.55 children per woman) and a low immigration (100,000 persons annually), the Canadian population is projected to be *below* current levels by the year 2041. As will become apparent, this occurs because the net natural increase becomes negative in the 2020s in most of the scenarios—a logical consequence, in part, of the Baby Boom of the 1950s. However, not all scenarios display this characteristic. The high fertility scenarios all show populations around 39 million persons by the year 2051—considerably higher than all of the remaining alternatives. It would appear, therefore, that long-run population futures are particularly sensitive to changes in fertility. In general, the *national* projections show relatively little sensitivity to interprovincial migration patterns (as might be expected), to changes in life expectancy, and, to a somewhat lesser degree, to levels of immigration.

A comparison of these projections with the Statistics Canada projections to the year 2001, summarized in Table 3-3, shows that, in

TABLE 3-2
ALTERNATIVE POPULATION FUTURES AND GROWTH FOR CANADA, 1981-2051

Projection Number[a]	Population (000's)				Growth (Average Annual Per Cent)		
	1981[b]	1991[b]	2001[b]	2051[b]	1981-91	1991-2001	2001-2051
1	24,187.3	26,748.0	28,480.7	28,931.9	1.01	0.63	0.03
2	24,187.3	26,802.5	28,622.5	29,367.9	1.03	0.66	0.05
3	24,180.4	26,501.0	27,851.1	25,041.5	0.92	0.50	-0.21
4	24,188.1	26,988.2	29,535.4	38,699.6	1.10	0.91	0.54
5	24,104.8	26,210.8	27,449.3	25,360.6	0.84	0.46	-0.16
6	24,187.3	26,743.0	28,463.6	28,720.3	1.01	0.63	0.02
7	24,187.3	26,749.8	28,486.5	29,014.2	1.01	0.63	0.04
8	24,188.1	27,043.0	29,679.2	39,202.5	1.12	0.93	0.56
9	24,098.0	25,968.6	26,838.8	21,732.7	0.75	0.33	-0.43
10	24,188.1	27,044.5	29,683.4	39,276.5	1.12	0.94	0.56
11	24,098.0	25,969.9	26,842.5	21,776.5	0.75	0.33	-0.42
12	24,187.3	26,749.0	28,484.0	28,977.8	1.01	0.63	0.03
13	24,187.3	26,748.8	28,483.2	28,968.3	1.01	0.63	0.03
14	24,053.1	25,865.1	26,783.6	22,985.7	0.73	0.35	-0.31

Notes: [a] See Table 3-1 for a brief description.
         [b] As at June 1.

Source: Projections by the author.

91

general, these population projections are slightly lower. This is the reflection of a mixture of lower fertility and higher emigration assumptions, but also a higher life expectancy assumption, which works in the opposite direction. It is not surprising, however, to find all projections with similar characteristics in the same "ball park."

The growth rate implications of these projections are also

TABLE 3-3
SUMMARY OF STATISTICS CANADA POPULATION
PROJECTIONS FOR CANADA, 1981-2001
(000's)

Projection Designation[a]	1981[b]	1991[b]	2001[b]
FIRST SERIES:			
1972-2001			
A	25,311.5	30,177.6	34,611.4
B	24,472.5	27,902.1	30,655.5
C	24,041.4	26,591.4	28,369.7
D	24,036.2	26,582.9	28,360.0
E	24,040.4	26,728.6	28,737.2
F	25,062.2	29,117.7	32,630.5
G	24,872.3	28,829.1	32,167.7
SECOND SERIES:			
1976-2001			
1	24,573.5	28,091.9	30,980.7
2	24,440.5	27,661.6	30,220.7
3	24,338.2	26,974.6	28,793.5
4	24,205.3	26,548.7	28,053.5
5	24,071.7	26,112.6	27,286.0
6	24,038.7	26,332.7	27,834.9
7	23,938.9	25,680.1	26,510.4

Notes: [a] For a description see Appendix, Table A-1.
     [b] As at June 1.

Sources: Statistics Canada, *Population Projections for Canada and the Provinces, 1972-2001* (Catalogue No. 91-514), and *Population Projections for Canada and the Provinces, 1976-2001* (Catalogue No. 91-520).

summarized in Table 3-2. Under a wide variety of assumptions, the average annual population growth rate is projected to be around 1 per cent in the 1980s and then to fall below 1 per cent in the 1990s for the first time in Canadian history. Even the most optimistic of these projections is for an average annual growth below 1 per cent, with most being closer to 0.5 per cent over the 1990s. Projecting these trends into the twenty-first century shows, basically, zero population growth. A range averaging between minus and plus 0.5 per cent per annum is projected under a wide variety of assumptions. It is clear from these results that the declining population growth experienced in Canada since the early 1960s can be expected to continue over the next two decades and beyond.

The same overall trend can be expected to a greater or lesser degree in each of the Canadian provinces. As can be seen from the results in Tables 3-4 and 3-5, population growth to the turn of the century is projected to be highest in Alberta and lowest in Quebec. It is also projected to be well above average in British Columbia and well below average in Manitoba. Increasing life expectancy (Projection 2) has very little impact on all growth rates.

Relative to the no change alternative (Projection 1),[28] increasing fertility to 2.25 children per woman by 2001 (Projection 4) has an overall impact of adding almost 0.2 per cent to average annual growth and has a slightly larger impact in the currently low fertility provinces (Quebec, Ontario and British Columbia). The impact of decreasing fertility to 1.55 children per woman by 2001 (Projection 3) reduces average annual growth by 0.1 per cent and has a slightly larger impact in the currently high fertility provinces (Newfoundland, Prince Edward Island, the Prairie provinces and the territories). Note, also, that this is sufficient for *negative* average annual growth to be experienced in Quebec, given the assumptions described above.

Reducing gross immigration from 140,000 to 100,000 persons per year (Projection 5) reduces the average annual growth rate by nearly 0.2 per cent, but has a much larger impact in Ontario and British Columbia than elsewhere. Manitoba and Alberta are also relatively more adversely affected by this development, as are the territories.

A return to the interprovincial migration patterns of 1966-75 (Projection 6) substantially reduces the growth rates of Saskatchewan and, to a lesser degree, Alberta and Prince Edward Island. The gainers in this scenario are Manitoba, Quebec, Ontario and the territories. Imposing a continued and more substantial westward drift on interprovincial migration (Projection 7) has a dramatic effect on the

TABLE 3-4
ALTERNATIVE POPULATION FUTURES FOR CANADA AND THE PROVINCES, 2001
(000's)

Projection Number	Can	Nfld	PEI	NS	NB	PQ	Ont	Man	Sask	Alta	BC	Yukon	NWT
1	28,480.7	678.9	154.0	1,007.3	850.4	6,338.0	10,196.1	1,087.6	1,218.7	3,300.7	3,578.2	22.6	48.2
2	28,622.5	682.3	154.4	1,011.6	853.9	6,362.7	10,259.2	1,093.7	1,226.3	3,317.2	3,590.1	22.7	48.5
3	27,851.1	650.4	149.3	985.6	831.4	6,220.9	10,007.6	1,060.1	1,173.9	3,201.5	3,504.1	21.7	44.7
4	29,535.4	695.0	158.6	1,045.8	882.6	6,590.1	10,597.6	1,123.5	1,248.7	3,410.7	3,711.1	23.3	48.6
5	27,449.3	669.8	150.7	987.6	834.2	6,169.2	9,728.8	1,047.3	1,189.7	3,175.3	3,428.1	21.8	46.7
6	28,463.6	677.2	148.7	987.7	826.3	6,626.4	10,545.8	1,168.7	1,012.9	2,833.1	3,546.9	29.9	60.0
7	28,486.5	643.7	143.4	943.8	796.9	6,228.3	9,835.1	1,110.0	1,218.8	3,642.2	3,863.0	19.6	41.7
8	29,679.2	698.3	159.0	1,050.1	886.2	6,615.0	10,661.5	1,129.7	1,256.4	3,427.5	3,723.2	23.4	48.9
9	26,838.8	641.6	146.1	966.3	815.6	6,054.9	9,547.7	1,020.7	1,145.9	3,079.2	3,356.6	21.0	43.3
10	29,683.4	662.0	148.0	983.6	830.2	6,499.9	10,282.5	1,153.2	1,256.5	3,783.3	4,021.8	20.3	42.3
11	26,842.5	608.5	136.1	905.7	764.6	5,950.0	9,205.2	1,042.0	1,146.0	3,401.6	3,627.1	18.2	37.4
12	28,484.0	660.0	147.5	966.1	815.7	6,285.4	10,003.5	1,096.0	1,220.7	3,489.3	3,734.5	20.9	44.4
13	28,483.2	662.6	149.9	985.0	831.5	6,281.4	10,028.4	1,102.3	1,217.7	3,451.7	3,706.1	21.2	45.5
14	26,783.6	674.5	149.0	982.0	829.0	6,260.8	9,362.4	990.1	1,163.6	2,995.3	3,310.4	21.5	45.2

Source: Projections by the author.

TABLE 3-5
ALTERNATIVE FUTURE POPULATION GROWTH FOR CANADA AND THE PROVINCES, 1981-2001
(Average Annual Per Cent)

Projection Number	Can	Nfld	PEI	NS	NB	PQ	Ont	Man	Sask	Alta	BC	Yukon	NWT
1	0.82	0.76	1.02	0.78	0.87	0.02	0.81	0.24	1.08	2.17	1.47	0.25	0.50
2	0.85	0.78	1.03	0.80	0.89	0.04	0.84	0.27	1.11	2.20	1.49	0.27	0.53
3	0.71	0.55	0.87	0.67	0.76	-0.08	0.71	0.11	0.89	2.02	1.37	0.06	0.13
4	1.00	0.88	1.17	0.97	1.06	0.21	1.00	0.40	1.20	2.34	1.66	0.40	0.54
5	0.65	0.70	0.92	0.68	0.78	-0.11	0.59	0.07	0.97	2.00	1.28	0.08	0.35
6	0.82	0.75	0.84	0.68	0.73	0.24	0.98	0.60	0.16	1.40	1.43	1.63	1.58
7	0.82	0.49	0.66	0.45	0.55	-0.07	0.63	0.34	1.08	2.67	1.86	-0.45	-0.22
8	1.03	0.90	1.18	0.99	1.08	0.23	1.03	0.43	1.23	2.37	1.68	0.43	0.57
9	0.54	0.48	0.76	0.58	0.67	-0.20	0.50	-0.06	0.78	1.84	1.18	-0.10	-0.02
10	1.03	0.63	0.82	0.66	0.75	0.14	0.85	0.53	1.23	2.87	2.07	-0.27	-0.15
11	0.54	0.22	0.41	0.25	0.35	-0.29	0.32	0.04	0.78	2.35	1.56	-0.80	-0.74
12	0.82	0.62	0.81	0.57	0.66	-0.02	0.71	0.28	1.09	2.45	1.69	-0.14	0.09
13	0.82	0.64	0.88	0.67	0.76	-0.03	0.72	0.31	1.08	2.40	1.65	-0.05	0.21
14	0.54	0.72	0.86	0.65	0.75	-0.04	0.42	-0.19	0.86	1.74	1.12	0.00	0.20

Sources: Tables 3-2 and 3-4.

provinces of Alberta and British Columbia, largely at the expense of the Atlantic provinces, Ontario, Manitoba and the territories.

Higher fertility rates, higher survival rates and gross immigration of 140,000 persons annually (Projection 8) increases average annual population growth to over 1 per cent in most provinces (including Ontario), exceptions being Quebec, Manitoba, Newfoundland and the territories. Conversely, lower fertility rates, unchanged survival rates and gross immigration of 100,000 persons annually (Projection 9) decreases population growth by almost 0.3 per cent per annum and results in negative average growth in Quebec, Manitoba and the territories.

The next two alternatives (Projections 10 and 11) repeat the previous two (Projections 8 and 9) but also include the westward drift interprovincial migration pattern. Under these conditions, average annual population growth for the high population alternative (Projection 10) approaches 3 per cent in Alberta and is greater than 2 per cent in British Columbia. In all other provinces (except Saskatchewan) average annual population growth is less than 1 per cent. The low population alternative (Projection 11) compounds the negative impacts on the population growth in all provinces east of Saskatchewan, with average population growth in Quebec falling to almost -0.3 per cent per annum.

Projections 12 and 13 display the sensitivity of provincial population growth to in-migration proportions and out-migration rates separately. The maintenance of current out-migration rates but with a westward orientation of the interprovincial migration pool (Projection 12) decreases average annual population growth in the provinces east of Manitoba by approximately 0.1 per cent and increases growth in Alberta and British Columbia by approximately 0.2 per cent. The maintenance of current in-migration proportions but with a change in out-migration rates that reduces out-migration in the western provinces (Projection 13) has a very similar impact.

Finally, setting net immigration at zero (Projection 14) (hence population change is determined solely by natural causes and interprovincial migration) quantitatively has a similar national impact to that of reducing net immigration to 100,000 persons annually and fertility to 1.55 children per woman by 2001 (that is, as Projection 9). The impacts of the former are, however, more favourable to the Atlantic provinces, Quebec, Saskatchewan and the territories, and less favourable to Ontario, Manitoba, Alberta and British Columbia.

Many of these results could have been expected from a careful analysis of the effects of the assumptions. However, the advantage of using a population projection model is not only to take explicit account of the different age structures of the provincial populations (see Figure 3-2), but also to be able to *quantitatively* assess the impacts of the alternative demographic assumptions. For example, given these assumptions for the remainder of the century, it is interesting to see:

- the *maximum* national average annual population growth for this period is around 1 per cent (Projection 8);
- the assumed improvements in life expectancy have a quantitatively negligible impact on provincial population growth (Projection 2);
- an increase in fertility has a proportionately smaller impact on population growth than a continuing decrease in fertility (Projections 3 and 4);[29]
- reducing gross immigration by 40,000 persons annually has only a slightly greater negative impact on average annual population growth than a continuing decrease in fertility to 1.55 children per woman by the year 2001 (Projections 3 and 5);
- changing interprovincial migration patterns can have a substantial impact on provincial population growth rates even though the national rate remains unaffected (Projections 6 and 7);
- a feasible range for average population growth for Canada and the provinces can be expected to be approximately between 0.5 and 1 per cent per annum (Projections 8 and 9);
- average population growth in Quebec could well be negative (Projections 3, 5, 6, 9, and 11 to 14);
- average annual growth could approach a provincial maximum of 3 per cent in Alberta (Projection 10), while the lowest provincial growth rate is −0.3 per cent per annum in Quebec (Projection 11);
- the assumed changes in in-migration proportions and out-migration rates have approximately the same quantitative impact on most provinces (Projections 12 and 13), but their combined effects are a little more than additive (compare Projection 7 with Projections 12 and 13);
- natural increase alone can be expected to account for annual population growth averaging around 0.5 per cent over the remainder of the century; and,
- a decrease in gross immigration of about 25,000 (from 100,000 to 75,000 persons annually) has approximately the same quantitative impact as gradually declining fertility of 0.2 children per woman (from 1.75 to 1.55) over this period (compare Projections 9 or 11 with Projection 14).

From these results it is also possible to confirm the likely continuing westward shift of the Canadian population. By the year 2001 the Prairie provinces are projected to account for between 17.6 per cent (Projection 6) and 21.0 per cent (Projection 7) of the Canadian population, up from 16.9 per cent in 1979. In addition, British Columbia, which accounted for 10.8 per cent of the Canadian population in 1979, is projected to increase its share to between 12.5 (Projection 6) and 13.6 per cent (Projection 7) by 2001. On the other hand, the two most populous provinces—Ontario and Quebec—are projected to decline in relative importance. In the no change scenario (Projection 1), Ontario's share declines slightly to 35.8 per cent (from 35.9 per cent in 1979), and Quebec's share declines noticeably to 22.3 per cent (from 26.5 per cent in 1979). The Atlantic provinces also suffer a decline in relative importance, from 9.5 per cent in 1979 to between 9.3 per cent and 8.9 per cent in 2001. All projections confirm the continuing westward shift of the Canadian population. Undoubtedly, numerous other similar quantitative assessments could be deduced from these results; this is an important advantage of quantitative population projection models.

Further, it can be deduced from these results that natural increase alone will account on average for 0.54 per cent annual population growth over the remainder of the century (Projection 14). A net intake of 25,000 immigrants (100,000 immigrants minus 75,000 emigrants) will account for an additional 0.11 per cent (Projection 5). A net intake of a further 40,000 immigrants (140,000 immigrants minus 75,000 emigrants) will contribute an additional 0.17 per cent (Projection 1). In fact, the addition of each 10,000 immigrants contributes a little over 0.04 per cent to average annual population growth in Canada over this period. Consequently, with a net intake of 65,000 persons annually over the remainder of the twentieth century, the natural increase will account for almost 66 per cent of population growth, and net international migration for the remaining 34 per cent, while a net intake of 25,000 persons annually implies figures of approximately 83 and 17 per cent respectively (see Table 3-6). Although closer to the historical average, this latter scenario (Projection 5) implies substantially reduced population growth through to the turn of the century and beyond. In summary, the importance of the net natural increase to population growth is likely to be reduced over the remainder of this century.

The reasons for the reduced importance of natural increase to population growth can be seen in Figure 3-3. Although the number of

TABLE 3-6
THE RELATIVE IMPORTANCE OF THE COMPONENTS OF
POPULATION GROWTH IN CANADA, 1981-2001
(%)

Projection Number	1981-1991		1991-2001	
	Net Natural	Net Migration[a]	Net Natural	Net Migration[a]
1	74.6	25.4	62.5	37.5
2	75.1	24.9	64.3	35.7
3	72.0	28.0	52.1	48.1
4	76.8	23.2	74.5	25.5
5	88.1	11.9	79.8	20.2
6	74.6	25.4	62.2	37.8
7	74.6	25.4	62.6	37.4
8	77.2	22.8	75.3	24.7
9	86.6	13.4	71.3	28.7
10	77.2	22.8	75.4	24.6
11	86.6	13.4	71.3	28.7
12	74.6	25.4	62.5	37.5
13	74.6	25.4	62.5	37.5
14	100.0	0	100.0	0

Note: [a] Net international migration.

Source: Projections by the author.

births are currently increasing (these are the children of the Baby Boom cohort), it is likely that a peak will be reached in the 1980s—early 1980s in the low fertility projection, mid-1980s in the no change projection, and late-1980s in the increased fertility projection—after which a decline is projected until the turn of the century. At the same time, the number of deaths is projected to increase along a somewhat increased trend line. The result is that the difference between births and deaths (the natural increase) narrows rapidly over the remainder of this century and becomes negative in the twenty-first century in most projections, the exact date depending on the characteristics of the projection.

This narrowing of the difference between the number of births and number of deaths is experienced to a lesser or greater degree in every province. By way of a summary, Table 3-7 shows the first year for

99

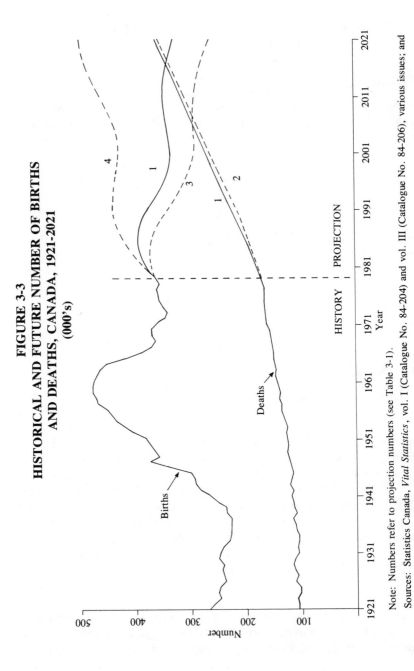

FIGURE 3-3
HISTORICAL AND FUTURE NUMBER OF BIRTHS
AND DEATHS, CANADA, 1921-2021
(000's)

Note: Numbers refer to projection numbers (see Table 3-1).

Sources: Statistics Canada, *Vital Statistics*, vol. I (Catalogue No. 84-204) and vol. III (Catalogue No. 84-206), various issues; and projections by the author.

TABLE 3-7
YEAR IN WHICH PROJECTED NET NATURAL INCREASE BECOMES NEGATIVE FOR CANADA AND THE PROVINCES[a]

Projec- tion Number	Can	Nfld	PEI	NS	NB	PQ	Ont	Man	Sask	Alta	BC	Yukon	NWT
1	2017	2027	2014	2012	2015	2002	2012	2019	2031	2042	2019	N	N
2	2018	2028	2015	2013	2016	2003	2013	2020	2032	2046	2020	N	N
3	2007	2015	2001	2001	2006	1999	2003	2004	2017	2024	2010	2038	2034
4	N	N	2031	N	N	2030[b]	N	N	N	N	N	N	N
5	2015	2026	2012	2010	2014	2001	2008	2017	2029	2037	2017	N	N
6	2017	2026	2011	2009	2013	2005	2014	2021	2023	2038	2018	N	N
7	2018	2025	2010	2007	2013	2002	2009	2020	2031	2043	2021	N	N
8	N	N	2031	N	N	2031[b]	N	N	N	N	N	N	N
9	2004	2015	2001	2000	2005	1998	2001	2002	2015	2022	2008	2033	2031
10	N	N	2028	N	N	2029[b]	N	N	N	N	N	N	N
11	2004	2013	1998	1999	2003	1998	2000	2003	2015	2023	2012	2033	2030
12	2017	2027	2013	2010	2014	2002	2011	2020	2031	2043	2020	N	N
13	2017	2026	2012	2010	2014	2002	2011	2020	2031	2042	2020	N	N
14	2014	2026	2011	2009	2013	2002	2005	2013	2027	2032	2015	N	N

Notes: [a] N means never over the period 1979-2051.
[b] Becomes positive again later in the period.

Source: Projections by the author.

which the net natural increase becomes negative for each province in each projection. A relatively early year implies that net natural increase will play a relatively reduced role in population growth. A relatively late year implies the opposite. As can be seen from Table 3-7, negative natural increases are very rarely projected for the remainder of this century. Needless to say, the earliest years when this may occur involve the low fertility alternatives (Projections 3, 9 and 11). Conversely, a higher fertility rate above replacement levels is generally sufficient to ensure that negative natural increases will never happen. In general, a negative natural increase occurs first in Quebec, then in Ontario and the Maritime provinces. It consistently occurs last in Alberta, but never in the (high fertility) territories.

Table 3-8 summarizes the contributions from each of the three net components of growth for the decades 1981-91 and 1991-2001 for each province under the no change scenario (Projection 1). The decreasing importance of natural increase is apparent across all provinces. Also apparent is the increasing importance of interprovincial migration. Over the period 1981-91, the natural increase remains the quantitatively most important component of population change in all provinces (except Manitoba), but by the 1991-2001 decade it is replaced by interprovincial migration in half of the provinces. International migration is important to Ontario and becomes a relatively more important component of population growth in the 1990s, when both the natural increase and interprovincial migration slow.

A similar analysis could be undertaken for each scenario, showing the relative importance of each of the components of population growth in each province. This would provide an almost bewildering array of information, much of which can be gleaned from the results discussed so far. For example, in Ontario the net natural increase always remains the most important component, followed by net international migration and net interprovincial migration. A reduction of 40,000 in international migration reduces total population change in Ontario by almost one-third. A return to the interprovincial migration patterns of 1966-75 has a quantitatively similar magnitude in Ontario to an increase in that province's fertility to 2.20 children per woman. Further westward movements result in substantial interprovincial losses for Ontario. In this latter regard, the effect in Alberta is, of course, the opposite. A return to the migration patterns of 1966-75 would make Alberta a net loser to interprovincial migration, whereas further westward movement would result in additional gains comparable to Ontario's additional losses. Moreover, these additional gains to

102

TABLE 3-8
PROJECTED COMPONENTS OF POPULATION GROWTH FOR CANADA AND THE PROVINCES, PROJECTION 1, 1981-2001
(000's)

Component	Can	Nfld	PEI	NS	NB	PQ	Ont	Man	Sask	Alta	BC	Yukon	NWT
1981-1991													
Net Natural	1,910.7	73.2	8.7	56.7	55.5	424.2	599.7	70.2	96.7	302.0	210.3	3.5	9.8
Net International	650.0	− 2.3	0.8	3.3	2.8	22.0	336.0	44.3	16.3	124.0	101.8	0.1	1.2
Net Interprovincial	0	−17.3	5.7	21.5	17.6	−318.3	− 49.3	−82.8	18.8	225.1	190.4	−3.2	−8.3
Total[a]	2,560.7	53.6	15.1	81.5	75.9	128.0	886.4	31.7	131.7	651.1	502.5	0.5	2.7
1991-2001													
Net Natural	1,082.8	56.8	4.4	28.3	32.4	146.4	308.4	37.6	70.8	256.2	130.9	2.7	8.1
Net International	650.0	− 2.3	0.8	3.3	2.8	22.0	336.0	44.3	16.3	124.0	101.8	0.1	1.2
Net Interprovincial	0	−12.8	8.0	31.7	24.1	−275.2	− 16.1	−62.5	16.8	122.2	173.2	−2.2	−7.4
Total[a]	1,732.8	41.7	13.2	63.2	59.3	−106.9	628.3	19.4	103.8	502.4	405.9	0.6	1.9

Note: [a] Totals may not be exact due to rounding.

Source: Projections by the author.

interprovincial in-migration would mean that net interprovincial migration gains would exceed those of the natural increase for Alberta. The results also verify the greater quantitative significance of interprovincial migration as compared to international migration in Alberta. Similar analyses can be carried out for the remaining provinces.

The final aspect of the population projections to be examined in this chapter is the age-sex compositions of the projected populations. Figure 3-4 summarizes the composition of the national population for the no change scenario (Projection 1) in 1991 and in 2001. Clearly, the relatively large number of teenagers of the late 1970s are in their late twenties and early thirties by the year 1991 and in their late thirties and early forties by the year 2001.

Of particular interest for public policy are the age groups at either end of the age spectrum. It is apparent that in spite of continued low average fertility rates (held constant at 1.75 children per woman), the relatively larger number of women in their childbearing years in the 1980s (a reflection of the Baby Boom) produces a baby "boomlet" (see Figure 3-3). This is reflected in an increase in the base of the population (see top half of Figure 3-4). However, this boomlet does not continue into the 1990s, since by this time the children of the "baby bust" period of the mid-1960s (see Figure 3-3) are entering their dominant childbearing years. Consequently, the number of young people declines. This decline is reflected in the base of the population "pyramid" (see bottom half of Figure 3-4). At constant fertility rates, the numbers in the youngest five-year group (0 to 4 years) in 2001 will be smaller than any other five-year group up to age 55 years. This will be a unique experience in Canadian demographic history. At the other end of the age spectrum, the numbers of elderly persons (65 years and over) are projected to expand rapidly. Their estimated number in 1979 was 2.2 million; by 1991 the number is projected to grow to over 3 million (an increase of 38 per cent), and by 2001 the number is projected to be around 3.5 million (a further increase of 21 per cent). In addition, this group is projected to become heavily female-dominant, a reflection of the difference in the life expectancy rates between males and females.

The decreasing numbers of the young and increasing numbers of the elderly over the next two decades reflect a continuation of the aging process throughout Canadian demographic history. The relatively more rapid aging of the 1970s can be expected to continue for the rest of this century and beyond. Moreover, this trend, if anything, is

FIGURE 3-4
THE FUTURE AGE-SEX COMPOSITIONS OF
THE CANADIAN POPULATION, 1991 AND 2001
(000,000's)

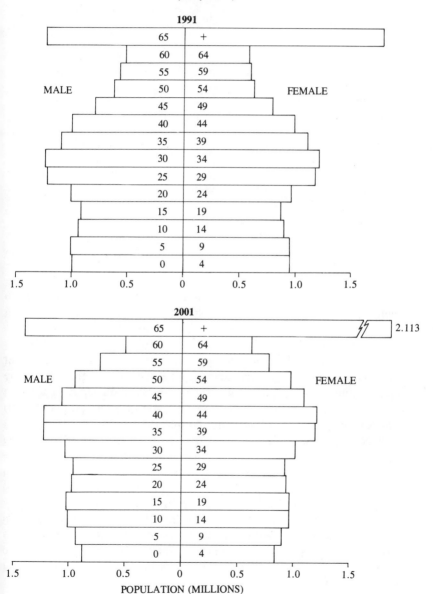

TABLE 3-9

SEX AND AGE COMPOSITION OF THE CANADIAN POPULATION, PROJECTION 1, 1981-2051

			Age Composition (%)			
Census Year	Sex Ratio[a]	Median Age (Years)	0-14 Years	15-64 Years	65+ Years	0-14 Years and 65+ Years
1981	0.984	29.5	22.5	67.8	9.7	32.2
1991	0.971	33.0	21.4	67.2	11.4	32.8
2001	0.962	36.9	19.4	68.3	12.3	31.7
2011	0.955	39.3	17.4	69.1	13.5	30.9
2021	0.945	40.5	17.2	66.2	16.6	33.8
2031	0.933	42.0	16.4	62.8	20.9	37.2
2041	0.927	42.4	16.2	63.1	20.8	36.9
2051	0.927	42.0	16.4	62.9	20.7	37.1

Note: [a] Ratio of males to females.

Source: Projections by the author.

accelerating. Table 3-9 shows that the median age is expected to increase from 29.5 years in 1981, to 33.0 years in 1991, and to 36.9 years in 2001. In other words, the median age of the Canadian population, which rose 3.2 years in the 1970s (see Table 1-2), is projected to rise 3.5 years over the 1980s and a further 3.9 years over the 1990s. Similarly, the modal age (the age or age group with the largest number of people) is also rising rapidly and is approaching the median, a situation that is also characteristic of an aging population. This process is projected to continue into the twenty-first century.

In addition, the Canadian population, expected in the 1981 census to show female dominancy for the first time, will become even more female-dominant. As shown in Table 3-9, the sex ratio drops from 0.984 males per female in 1981, to 0.962 by the year 2001, and to 0.927 by the year 2051. This is especially apparent in the elderly population, where the sex ratio falls from 0.75 in 1981, to 0.66 in 2001, and to 0.65 in 2051. In other words, there are currently three elderly males for every four elderly females, but by the turn of the century the ratio will be two elderly males for every three elderly females.

106

One feature of Table 3-9 is worth noting, even if it is largely hypothetical. The aging process is projected to come to an end around 2041. All the indicators show a population beginning to get younger by 2051! This occurs primarily because the large cohorts associated with the Baby Boom generation will have largely passed away by the 2040s and the age composition of the population will no longer be dominated by this cohort under the assumed conditions. This hypothetical scenario emphasizes that this feature of the current Canadian population can be expected to have continuing effects on future demographic history—at least until the 2040s.

These projected compositional features are largely unaffected by the choice of assumptions. Table 3-10 outlines the summary compositional

TABLE 3-10
ALTERNATIVE SEX AND AGE COMPOSITIONS OF THE CANADIAN POPULATION, 1979 AND 2001

Year and Projection Number	Sex Ratio[a]	Median Age (Years)	Age Composition (%)			
			0-14 Years	15-64 Years	65 + Years	0-14 Years and 65 + Years
1979	0.987	28.8	23.5	67.2	9.3	32.8
2001						
1	0.962	36.9	19.4	68.3	12.3	31.7
2	0.958	37.0	19.3	68.1	12.6	31.9
3	0.960	37.6	17.9	69.5	12.6	30.5
4	0.965	35.8	22.1	66.0	11.9	34.0
5	0.964	37.2	19.2	68.3	12.5	31.7
6	0.962	36.9	19.3	68.3	12.3	31.7
7	0.962	36.9	19.4	68.3	12.3	31.7
8	0.962	35.9	22.0	65.8	12.2	34.2
9	0.962	37.8	17.7	69.5	12.8	30.5
10	0.962	35.9	22.0	65.8	12.2	34.2
11	0.962	37.8	17.7	69.5	12.8	30.5
12	0.962	36.9	19.4	68.3	12.3	31.7
13	0.962	36.9	19.4	68.3	12.3	31.7
14	0.964	37.5	19.1	68.4	12.5	31.6

Note: [a] Ratio of males to females.
Sources: Statistics Canada and projections by the author.

measures for each of the fourteen projections for the year 2001. A comparison of this year with 1979 (or 1981—see Table 3-9) shows that regardless of the alternative chosen, the male proportion of the population will decline, resulting in a decline of the sex ratio from a 1979 value of 0.987 to one of around 0.96 by the year 2001. In general, higher fertility (for example, Projection 4), which tends to be male-dominant, and lower immigration (for example, Projection 5), which tends to be female-dominant, slightly increases the proportion of males and hence the sex ratio.

The median age is slightly more sensitive to the assumptions, but regardless of the chosen projection one conclusion is inescapable. The median age will increase from 28.8 years in 1979 to over 35.8 years (Projection 4) by 2001, an increase of almost 25 per cent. In fact, the actual increase could be even more—perhaps to a high of 37.8 years by 2001 (Projection 9), an increase of over 30 per cent. Not surprisingly, increases in fertility (Projections 4, 8 and 10) tend to moderate the increase, while decreases in mortality (Projection 2) tend to increase the median age. Since immigrants tend, on average, to be younger than the Canadian population, decreases in immigration (Projections 5, 9, 11 and 14) also tend to increase the median age.

Perhaps the most sensitive of the three summary measures in Table 3-10 to the assumptions is the age composition of the population, but even here the trends are inescapable. The percentage of the elderly (65 years and over) members of the population, at 9.3 per cent in 1979, is projected to increase to over 12 per cent by the year 2001—an increase of almost one-third over the remainder of the century. Obviously, this figure will be even further increased by improved survival rates (Projection 2) and by decreased fertility rates (Projections 3, 9 and 11). It is also increased slightly by lower immigration (Projections 5, 9, 11 and 14). However, the overall range is relatively narrow.

At the other end of the age spectrum, the sensitivity of the percentage of young persons to fertility rates is readily apparent from these results. However, once again an inescapable conclusion is evident from data in Table 3-10. The percentage of young, pre-working-age (0 to 14 years) members of the population in 2001 is projected to be *below* the estimated 1979 value of 23.5 per cent—*even if* fertility rises to above replacement levels (Projections 4, 8 and 10). With further declines in fertility (to 1.55 children per woman by 2001) this group may comprise as little as 17.7 per cent of the Canadian population (Projections 9 and 11). Although primarily dictated by Canadian fertility, this percentage is decreased slightly by reduced

108

immigration, which tends to be of a higher proportion of working-age persons than the Canadian population.[30]

The decreasing percentage of the young and the increasing percentage of the elderly underscore the projected aging of the Canadian population. They also provide conflicting trends within the non-working-age population. In 1979 these two groups together comprised 32.8 per cent of the Canadian population. The projection results show that unless fertility rises to above-replacement levels (Projections 4, 8 and 10), this dependent population will likely be relatively *smaller* by 2001. Over the remainder of this century, the decline in the number of the young is likely to more than offset the increase in the number of the elderly.[31] This means that there will be relatively more people of working age (15 to 64 years) than has ever been experienced in Canadian demographic history (see Table 1-2). Moreover, *even if* fertility rises to above replacement levels, the percentage of working-age persons is projected to be higher than had ever been experienced before the mid-1970s.

In summary, the wide variety of population futures shows some inescapable conclusions. The Canadian population is very likely to continue to become more female-dominant, to age substantially, and to have relatively more people of working age over the balance of this century and beyond. The new levels suggested by these trends have never been experienced before in Canadian demographic history.

All of these trends can be expected to be experienced in each of the Canadian provinces and territories, to a greater or lesser degree. Table 3-11 outlines the sex ratios in each of the provinces for each of the projections for 1979 (estimated) and 2001 (projected). The decline in sex ratios, with one exception, is apparent throughout.[32] The populations of Ontario and Manitoba are projected to surpass Quebec as the most female-dominant populations, while those of Saskatchewan and Prince Edward Island are projected to surpass Newfoundland and Alberta as the most male-dominant populations. These trends primarily reflect the combinations of assumed out-migration rates and in-migration proportions and the associated age-sex compositions of these interprovincial migration flows (see the Appendix). In general, Quebec, Ontario and Manitoba are projected to have below-average sex ratios, Nova Scotia and British Columbia are projected to have approximately average sex ratios, and Newfoundland, Prince Edward Island, Saskatchewan and Alberta are projected to maintain male-dominant populations. New Brunswick, although with an above-average sex ratio, is projected to become a female-dominant

TABLE 3-11
ALTERNATIVE SEX RATIOS FOR CANADA AND THE PROVINCES, 1979 AND 2001
(Ratio of Males to Females)

Year and Projection Number	Can	Nfld	PEI	NS	NB	PQ	Ont	Man	Sask	Alta	BC	Yukon	NWT
1979	0.987	1.030	1.010	0.993	1.000	0.977	0.977	0.982	1.016	1.027	0.990	1.107	1.047
2001													
1	0.962	1.008	1.013	0.969	0.987	0.958	0.942	0.941	1.011	1.004	0.960	1.055	0.928
2	0.958	1.010	1.013	0.968	0.987	0.958	0.935	0.936	1.013	1.000	0.957	1.045	0.929
3	0.960	1.006	1.012	0.967	0.986	0.957	0.941	0.939	1.009	1.002	0.959	1.047	0.927
4	0.965	1.009	1.015	0.972	0.989	0.962	0.946	0.945	1.011	1.005	0.963	1.044	0.929
5	0.964	1.009	1.015	0.969	0.988	0.959	0.944	0.943	1.012	1.006	0.963	1.057	0.930
6	0.962	1.009	1.015	0.968	0.987	0.962	0.945	0.947	1.009	0.998	0.958	1.048	0.958
7	0.962	1.007	1.011	0.965	0.984	0.957	0.939	0.943	1.011	1.007	0.966	1.053	0.922
8	0.962	1.011	1.015	0.971	0.989	0.961	0.939	0.940	1.014	1.002	0.960	1.053	0.929
9	0.962	1.007	1.012	0.967	0.986	0.958	0.942	0.940	1.010	1.005	0.961	1.059	0.924
10	0.962	1.009	1.014	0.967	0.986	0.960	0.935	0.942	1.014	1.005	0.966	1.051	0.923
11	0.962	1.005	1.010	0.963	0.983	0.957	0.938	0.942	1.011	1.008	0.967	1.045	0.918
12	0.962	1.007	1.012	0.966	0.985	0.958	0.941	0.942	1.011	1.006	0.963	1.049	0.926
13	0.962	1.008	1.013	0.967	0.986	0.958	0.941	0.943	1.011	1.005	0.963	1.048	0.928
14	0.964	1.007	1.014	0.968	0.987	0.957	0.945	0.944	1.012	1.011	0.963	1.048	0.932

Notes: [a] See note 32 in the text.
[b] See note 33 in the text.

Sources: Statistics Canada and projections by the author.

population. The Yukon is projected to remain male-dominant, but under these assumptions, the Northwest Territories are projected to become a female-dominant population.[33]

Once again high fertility rates (Projection 4) and low immigration (Projections 5 and 14) generally increase the sex ratios. In addition, a return to 1966-75 interprovincial migration patterns tends to increase the sex ratios of all provinces east of Saskatchewan (Projection 6) and to decrease the sex ratios of the remaining provinces, whereas a further westward movement of interprovincial migrants tends to have the opposite impacts (Projection 7). These impacts are, however, relatively slight, especially in comparison to the overall downward trend of the sex ratio over the projection horizon.

Table 3-12 presents the projected median age in the year 2001 for each of the provinces, under each of the alternative projections. The overall trend of a rapidly rising median age is apparent in all provinces and in all projections. Newfoundland is projected to remain the youngest province,[34] while Quebec is projected to replace British Columbia as the oldest province. Ontario is also projected to surpass British Columbia in median age, which largely reflects the assumed age composition of interprovincial migrants.[35] Quebec and Ontario display lower than average out-migration rates and, relative to their populations, lower in-migration proportions, while British Columbia displays a higher than average out-migration rate and receives more than its population share of in-migrants. Since the median age of interprovincial migrants tends to be lower than that of the population at large,[36] British Columbia's population is rejuvenated more than those of Quebec and Ontario and hence does not age as rapidly.[37]

With regard to the alternative projections, decreases in fertility (Projections 3, 9 and 11) and immigration (Projections 5, 9, 11 and 16) tend to increase the median age, as do increases in survival rates (Projection 2). In addition, a return to recent (1966-75) interprovincial migration patterns tends to increase the median age in the Atlantic provinces and in the western provinces of Saskatchewan, Alberta and British Columbia (Projection 6). A further westward movement of interprovincial migrants tends to increase the median age for every province east of Manitoba and reduce it for the remaining provinces (Projection 7). Again these results are a reflection of the combinations of migration assumptions.

Finally, Tables 3-13 to 3-15 show the age compositions of the projected provincial populations for each of the projections. Table 3-13 shows the projected percentages of the non-working-age young (0 to

111

TABLE 3-12
ALTERNATIVE MEDIAN AGE FOR CANADA AND THE PROVINCES, 1979 AND 2001
(Years)

Year and Projection Number	Can	Nfld	PEI	NS	NB	PQ	Ont	Man	Sask	Alta	BC	Yukon	NWT
1979	28.8	24.1	27.7	28.2	26.9	28.9	29.6	29.0	28.3	26.9	30.2	25.0	20.7
2001													
1	36.9	33.8	36.8	37.0	36.5	38.1	37.5	36.8	35.5	34.0	37.2	29.6	24.3
2	37.0	33.9	36.8	37.1	36.5	38.2	37.6	36.8	35.6	34.1	37.2	29.7	24.3
3	37.6	35.2	37.7	37.6	37.1	38.7	38.0	37.5	36.7	34.9	37.8	30.7	26.4
4	35.8	33.0	35.9	35.9	35.3	37.0	36.3	35.7	34.7	32.9	36.1	28.7	24.1
5	37.2	33.9	36.9	37.1	36.6	38.3	37.8	37.0	35.7	34.2	37.5	29.7	24.3
6	36.9	34.0	37.1	37.2	36.7	37.8	37.3	36.4	36.8	34.4	37.3	29.8	24.7
7	36.9	34.1	37.2	37.4	36.8	38.2	37.7	36.6	35.5	33.8	36.8	29.6	24.2
8	35.9	33.1	35.9	36.0	35.4	37.0	36.5	35.8	34.8	33.0	36.1	28.8	24.1
9	37.8	35.2	37.8	37.8	37.2	38.9	38.3	37.8	36.8	35.1	38.1	30.8	26.4
10	35.9	33.4	36.4	36.4	35.8	37.2	36.7	35.6	34.8	32.8	35.7	28.7	24.0
11	37.8	35.5	38.3	38.1	37.6	39.0	38.6	37.7	36.8	34.9	37.6	30.7	26.3
12	36.9	33.9	37.0	37.2	36.7	38.2	37.6	36.7	35.5	33.9	37.0	29.7	24.2
13	36.9	34.0	37.0	37.1	36.6	38.2	37.6	36.7	35.5	33.9	37.0	29.6	24.3
14	37.5	33.9	37.1	37.3	36.7	38.4	38.2	37.5	35.9	34.5	37.8	29.8	24.3

Sources: Statistics Canada and projections by the author.

112

TABLE 3-13
ALTERNATIVE PERCENTAGES OF YOUNG PEOPLE (0 TO 14 YEARS) IN THE POPULATIONS OF CANADA AND THE PROVINCES, 1979 AND 2001
(%)

Year and Projection Number	Can	Nfld	PEI	NS	NB	PQ	Ont	Man	Sask	Alta	BC	Yukon	NWT
1979	23.5	31.3	25.9	24.5	26.0	22.7	23.0	24.1	25.2	25.3	22.2	27.3	36.6
2001													
1	19.4	23.4	20.7	19.4	19.7	18.5	18.6	19.8	21.8	21.7	19.0	23.9	31.7
2	19.3	23.3	20.7	19.3	19.7	18.4	18.6	19.8	21.8	21.6	18.9	23.8	31.7
3	17.9	20.6	18.7	17.9	18.2	17.2	17.4	18.1	19.3	19.7	17.6	21.7	27.3
4	22.1	25.1	22.9	22.2	22.5	21.4	21.6	22.2	23.6	24.1	21.7	26.2	32.1
5	19.2	23.4	20.6	19.3	19.6	18.3	18.4	19.6	21.7	21.6	18.8	23.9	31.6
6	19.3	23.3	20.5	19.2	19.5	18.7	18.8	20.0	20.9	21.3	18.9	24.2	31.7
7	19.4	23.3	20.4	19.1	19.5	18.4	18.5	19.9	21.8	21.9	19.3	24.0	31.7
8	22.0	25.0	22.9	22.1	22.4	21.3	21.5	22.2	23.6	24.0	21.7	26.1	32.2
9	17.7	20.6	18.5	17.8	18.1	17.1	17.2	17.9	19.2	19.6	17.4	21.4	27.0
10	22.0	24.8	22.6	21.8	22.2	21.2	21.3	22.3	23.6	24.3	22.0	26.1	32.2
11	17.7	20.4	18.3	17.6	17.9	17.0	17.0	18.0	19.2	19.8	17.7	21.4	27.1
12	19.4	23.4	20.5	19.2	19.5	18.4	18.6	19.8	21.8	21.8	19.1	23.9	31.8
13	19.4	23.3	20.6	19.3	19.6	18.4	18.6	19.9	21.8	21.8	19.1	24.1	31.7
14	19.1	23.4	20.5	19.2	19.5	18.3	18.2	19.4	21.6	21.4	18.6	23.8	31.6

Sources: Statistics Canada and projections by the author.

TABLE 3-14
ALTERNATIVE PERCENTAGES OF WORKING-AGE PEOPLE (15 TO 64 YEARS) IN THE POPULATIONS OF CANADA AND THE PROVINCES, 1979 AND 2001

(%)

Year and Projection Number	Can	Nfld	PEI	NS	NB	PQ	Ont	Man	Sask.	Alta	BC	Yukon	NWT
1979	67.2	61.6	62.4	65.1	64.5	68.9	67.5	64.7	63.3	67.1	67.3	69.4	60.1
2001													
1	68.3	66.6	66.7	68.2	68.6	68.9	68.2	66.3	65.8	69.2	68.6	69.9	61.2
2	68.1	66.4	66.6	68.0	68.5	68.7	67.8	66.1	65.6	69.0	68.6	70.0	61.2
3	69.5	69.0	68.3	69.4	69.8	69.9	69.2	67.6	67.8	70.9	69.8	71.9	65.1
4	66.0	65.1	64.9	65.9	66.2	66.4	65.7	64.3	64.3	67.1	66.3	67.8	60.9
5	68.3	66.6	66.7	68.2	68.6	68.9	68.1	66.2	65.8	69.2	68.6	70.2	61.3
6	68.3	66.6	66.5	68.0	68.4	69.0	68.3	66.6	65.3	68.9	68.6	70.1	61.8
7	68.3	66.5	66.4	67.9	68.3	68.8	68.0	66.4	65.8	69.5	68.9	69.9	61.2
8	65.8	64.9	64.8	65.7	66.1	66.3	65.4	64.1	64.1	66.9	66.3	67.9	60.9
9	69.5	69.0	68.3	69.3	69.8	69.9	69.1	67.5	67.8	70.9	69.7	72.4	65.4
10	65.8	64.8	64.5	65.4	65.9	66.2	65.3	64.2	64.1	67.1	66.5	68.0	60.5
11	69.5	68.8	68.0	69.0	69.5	69.8	68.9	67.7	67.8	71.2	70.1	72.0	65.1
12	68.3	66.5	66.5	68.1	68.4	68.9	68.1	66.3	65.8	69.3	68.8	69.9	61.2
13	68.3	66.5	66.5	68.1	68.5	68.9	68.1	66.3	65.8	69.3	68.8	69.8	61.2
14	68.4	66.6	66.7	68.2	68.6	69.0	68.2	66.2	65.8	69.4	68.7	70.1	61.4

Sources: Statistics Canada and projections by the author.

TABLE 3-15

ALTERNATIVE PERCENTAGES OF ELDERLY PEOPLE (65 YEARS AND OVER) IN THE POPULATIONS OF CANADA AND THE PROVINCES, 1979 AND 2001

(%)

Year and Projection Number	Can	Nfld	PEI	NS	NB	PQ	Ont	Man	Sask	Alta	BC	Yukon	NWT
1979	9.3	7.2	11.5	10.4	9.5	8.4	9.6	11.2	11.5	7.6	10.5	3.7	3.2
2001													
1	12.3	10.0	12.6	12.4	11.7	12.7	13.2	13.9	12.4	9.1	12.4	6.2	7.1
2	12.6	10.3	12.7	12.7	11.9	12.9	13.6	14.2	12.6	9.3	12.5	6.2	7.1
3	12.6	10.4	13.0	12.7	12.0	12.9	13.4	14.3	12.9	9.4	12.7	6.5	7.6
4	11.9	9.7	12.2	12.0	11.3	12.2	12.7	13.5	12.1	8.8	12.0	6.0	7.0
5	12.5	10.0	12.7	12.5	11.8	12.8	13.5	14.2	12.5	9.2	12.6	6.0	7.1
6	12.3	10.0	13.0	12.7	12.1	12.3	12.9	13.3	13.8	9.8	12.5	5.7	6.5
7	12.3	10.3	13.2	13.0	12.2	12.8	13.5	13.7	12.4	8.7	11.8	6.1	7.2
8	12.2	10.1	12.3	12.2	11.4	12.4	13.1	13.7	12.3	9.0	12.0	6.0	7.0
9	12.8	10.5	13.1	12.8	12.1	13.0	13.7	14.5	13.0	9.5	12.9	6.2	7.6
10	12.2	10.4	12.9	12.7	11.9	12.5	13.4	13.5	12.3	8.6	11.5	5.9	7.3
11	12.8	10.8	13.7	13.4	12.6	13.2	14.0	14.3	13.0	9.1	12.3	6.6	7.8
12	12.3	10.1	13.0	12.7	12.0	12.7	13.4	13.9	12.4	8.9	12.1	6.2	7.0
13	12.3	10.1	12.9	12.6	11.9	12.7	13.3	13.8	12.4	9.0	12.1	6.1	7.0
14	12.5	10.0	12.8	12.6	11.9	12.6	13.5	14.4	12.6	9.2	12.7	6.1	7.1

Sources: Statistics Canada and projections by the author.

14 years), Table 3-14 shows the projected percentages of working-age persons (15 to 64 years), and Table 3-15 shows the projected percentages of the non-working-age elderly (65 years and over). The projected declining percentage of the young is apparent in *all* provincial populations, *even* in the high fertility scenarios (Projections 4, 8 and 10). The low fertility provinces of Quebec and Ontario are projected to replace British Columbia as the provinces with the lowest percentages of the young, while high fertility Newfoundland and territories are projected to continue with the highest percentages. In general, Quebec, Ontario and British Columbia have below-average percentages of the young and all other provinces have above-average percentages. As expected, these percentages rise with increased fertility (Projections 4, 8 and 10) and fall with increased life expectancy (Projection 2) and decreased immigration (Projections 5, 9, 11 and 14). A return to the migration patterns of 1966-75 (Projection 6) increases these percentages in Quebec, Ontario, Manitoba and the territories, and reduces them everywhere else. However, a continuation of the westward movement of interprovincial migrants increases the percentages west of Ontario, particularly in Alberta and British Columbia. This occurs because the foremost age for interprovincial migration is the twenties (see Figure 2-3), and people of this age often have young children.

At the other end of the age spectrum (Table 3-15), the percentage of the elderly is projected to increase in *every* province, especially in Quebec and, to a lesser extent, in Ontario. Alberta is projected to replace Newfoundland as the province with the lowest percentage of the elderly, while Manitoba is projected to replace Saskatchewan as the province with the highest percentage (except in the case of a return to the interprovincial migration patterns of 1966-75 [Projection 6]). As before, these percentages are increased by improved life expectancy (Projection 2), by decreased fertility (Projections 3, 9 and 11) and by decreased immigration (Projections 5, 9, 11 and 14). A recurrence of the 1966-75 interprovincial migration patterns (Projection 6) generally increases these percentages in the Maritimes and in the three westernmost provinces, and decreases them in Quebec, Ontario and Manitoba. If interprovincial migration continues to move westward (Projections 7, 10 and 11), the percentages increase in all provinces except Alberta, British Columbia and, perhaps, Manitoba.

The general downward trend in the proportion of the young and general upward trend in the proportion of the elderly in every province confirm the aging process summarized previously. It is interesting to discover that, generally, in *all* provinces the declining percentages of young people more than offset the increasing percentages of the elderly. Therefore, by the year 2001 there is a higher percentage of the provincial populations of working age (see Table 3-14). The only exceptions are to be found in the increasing fertility projections (Projections 4, 8 and 10), and only then in the provinces of Quebec, Ontario, Manitoba and British Columbia. Even in these cases, the resulting percentages of working-age persons are still well above the 1971 percentages (see Table 1-8). These percentages, however, are decreased by improving life expectancy—primarily of benefit to the young and the old (Projection 2) and by increasing fertility (Projections 4, 8 and 10). They are largely unaffected by changes in immigration (Projections 5 and 14). This latter finding is quite interesting and suggests that in spite of a trend to more dependency in Canadian immigration flows, the current age composition is very similar to the average age composition of the Canadian population over this period. Finally, these percentages are also relatively unaffected by alternative interprovincial migration patterns (see Projections 6 and 7). These findings will be important in the analysis of labour force growth, to be undertaken in chapter 6.

An unavoidable conclusion from this synopsis of Canada's population futures is the relative insensitivity of population aging to a wide range of alternative demographic futures. From the results presented in this chapter, it appears that the Canadian population can be expected to age, on average, between seven and nine years by the turn of the century (see Table 3-12). This is more than it aged throughout the whole of the twentieth century to date (see Table 1-2). In other words, the Canadian population can be expected to age at least as much in the last twenty years of the twentieth century as it did over the first eighty years, *and* this result is insensitive to a wide range of alternative population futures. These conclusions produce a number of unalterable consequences. Declining population growth, increasing female dominancy, and historically low dependency ratios are clear examples. These results form the basis for the economic and policy analysis of Canada's population futures that are presented in Part 2 of this study.

Since the major orientation is on population aging, the results outlined above for the three age groups provide a useful focus for the analyses presented in Part 2. Chapter 4 provides an overview by examining, with the use of dependency ratios, the economic implications and policy challenges posed by the changing age

117

composition. The major impacts of the demographic trends for the young are on future educational enrolments and policies. These are analyzed in chapter 5. Chapter 6 is devoted to an analysis of the demographic trends of the working-age population on the future labour force, and hence on potential output (GNP) growth in Canada and the provinces. The effects of the increased number of the elderly on pensions are briefly reviewed in chapter 7, along with various other economic implications and challenges posed by population aging in Canada's demographic future.

Summary

The technical methodology underlying all population projection models is the standard population identity, which relates the change in population to its three main components—natural increase, net international migration and, for provincial populations, net interprovincial migration. With simplifying assumptions and appropriate parametrization, these models can generate the familiar exponential-type population growth. They can be used for either *ex ante* or *ex post* projections. The generation of population futures represents the latter type of application.

The Statistics Canada model used in this study has been parametrized for simplification and expanded to include the age and sex compositions of Canada's provincial and territorial populations. As a result, the national population is an aggregation of these populations. A rate approach is used for fertility, mortality and interprovincial migration, while a level approach is used for international migration. The rate approach is in line with the general principle of relating the component of population change to the population "at risk." In the case of emigration, there is insufficient information available to adopt a rate approach.

To develop alternative population futures, it is necessary to adopt future values for these rates and levels. Each future scenario is then conditional on these underlying assumptions. In the absence of well-developed, empirically tested theories of population change, alternative future scenarios or projections based on various combinations of the chosen assumptions have been developed to represent a feasible range of possible outcomes. This approach also facilitates an analysis of the sensitivity of the results to the assumptions. The various assumptions and combinations adopted in this study are based on recent data and follow in the "spirit" of the second generation of Statistics Canada projections, with some modifications. However, they

118

provide additional sensitivity analysis for the various assumptions. In total, fourteen alternative projections are presented. All projections have 1979 as their starting point and continue to the year 2051, although the analysis is largely confined to the last twenty years of the twentieth century.

The wide variety of results shows some inescapable conclusions. Population aging in Canada and the provinces is very likely to continue at an even more rapid pace, with the consequence that the Canadian and provincial populations are very likely to continue to grow slowly, to become more female-dominant, and to have relatively more people of working age over the remainder of this century and beyond. Levels never before experienced in Canadian demographic history are suggested by these results.

The continuation of the projections into the twenty-first century shows possible future population *decreases* after the 2020s—a result of negative natural increases—and a reversal of the aging process after the 2040s—a consequence of the passing of the Baby Boom generation. The results show the continuing damped wave-like impact of this generation on births. Further, with declining natural increases, interprovincial migration patterns can be expected to have a relatively greater impact on provincial population growth in the years ahead. The results of the projections also outline the implications of the likely continuing westward drift of the Canadian population.

The general conclusion from these results is that many of these future trends are largely insensitive to the choice of a wide variety of assumptions. In this sense, they are almost "inevitable." The chapters in Part 2 of this study explore some of the economic and policy implications and challenges posed by these largely inevitable trends.

119

Part 2

The Future Economic and Policy Challenges

Population Aging
and Public Policies

4

Introduction to Part 2

It could be argued that many, but not all, of the underlying trends in past Canadian demographic developments (as reviewed in Part 1) could have been largely anticipated by those concerned with the development and implementation of public policies. Notable exceptions may have been the immigration waves preceding the First World War and following the Second World War and the height of the Baby Boom in the 1950s. Nonetheless, as such new information came to light, many of the subsequent demographic developments could have been foreseen. However, many of the trends outlined in Part 1 appear to have been largely unanticipated (or perhaps ignored) in the policy milieu, with the result that policy makers appear to have been largely unprepared for the demographically inevitable events that have characterized at least recent Canadian demographic history.

Over the 1970s, for example, the decline in elementary school enrolments resulting from the "baby bust" of the 1960s became well established, and the logical implications for enrolments at the secondary and post-secondary levels were explored. However, coordinated policy development in the educational sector is still not well established. The education system seems no more ready for the departure of the Baby Boom generation than it was for its arrival.[1] The high levels of youth unemployment in the latter half of the 1970s also reflect demographically inevitable consequences for which employers, labour force participants and policy makers appear to have been largely unprepared. Whether and how these unemployment rates can be lowered continues to be a debate in current policy,[2] but the fact that even the inevitable arrives as a surprise[3] is largely a reflection of the paucity and ineffectiveness of the work in this area.

As outlined in Part 1 of this study, Canada's population futures will similarly contain a number of inevitable developments. In particular,

123

population aging, with all its attendant consequences, is likely to take place at an even more rapid pace in future years. It can only be hoped that if familiarized with some of the economic implications and consequent policy challenges of these future trends, policy makers will be better prepared for the inevitable surprises that lie in Canada's demographic future. It is to this objective that this part of the study is devoted.

By way of an overview, the general economic implications and policy challenges posed by the changing age composition within Canada's population futures are considered in this chapter, followed by two detailed case studied, where new insights into familiar problems are presented, and by an outline of areas where similar methodology may be usefully applied. The major effects of the trends in the young population are in educational enrolments and policies; these are examined, for all three levels of the education system, in chapter 5. Chapter 6 is devoted to the working-age group and the implications for the future labour force, and hence potential output (GNP) growth in Canada and the provinces. Since the impacts of the increased numbers of the elderly on Canada's pension and health care systems have been outlined in detail elsewhere, chapter 7 is devoted only to a brief review of these developments, along with examples of further economic challenges of population aging in the areas of housing, justice, savings and voting behaviour. This is an illustrative rather than an exhaustive list of possible useful applications. The economic challenges posed by Canada's population futures are numerous and widespread. The resulting analyses and policies will need to be just as numerous and widespread if Canada is to avoid the inevitable surprises that have characterized its recent demographic history and public policies.

Population Aging and Numerical Dependency

As noted in Part 1, population aging is *not* a new phenomenon in Canada. Perhaps the single most common index of population aging is the median age of the population. Figure 4-1 outlines the past and projected future median age of the Canadian population under the no change scenario (Projection 1). It shows that the median age has already reached historically high levels and is projected to increase dramatically in the years ahead. The population will age approximately as much over the next 70 years as it did over the previous 130 years.[4] Within this time profile, the transitory character of the reversal caused by the Baby Boom of the 1950s is clearly apparent. Also apparent is

124

the increasingly upward trend of the 1930s (another period of rapid aging in Canada), which was reestablished in the 1970s and is projected to continue until the turn of the century and beyond. The maximum median age in this scenario is over 42 years for the year 2041,[5] after which the median age declines. This is a logical consequence of the passing of the Baby Boom generation by that time.

Although the median age is a very useful summary indicator of population aging, it does not detail some of the important compositional changes so crucial to public policy formulation and implementation — in particular, the decreasing proportion of the young and the increasing proportion of the elderly usually characteristic of an aging population. It is useful and convenient for later analysis to define these as the non-working-age groups of 0 to 14 years and 65 years and over.

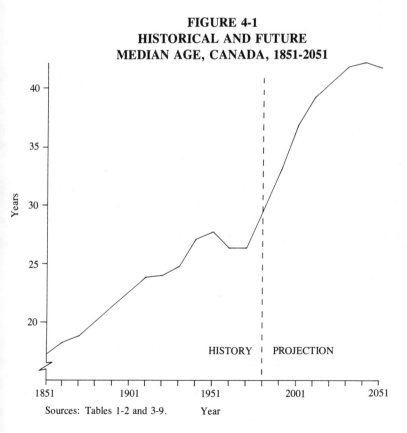

FIGURE 4-1
HISTORICAL AND FUTURE
MEDIAN AGE, CANADA, 1851-2051

Sources: Tables 1-2 and 3-9.

125

The historical and projected time profiles of these two non-working-age groups in Canada for the 200-year period 1851-2051 are summarized in Figure 4-2 (with future projections based on the no change scenario — Projection 1).

The general trends underlying an aging population are clearly apparent from these results. The proportion of elderly persons in the Canadian population has been increasing while the proportion of young persons has been decreasing, and both of these trends are projected to characterize Canada's population futures. Of particular interest is the fact that the rising trend of the elderly's proportion is projected to increase more rapidly in the future, while the declining trend of the youth proportion is expected to level out over the projection horizon. For the first time in Canadian demographic history, the two proportions will be approximately the same in the year 2021, after which the elderly will comprise a greater proportion of the Canadian population than the young. It is worth noting again that the massive pre-First World War immigrant inflow and the post-Second World War Baby Boom had transitory impacts on these general trends.

Of particular importance to public policy are the *magnitudes* of the trends portrayed in Figure 4-2. The percentage of the population aged 65 years and over has been gradually increasing (see Table 1-2) from 2.7 per cent in 1851, to 5.0 per cent at the turn of the century, and to 8.1 per cent in 1971. Projections of future population (see Tables 3-9 and 3-15) show that this upward trend will accelerate to a figure around 12.3 per cent in 2001 and will rise to over 20 per cent by 2031. The future pattern is relatively insensitive to the alternative assumptions — for example, the projected figures for 2001 vary between 11.9 per cent and 12.8 per cent, all well above the 1979 figure of 9.3 per cent (see Table 3-15). As previously noted (in chapter 3), the aging process is projected to cease around 2031 to 2041 when the effect of the Baby Boom ceases to have any further impact on the age composition. Beyond that point the percentage of elderly persons stabilizes, and the Canadian population is projected to get slightly younger (see Table 3-9).

The percentage of the population aged 0 to 14 years has been declining (see Table 1-2) from almost 50 per cent in 1851, to around 34.4 per cent at the turn of the century, and to 29.6 per cent in 1971. Projections of future population (see Tables 3-9 and 3-13) show that this downward trend will gradually slow down, reaching figures of around 19.4 per cent in 2001 and 16.2 per cent by 2031. This future pattern is somewhat less insensitive to alternative assumptions. For

126

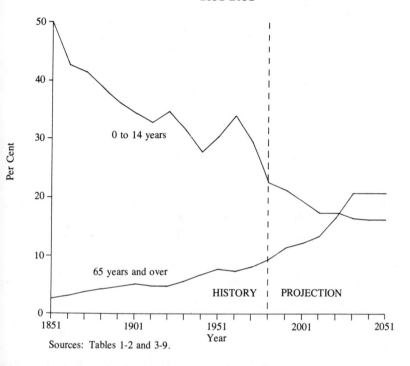

FIGURE 4-2
HISTORICAL AND FUTURE
AGE COMPOSITION, CANADA,
1851-2051

Sources: Tables 1-2 and 3-9.

example, the projected figures for 2001 vary between 17.7 per cent and 22.1 per cent, *all* of which are below the 1979 figure of 23.5 per cent (see Table 3-13). The cessation of population aging around 2031 reflects a stabilization of the youth percentage over the latter part of the future projection.

From these two comparisons (and Figure 4-2) it is clear that the secular decline in the percentage of the young has been greater than the secular increase in the percentage of the elderly. Moreover, this trend is projected to continue, albeit at a slower pace, into the twenty-first century. The economic and policy implications of this trend are far-reaching, for it implies that the composition of the non-working-age (or dependent) population is changing dramatically.[6]

To assess the numerical magnitude of this latter effect, the two dependent age groups can be combined and expressed as a proportion

127

of the total population. This is sometimes referred to as the dependency proportion. A numerical *total* dependency ratio that takes account of the trends in both dependent groups in the population can then be constructed by taking the ratio of this combined proportion to the working-age (15 to 64 years) proportion.[7] The total dependency ratio, therefore, takes account of the differing trends in *all* of the different age groups that comprise the total population. It provides a general indication of the average number of persons of non-working age that must be "supported" by each person of working age in the population. Since an aging population generally will have a declining percentage of young and an increasing percentage of elderly persons (both of which are in the numerator), there is no *a priori* expectation as to the impact of population aging on this ratio. However, if the percentage of young has been declining faster than the percentage of elderly has been increasing, there will be a secular decline in the total dependency ratio.

These calculations are set out in Table 4-1. The historical and projected dependency proportion (for the no change scenario, Projection 1) and the total dependency ratio and its inverse for Canada from 1851 to 2051 are presented. The total dependency ratio is illustrated in Figure 4-3. In 1851, 47.6 per cent of the Canadian population were aged 0 to 14 years and 65 years and over. This gradually declined over the years to an estimated 32.8 per cent in 1969. This downward secular trend, which implies *decreasing* numerical dependency, is projected to continue well into the twenty-first century. Only after approximately 2011 is it projected to increase, reaching a level around 37 per cent for the period 2031 to 2051. In other words, the increasing proportion of the elderly has been more than offset by the decreasing proportion of the young throughout Canadian history. This is expected to continue well into the twenty-first century. Note the transitory aberrations on the secular decline introduced by the immigration waves and the increased numbers of births preceding the First World War and following the Second World War, with the consequent echo effects (see Figure 3-3) in the 1980s. It is not until into the next century that the trend is reversed on a more permanent basis.[8]

Since the dependency proportion has been on a secular decline, the working-age proportion must have been on a secular increase. Consequently, the ratio of the dependency proportion to the working-age proportion (that is, the total dependency ratio) must be declining, a decline which is projected to continue into the twenty-first century. The subsequent increase is to the levels of the 1930s or early

128

TABLE 4-1
HISTORICAL AND PROJECTED DEPENDENCY PROPORTION, TOTAL DEPENDENCY RATIO AND INVERSE TOTAL DEPENDENCY RATIO FOR CANADA, 1851-2051

Census Year	Dependency Proportion[a]	Total Dependency Ratio[b]	Total Inverse Dependency Ratio[c]
History			
1851	0.476	0.909	1.10
1861	0.455	0.834	1.20
1871	0.453	0.828	1.21
1881	0.428	0.749	1.34
1891	0.409	0.692	1.44
1901	0.394	0.651	1.54
1911	0.376	0.603	1.66
1921	0.392	0.644	1.55
1931	0.372	0.592	1.69
1941	0.345	0.526	1.90
1951[c]	0.381	0.615	1.62
1961	0.415	0.712	1.41
1971	0.377	0.604	1.65
Projection[d]			
1981	0.322	0.475	2.10
1991	0.328	0.489	2.05
2001	0.317	0.464	2.15
2011	0.309	0.446	2.24
2021	0.342	0.519	1.92
2031	0.372	0.593	1.69
2041	0.369	0.586	1.71
2051	0.371	0.590	1.69

Notes: [a] Number of persons aged 0 to 14 years and 65 years and over divided by the total population.

[b] Number of persons aged 0 to 14 years and 65 years and over divided by the number of persons aged 15 to 64 years.

[c] Inverse of note[a] (Number of persons of working age per "dependent" person).

[d] Projection 1.

[e] Includes Newfoundland. (Figures without Newfoundland are 0.610 and 1.64 respectively.)

Sources: Tables 1-2 and 3-9.

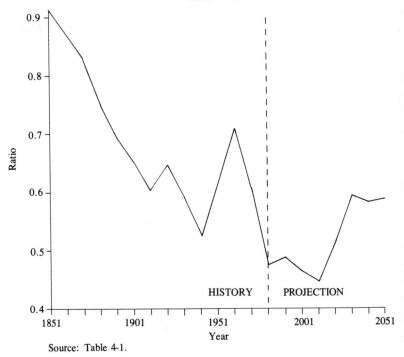

FIGURE 4-3
HISTORICAL AND FUTURE
DEPENDENCY RATIO, CANADA,
1851-2051

Source: Table 4-1.

1960s. The inverse of the total dependency ratio shows that there were 1.1 persons of working age for every person of non-working age in 1851;[9] by 1941 this had risen to 1.9 persons; and with the postwar Baby-Boom it fell to a low of 1.4 persons in 1961. The 1979 figure is estimated to be 2.0 persons, an all-time high in Canadian demographic history, and similar high levels are projected for the remainder of this century and into the first two decades of the next. Never before have there been so many people of working age relative to the number of people of non-working age in Canada. Although the proportion of the elderly is projected to increase in Canada over the next forty years, the declining proportion of young more than offsets this increase, thus keeping the total dependency ratio at historically low levels (or its inverse at historically high levels).

These conclusions are almost totally insensitive to the alternative

130

TABLE 4-2
ALTERNATIVE DEPENDENCY PROPORTION, TOTAL DEPENDENCY RATIO AND INVERSE TOTAL DEPENDENCY RATIO, 1979 AND 2001, AND PEAK DEPENDENCY RATIO, 1981-2051[a]

Year and Projection Number	Dependency Proportion	Total Dependency Ratio	Inverse Total Dependency Ratio	Peak	
				Year	Inverse Total Dependency Ratio
1979	0.328	0.489	2.04	—	—
2001					
1	0.317	0.464	2.15	2007	2.27
2	0.319	0.469	2.13	2006	2.23
3	0.305	0.439	2.28	2007	2.40
4	0.340	0.515	1.94[b]	1983	2.12
5	0.317	0.465	2.15	2007	2.27
6	0.317	0.464	2.16	2007	2.27
7	0.317	0.465	2.15	2007	2.27
8	0.342	0.520	1.92[b]	1983	2.12
9	0.305	0.439	2.28	2007	2.40
10	0.342	0.520	1.92[b]	1983	2.12
11	0.305	0.439	2.28	2007	2.40
12	0.317	0.464	2.15	2007	2.27
13	0.317	0.464	2.15	2007	2.27
14	0.316	0.462	2.16	2007	2.29

Notes: [a] See notes to Table 4-1.

[b] This is a trough between peaks in 1983 and 2007 at values around 2.12 and 2.00 respectively.

Sources: Table 3-10 and calculations by the author.

population futures (see Table 4-2). Their insensitivity to alternative interprovincial migration assumptions is not surprising. What is surprising is their insensitivity to alternative immigration assumptions. Although somewhat more sensitive to fertility assumptions, the total dependency ratio (or its inverse) reaches and stays at historically low (high) levels for the rest of this century and into the twenty-first.[10] In almost all cases, a local (if not global) peak for the inverse dependency ratio is reached around 2007 at a value of 2.27 persons of working age

131

for every person of non-working age. The range is a relatively narrow 2.12 to 2.40, with the low level being well *above* any value experienced historically in Canada.

Table 4-3 presents a similar summary for each of the provinces. Historically the Atlantic provinces have experienced below-average inverse total dependency ratios. This position generally continues into the projection period.[11] Newfoundland has a relatively higher percentage of young people but relatively lower percentages of elderly and working-age people (see Tables 3-13 to 3-15). The percentages of the elderly are higher in the remaining Atlantic provinces — this accounts for the region's somewhat higher inverse total dependency ratios. Currently Quebec and Ontario have the highest ratios, largely a reflection of their relatively lower fertility rates. However, the loss of working-age persons to interprovincial migration gradually erodes this relative position. This is in contrast to the provinces of Alberta and British Columbia, which, although facing an aging population, gain

TABLE 4-3

HISTORICAL AND PROJECTED INVERSE TOTAL DEPENDENCY RATIO[a] FOR CANADA AND THE PROVINCES, 1901-2041

Province	*History*				*Projection*[b]			
	1901	*1921*	*1941*	*1961*[c]	*1981*	*2001*	*2021*	*2041*
Nfld	—	—	—	1.09	1.32	1.99	1.80	1.56
PEI	1.37	1.39	1.53	1.15	1.74	2.00	1.77	1.53
NS	1.47	1.43	1.68	1.30	1.94	2.15	1.91	1.66
NB	1.42	1.37	1.57	1.18	1.90	2.18	1.94	1.66
PQ	1.30	1.34	1.69	1.42	2.28	2.21	1.89	1.72
Ont	1.71	1.77	2.09	1.48	2.14	2.14	1.94	1.71
Man	1.46	1.51	2.08	1.40	1.87	1.96	1.82	1.63
Sask	1.41	1.38	1.85	1.31	1.77	1.92	1.83	1.61
Alta	1.45	1.59	1.95	1.37	2.09	2.25	2.03	1.80
BC	2.65	2.13	2.36	1.41	2.09	2.19	1.95	1.71
Can[d]	1.54	1.55	1.90	1.41	2.10	2.15	1.92	1.71

Notes: [a] Ratio of persons aged 15 to 64 years to remaining population.
       [b] Projection 1.
       [c] Includes Newfoundland.
       [d] Includes the territories.

Sources: Tables 1-8, 3-13, 3-14 and 3-15 (for 2001) and projections by the author.

working-age persons from interprovincial migration, and hence experience relative upward movement in their inverse ratios. The remaining western provinces of Manitoba and Saskatchewan, which currently have the highest percentages of elderly persons in their populations and above-average percentages of the young (and hence relatively low ratios), are projected to continue in this position throughout the projection horizon.

In summary, Alberta and British Columbia are projected to gradually replace Ontario and Quebec as the provinces in the most favourable position from this viewpoint. The remaining six provinces (with the possible exception of New Brunswick) are projected to continue in the more unfavourable positions.

It is important to recognize, however, that in all provinces the position is projected to improve, even beyond the current historically favourable position, throughout much of the projection horizon. Moreover, even upon the retirement of the Baby Boom generation, the dependency ratios return to levels experienced in Canada in recent history. In other words, in all provinces the reduced proportion of the young more than offsets (numerically) the increased proportion of the elderly throughout this and into the next century. And even when this is no longer the case (beyond approximately 2007), the tendency is towards dependency levels that have been experienced in Canada's recent past history (late 1940s and early 1970s).

In summary, the secularly declining trend in the total dependency ratio (or secularly increasing trend in its inverse) over much of the historical period suggests that there has been a secular decline in the "responsibilities or burdens" on the working-age population in Canada. This trend can be expected to continue into the twenty-first century, over which time there will be more than two persons of working age for every person of non-working age in the Canadian population — a historically high figure. Beyond the year 2007, approximately, the reversal will be to "responsibilities or burdens" that approach levels experienced within recent demographic history.

It should be abundantly clear from these results that the locus of dependence (or responsibility) is moving from the young to the elderly throughout the entire projection period. Canadians will be required to devote relatively more of their time and resources than ever before to supporting the elderly in the years ahead and relatively less time and resources to supporting the young. Of course, this will become particularly apparent in the twenty-first century when the proportion of the young ceases to be higher than the proportion of the elderly in Canadian society.

The above discussion is purely in terms of the *numbers* of people. However, as has been noted, the composition of the dependent population is changing as a result of the aging of the Canadian population. There will be fewer young and more elderly people in this population. If these two age groups are treated somewhat differently, at least in terms of public programs, then a *numerical* dependency ratio may be an inadequate way of conveying the impacts on public policies of the changing age composition. For this reason, effective or expenditure dependency ratios, which take into account the relatively greater cost per capita of servicing the aged, have been developed. These are analyzed in the next section.

Expenditure Dependency Futures

The results from the numerical dependency futures imply that for the rest of this century and into the next, there will be relatively more people of working age than ever before in Canadian history. This *suggests* that the total potential per capita cost of servicing the young and elderly populations in Canada could well be *reduced* in the years ahead. However, implicit in this observation are the assumptions that resources can and will be transferred from programs used primarily by the young (such as education) to those used primarily by the elderly (such as pensions and health care) and that the costs of provision of these different services are not *only* proportional to the numbers involved, but are also comparable in the different programs.

Whether or not per capita costs are related to the size of a program remains an issue to be examined at the level of each program. If there are economies of scale in the provision of some public programs, then it is likely that the per capita costs associated with that program will decline as increased numbers of persons are serviced. Similarly, per capita costs will increase for programs of decreasing size. There is little empirical evidence currently available on this issue, so it is not possible to incorporate any figures into the general calculations reported in this section. However, note that within the dependent population there will be a greater number of elderly people in the years ahead and a reduced proportion (but not necessarily a reduced number) of young. This means that if there are economies of scale to be gained in the provision of public services to the elderly, the increases in costs of these programs could be less than proportional to the increases in population numbers, as suggested by the numerical dependency calculations. The opposite may be true of programs oriented towards the young.

134

It is becoming evident that the relative cost of the provision of public services is not the same for different groups of the population. For example, such public services as education, transportation and justice services may not be particularly directed towards the elderly (education certainly is not — see chapter 5), but health care and pensions certainly are.[12] Since these latter programs comprise a relatively large proportion of total government expenditures in Canada, it might be expected that the cost of the provision of public services for the elderly is relatively greater than for other members of the population. In fact, a study by the federal Treasury Board concluded that in Canada in 1976 per person total government expenditures were approximately two and a half times as great for the elderly (persons 65 years and over) as for the young (aged 0 to 17 years).[13] This figure is corroborated in the United States, where research has indicated that the figure may be as high as three times as great for the elderly compared to the younger members of the population.[14] Whatever the exact figure, it certainly appears that it is relatively more expensive in terms of existing public programs in North America to support an elderly person than to support a young person, or a person of working age. This means that even if an aging population did not increase in size, the relatively larger proportion of elderly will lead to an increase in public expenditures, and hence to a potentially increased tax burden on the possibly reduced proportion of those of working age.

This potentially increasing tax burden on those of working age, especially in an aging population, is also predicated on the notion that, in general, this group bears the greatest share of the costs of and receives the least share of the benefits from public services. That the greatest burden of taxation falls on the working-age population would appear to be an indisputable hypothesis. Most taxation is collected on current income, and most current income is earned by those of working age. Pre-working-age members of the population attend educational institutions and seldom earn current income, while the private income of the elderly is usually generated by part-time labour force positions and from the investment income of assets accumulated over their working ages. Although for any single individual this income may be relatively high, the general observation is a marked decline in people's private incomes upon their retirement.[15]

Finally, it may be unrealistic to assume that resource transfers from programs used primarily by the young to those used primarily by the elderly can and will be effected. Groups or organizations, whether private or public, do not give up resources easily, even if those resources are required elsewhere within the organization or within society. However, as is well known by any manager, *relative* resource transfers can be effected by freezing the budget of one group and adding all budgetary increments to those of other groups. This process can be further facilitated by inflation, where nominal budgetary increments are likely to be larger.[16] In short, relative resource transfers are a difficult but not an impossible task.

Given these considerations, numerical dependency ratios are of limited usefulness for public policy considerations, since they do not consider the cost implications of the changing composition of the non-working-age population in an aging environment. Not only do these ratios fail to take into account the possible impacts of economies and diseconomies of scale in the provision of public services and the difficult administrative (and political) issue of effecting resource transfers, they also ignore the implications of the higher relative per capita cost of providing public services for the elderly.

The emerging evidence on the non-similarity of the relative costs of providing public services to the elderly as compared to to the young, at least in North America in the 1970s, seems clearly to suggest that the elderly are between two and three times as expensive to maintain on public services as the young. In terms of the dependent population, this implies that for every additional elderly member there must be a reduction of *two to three* young members if the real level of public services is to be maintained. The analysis in the previous section has indicated that for much of the projection period in all provinces there is a greater reduction in the number of the young than there is an increase in the number of the elderly. What is not clear from that analysis, however, is whether or not the numbers are sufficient to maintain a constant real level of public services to all groups, given the difference in the servicing cost between the young and the elderly.

Rather than embark on a detailed analysis at the program level, it is possible to obtain an overview of the likely *demographic* impact on public expenditures in Canada over the projection horizon by constructing a weighted dependency ratio, where the weights reflect the relative costs of servicing the different segments of the population — in this case, the different age groups. Using the notation employed previously,[17] this can be defined as:

$$\frac{(POPY/POP) + \omega(POPE/POP)}{(POPW/POP)} = \frac{POPY + \omega POPE}{POPW}$$

where ω denotes the relative cost of servicing the elderly compared to the young. This measure has been referred to as the effective or expenditure dependency ratio.[18] For Canada, ω would appear to be approximately two and a half, or, most likely, would lie between two and three.[19] Assuming a constant value for ω implies not only that per capita program costs are independent of size,[20] but also that the *relative* per capita costs of various public services (for example, public education and health services) remain unchanged over the projection horizon. Whether realistic or not, this procedure does have the desirable effect of isolating the impacts of population aging on public programs, and for this reason ω will be held fixed throughout the projection horizon.[21] However, since the estimates of ω are tentative at best, the sensitivity of the results to the value of ω will be explored. For this reason, Tables 4-4 and 4-5 show the calculations with $\omega=2$ and $\omega=3$ respectively. (Note that the comparable calculations with $\omega=1$ are contained in Table 4-2.) Since the normalization in the above definition is arbitrary (see note 19), the results are expressed as an index relative to 1979. A number greater than 1 implies increased pressure on public expenditures relative to 1979 (since the expenditure dependency ratio is relatively higher), while a number less than 1 implies decreased pressure on public expenditures relative to 1979.

These results, summarized in Figure 4-4, suggest that if the public programs currently in place in Canada had been in place throughout Canadian history, the late 1970s would have represented a period when the demographic pressures on public expenditures would have been at a historically *low* level. Only in the early 1900s when the immigration wave swelled the working-age population, and in the 1930s when significant aging increased the working-age population, have there been comparably reduced pressures on public programs, when viewed from today's vantage point. In contrast, during the last half of the nineteenth century when there was a high proportion of young people in the population, and again during the Baby Boom decade of the 1950s, the pressures on public programs were comparably much greater (the figures suggest by between one-quarter and one-half). Note, however, that these pressures came from the need to provide public services to the young (education services in particular).

As has been demonstrated above, in the decades ahead the pressures are projected to come from the provision of public services to the elderly (primarily, health care and pensions). However, the figures in Tables 4-4 and 4-5 suggest that these demographic pressures are unlikely to be manifested in the next few years (since the proportion of

137

TABLE 4-4

HISTORICAL AND PROJECTED EXPENDITURE DEPENDENCY RATIO FOR CANADA, 1851-2051, FOR $\omega=2$

Census Year	Young Person Equivalents[a]	Working-Age Population (000's)	Expenditure Ratio[b]	Dependency Index[c] (1979=1.0)
History				
1851	1,225	1,276	0.960	1.53
1861	1,567	1,761	0.890	1.42
1871	1,806	2,018	0.895	1.43
1881	2,030	2,473	0.821	1.31
1891	2,197	2,856	0.769	1.23
1901	2,389	3,254	0.734	1.17
1911	3,047	4,495	0.678	1.08
1921	3,864	5,344	0.723	1.15
1931	4,434	6,519	0.680	1.08
1941	4,734	7,540	0.628	1.00
1951[d]	6,423	8,672	0.741	1.18
1961	8,974	10,655	0.842	1.34
1971	9,870	13,443	0.734	1.17
Projection[e]				
1981	10,130	16,396	0.618	0.98
1991	11,828	17,967	0.658	1.05
2001	12,546	19,448	0.645	1.03
2011	13,133	20,480	0.641	1.02
2021	15,543	19,967	0.778	1.24
2031	17,612	19,025	0.926	1.47
2041	17,158	18,746	0.915	1.46
2051	16,717	18,196	0.919	1.46

Notes: [a] Number of persons aged 0 to 14 years plus two times the number of persons aged 65 years and over.

[b] Young person equivalents divided by working-age population.

[c] Ratio divided by 0.628 (the 1979 level).

[d] Includes Newfoundland (excluding Newfoundland, Index=1.17).

[e] Projection 1 (no change scenario).

Sources: Calculations by the author from census data. Data for pre-1901 taken from M. C. Urquhart, *Historical Statistics of Canada* (Toronto: Macmillan, 1965), p. 16. (See also Table 1-2).

TABLE 4-5
HISTORICAL AND PROJECTED EXPENDITURE DEPENDENCY
RATIO FOR CANADA, 1851-2051, FOR $\omega=3$

Census Year	Young Person Equivalents[a]	Working Age Population (000's)	Expenditure Ratio[b]	Dependency Index[c] (1979=1.0)
History				
1851	1,290	1,276	1.011	1.32
1861	1,665	1,761	0.945	1.23
1871	1,941	2,018	0.962	1.26
1881	2,208	2,473	0.893	1.17
1891	2,417	2,856	0.846	1.10
1901	2,660	3,254	0.818	1.07
1911	3,382	4,495	0.753	0.98
1921	4,284	5,344	0.802	1.05
1931	5,010	6,519	0.769	1.00
1941	5,502	7,540	0.730	0.95
1951[d]	7,510	8,672	0.866	1.13
1961	10,366	10,655	0.973	1.27
1971	11,614	13,443	0.864	1.13
Projection[e]				
1981	12,469	16,396	0.760	0.99
1991	14,875	17,967	0.828	1.08
2001	16,059	19,448	0.826	1.08
2011	17,127	20,480	0.836	1.09
2021	20,714	19,967	1.037	1.35
2031	23,936	19,025	1.258	1.64
2041	23,331	18,746	1.245	1.62
2051	22,699	18,196	1.247	1.63

Notes: [a] Number of persons aged 0 to 14 years plus three times the number of persons aged 65 years and over.

[b] Young person equivalents divided by working-age population.

[c] Ratio divided by 0.766 (the 1979 level).

[d] Includes Newfoundland (excluding Newfoundland, Index=1.12).

[e] Projection 1 (no change scenario).

Sources: Calculations by the author from census data. Data for pre-1901 taken from M. C. Urquhart, *Historical Statistics of Canada* (Toronto: Macmillan, 1965), p. 16. (See also Table 1-2).

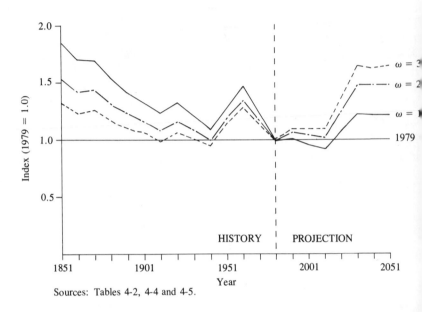

FIGURE 4-4
HISTORICAL AND FUTURE EXPENDITURE
DEPENDENCY RATIO INDEXES, CANADA,
1851-2051

Sources: Tables 4-2, 4-4 and 4-5.

young people continues to decline sufficiently to offset the increasing
proportion of the elderly). For the remainder of this century and into
the twenty-first, these pressures will attain levels largely within
previous historical experience,[22] and until around the mid-2020s, they
will be below the pressures exerted on public programs by the Baby
Boom generation. For example, Table 4-4 (with $\omega=2$) suggests that
over the remainder of the twentieth century these pressures will be no
more than 5 per cent *above* the 1979 levels, compared to a 34 per cent
difference in 1961. Further, Table 4-5 (with $\omega=3$) suggests these
pressures will be around 8 per cent higher compared to a 27 per cent
difference in 1961. Beyond the 2020s the ratios do increase
substantially, suggesting an increasing burden on the working-age
populations of that period. In summary, these calculations show that
demographic pressures on public expenditures resulting from population aging are currently at historically low levels and, after a brief
hiatus, can be expected to gradually increase in the 1980s and beyond,
at least until the 2020s, to levels that are within recent historical

140

experience and generally below the pressures exerted by the Baby Boom generation.

These conclusions do underscore the need to orient current policy towards the gradual transference of resources from the young to the elderly in Canada in the years ahead. The most obvious transfers would be a relative reduction in education expenditures and a relative increase in health care, housing for the elderly and pension expenditures. Of special concern to the current policy-maker is how long these demographic pressures will remain at historically low levels, or exactly when the increased pressures from population aging will start to appear. In other words, when will the projected increased proportion of elderly no longer be compensated for by a projected decreased proportion of young in terms of both numbers and public expenditure pressures?

Figure 4-5 outlines the historical and future annual movements in the

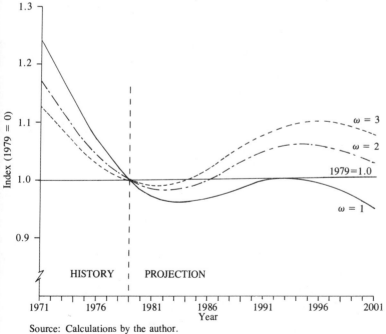

FIGURE 4-5
HISTORICAL AND FUTURE EXPENDITURE
DEPENDENCY RATIO INDEXES, CANADA,
1971-2001

Source: Calculations by the author.

141

expenditure dependency ratio index (1979=1.0) for the period 1971 to 2001. These calculations suggest that the current hiatus will likely be comparatively short lived. The indexes reach minimum values in the early 1980s before commencing a gradual upward movement.[23] The period from the present to around 1985 would appear to be one when the demographic pressures on public programs will be no greater than in 1979.[24] Since this period is so early in the projection horizon, this conclusion is insensitive to the alternative assumptions (results not presented). Moreover, as indicated in Table 4-6, the length of the hiatus is quite similar in most provinces, its duration being shortest in Quebec, Manitoba, Saskatchewan and British Columbia, and longest in Newfoundland and Prince Edward Island.[25] In level terms, Prince Edward Island and Saskatchewan currently have the highest expendi-

TABLE 4-6

PROJECTED YEAR OF MINIMUM EXPENDITURE DEPENDENCY RATIO INDEX FOR CANADA AND THE PROVINCES, 1979-2001[a]

(1979=1.0)

	$\omega=2$			$\omega=3$		
Province	1979 Value	Minimum Year	Minimum Index	1979 Value	Minimum Year	Minimum Index
Nfld	0.740	1990	0.903	0.856	1990	0.941
PEI	0.785	2001[c]	0.877	0.970	2001[c]	0.904
NS	0.695	1983	0.970	0.854	1982	0.982
NB	0.698	1986	0.950	0.845	1983	0.970
PQ	0.574	1981	0.985	0.696	1980	0.995
Ont	0.623	1983	0.979	0.765	1982	0.991
Man	0.719	1981	0.995	0.892	1979	1.000
Sask	0.762	1981	0.987	0.944	1981	0.993
Alta	0.605	1984	0.972	0.718	1983	0.979
BC	0.642	1981	0.996	0.798	1979	1.000
Can[b]	0.628	1982	0.982	0.766	1981	0.992

Notes: [a] Projection 1.
         [b] Includes the territories.
         [c] Decreasing throughout the period.

Source: Calculations by the author.

ture dependency ratios, and Quebec and Alberta the lowest. This quite substantial interprovincial variation reflects the different age distributions of the provincial populations (see Figure 3-2). In summary, policy makers in Canada can enjoy a hiatus of no more than five years (depending on the province) in the early 1980s before the demographic pressures of population aging can be expected to place upward pressure on public expenditures.

The early 1980s, therefore, provide a unique period in Canada for those concerned with the development and implementation of policies and programs appropriate for an aging population. The trend of reduced pressures on public expenditures for the dependent population that characterized the 1970s will end. An increase in these pressures will begin to emerge in the mid-1980s as a result of continued population aging.

Summary

The level of public expenditures and the burden of taxation in an economy reflect in part the relative proportion of the productive, or working-age, population to the non-working-age, or dependent, population. The non-working-age population is composed of the young and the elderly. By examining the trends in these relative proportions, one can isolate the demographic pressures on public expenditures and the movements in the implied burden of taxation on the population at large, or on the population of working age. Such measures are called dependency ratios.

Total dependency includes the young as well as the elderly in the non-working-age group. In an aging population, it might be expected that the number or percentage of elderly will be increasing while the number or percentage of the young will be decreasing. If the latter trend more than offsets the former trend, then total dependency will decline. This has been the secular trend in Canada, notably in the 1960s and 1970s. Currently, total dependency is at a historically low level and is projected to remain so for the rest of-this century and into the next. This conclusion is insensitive to alternative projections and applies in all provinces. In other words, there will be relatively more people of working age than ever experienced in Canadian history. The reduced proportion of the young more than offsets (numerically) the increased proportion of the elderly in all provinces into the twenty-first century. And even when this is no longer the case (beyond approximately 2007), the trends are towards total dependency levels within recent historical experience. Hence, the potential transfer of

143

resources from the young to the elderly, implied by the increasing proportion of elderly in Canada's population futures, could substantially reduce the burden on the working-age population.

The level of public expenditures and the implied burden of taxation are, however, also influenced by the relative costs of programs for the different dependent populations. Recent research in Canada and the United States suggests that it costs approximately two and a half to three times as much to support an elderly person on public programs as it does a young person. Consequently, the numerical dependency ratios do not provide a sufficient indication of the impact of population aging on public expenditures and on the associated tax burden. Effective or expenditure dependency ratios reflect the greater relative per capita cost of the public servicing of the elderly. These calculations show that the late 1970s represented a period when the demographic pressures on public expenditures declined to a historically low level. This is projected to continue into the *early* 1980s, after which the increased proportion of the relatively more costly elderly is projected to more than offset the decreased proportion of the relatively less costly young, resulting in increased pressures on government expenditures. However, these pressures are projected to rise to levels in the remainder of this century and the first two decades of the next century that are well within previous historical experience and generally below the pressures exerted on public programs by the Baby Boom generation. Thus, the early 1980s provide a unique opportunity to establish and consolidate the policies and programs necessary for an aging population in Canada and the provinces.

Future Enrolments and Education Policy

5

Introduction

The education sector in Canada is perhaps the most notable area where public policies can be considerably influenced by the impacts of demography. Elementary and secondary school enrolments over the 1960s and 1970s largely reflected the aging of the Baby Boom generation. In recent years, these impacts have been experienced in the enrolments of post-secondary educational institutions. Yet even though the declines in elementary and secondary school enrolments have been explored,[1] the educational system seems no more ready for the departure of the Baby Boom generation than it was for its arrival. The demographically induced inevitable surprises appear to be lingering on! Moreover, current educational planning and policy at the post-secondary levels of instruction appear quite misguided when the elementary-secondary patterns are projected unchanged into the post-secondary system.[2] The purpose of this chapter is to reexamine existing educational enrolment projections (with the population futures detailed in chapter 3 as a base), and to outline the challenges to future education policy in the context of these enrolment projections and the general trends discussed in chapter 4.

Since school attendance is compulsory for those aged between 6 and 15 years in most Canadian provinces, it can be expected that school enrolments for these ages will very closely mirror the size of this population. Even beyond the compulsory school attendance ages — the higher levels of secondary education and all post-secondary education — it might be expected that enrolments closely follow the size of the relevant populations, both historically and into the future.

This relationship between school enrolments and the population can be summarized in a manner analogous to that used for births and deaths (see chapter 3); that is, by defining an enrolment rate for each age-sex group in the student population as the ratio of total enrolments at the beginning of the academic year in that group to the total population of that group.[3] Following the principles outlined in chapter 3, the relevant population measure in the denominator should represent the population "at risk"; that is, the catchment (or "reservoir" of those of relevant age) from which the respective educational institutions draw their enrolments. Thus, for example, elementary enrolments should be primarily related to the populations in age groups 6 through 15 years; secondary enrolments, to the populations in age groups 14 through 19 years; and post-secondary enrolments, to the groups in the population aged 18 years and over. Since education is the responsibility of provincial governments in Canada, the exact ages chosen for each enrolment type may vary from province to province. For those age groups where school attendance is compulsory, the rate will approximately equal 100 per cent.[4] Moreover, the enrolment rate can be made institution-specific so that enrolments by institutional type can be obtained. Consequently, enrolment rates for 17-year-olds could conceivably be calculated for elementary, secondary and perhaps post-secondary institutions, although the expectation would be that the former and the latter would be close to zero. However, this does become an important consideration when measuring the educational participation of mature-age students.

Projections of future enrolments for any institutional type that are linked to population futures can be obtained by first rewriting the enrolment rate definition so that enrolments are the product of the enrolment rate and the relevant future population in each age-sex group, and then aggregating across all appropriate age-sex groups for that type of institution.[5] In this way future enrolment rates become the parameters of the model in much the same way as, for example, the out-migration rates are in the generation of population futures (see chapter 3).

The specification of future age-sex-specific enrolment rates remains a largely unresearched problem. For the younger age groups where school attendance is compulsory, rates approximately equal to 100 per cent can be safely assumed. However, for age groups beyond approximately 15 years, numerous factors determine the observed enrolments rates. Attitudes to education, opportunities for education, and the state of the job market are likely to be the most important determinants, although numerous other sociological and economic factors could also be important. Once again, in the absence of a well-developed, empirically validated theory of enrolment rate

146

determination, the approach adopted in this study is to develop a set of enrolment rates based on recent historical experience and then to test the sensitivity of the results to alternative assumptions. Note that the assumption of *constant* rates throughout the projection period isolates the impacts of demographic developments on enrolments, since under these conditions enrolments are influenced solely by the aging of the underlying population.

In summary, the methodology to be followed in the remainder of this chapter is to use the enrolment rate approach to obtain enrolment futures by type for each province. The enrolment rates are calculated for age-sex-specific groups within each major institutional type for each province and are held constant throughout the projection horizon. In this way the enrolment implications of future demographic developments can be examined. For the younger age groups, where enrolment is compulsory, no sensitivity analysis is necessary, but for the more senior age groups sensitivity to alternative rate assumptions can be examined.

In the sections that follow, three types of enrolments are considered: total elementary and secondary, post-secondary university and post-secondary non-university.[6] Like the population projections, assumptions are developed at the provincial level, with the Canada-wide implications following from an aggregation of the provincial totals. For each type of enrolment, assumptions are based on a brief historical overview of recent trends. Then follows a review of the results, which are consistent with the population futures outlined in chapter 3. The challenges posed by these results are examined in a concluding section.

Elementary-Secondary Enrolments: A Historical Overview

In Canada children enter the school system at the elementary level, usually at around six years of age.[7] From there they proceed to the secondary level at an age largely dependent on the policies of the province involved. Currently most provinces have six elementary grades, followed by six secondary grades (or years).[8] Consequently, a student entering at age 6 will generally have left the elementary-secondary system by age 18 in most provinces. Enrolment in this system is compulsory to age 15 or 16 years, depending on the province.[9] Thus, it might be expected that enrolment rates will be around 100 per cent up to these ages.

Because of the interprovincial differences in the elementary-secondary levels of education, it is useful, and probably appropriate for comparative purposes, to combine the two levels into a single entity. In this way only the different entry and exiting ages have to be considered when examining the enrolment data, not the divisions between the elementary and secondary levels. At this time Ontario has the most years of elementary-secondary education (thirteen), and Newfoundland and Quebec the fewest (eleven). All other provinces have twelve years of elementary-secondary education.[10]

Of course, these arrangements have not always been in force, but the mammoth task of providing a historical review of the evolving educational requirements for each province is not attempted here. Instead, Table 5-1 provides a historical summary of elementary and secondary enrolment in public schools for each of the provinces over the past century. Recall that these numbers reflect not only the underlying demographic patterns, but also the changing enrolment rate (or participation) patterns, which among other things will embody the impacts of many of the changing educational arrangements (compulsory ages, grade offerings, and so on) that have taken place in the provinces over this period.

Over the century 1870-1970, elementary-secondary enrolment in public schools grew from over three-quarters of a million to over five and a half million students — a more than sevenfold increase. Over the same period the total population increased almost sixfold (see Table 1-1). The first conclusion from these data is that enrolment growth has exceeded population growth over the century (see Table 5-2). This implies an increasing enrolment (or participation) rate, especially when the changing age composition of the population is accounted for (see Table 5-2).[11] That most of the enrolment rate increases have occurred in the postwar period, especially during the 1960s, is of particular interest.

Since Table 5-3 provides annual data for the postwar period, a more detailed analysis of elementary-secondary enrolment growth is possible for this period. During the 1950s annual growth averaged approximately 5.3 per cent, while in the 1960s the average annual growth was 3.3 per cent. In the 1970s there was a *negative* average annual growth with the peak enrolment of over 5.8 million students having been reached in the 1970-71 academic year. Since the general trend of declining enrolment growth over the 1950s and 1960s was masked by the ever-increasing numbers of students, the negative growth in the 1970s arrived as a "surprise" in many jurisdictions.

The provincial distribution of the above pattern is summarized in Table 5-4. From these data it is apparent that the peak enrolment

TABLE 5-1
TOTAL ENROLMENT IN PUBLIC ELEMENTARY AND SECONDARY SCHOOLS FOR CANADA AND THE PROVINCES, 1870-1975
(000's)

School Year Beginning in	Can	Nfld	PEI	NS	NB	PQ	Ont	Man	Sask	Alta	BC	Territories and Overseas
1870	767.5	—	14.0	77.2	32.0	200.5	443.0	0.8	—	—	—	—
1880	852.3	—	21.6	80.2	49.6	204.0	489.4	4.9	—	—	2.6	—
1890	942.5	—	22.5	85.6	59.6	227.6	514.0	23.9	—	—	9.3	—
1900	1,054.5	—	21.0	98.4	66.7	276.6	492.5	51.9	23.8	—	23.6	—
1910	1,318.4	—	17.7	102.9	69.0	350.5	518.6	80.8	72.3	61.7	44.9	—
1920[a]	1,834.3	55.6	17.5	109.5	73.8	458.0	637.5	129.0	184.8	138.2	86.0	—
1930	2,099.2	60.6	17.5	115.5	88.8	542.6	668.1	153.6	230.5	168.7	113.9	—
1940	2,075.0	67.2	18.2	116.9	92.0	588.2	643.6	131.6	201.4	163.4	119.6	—
1950	2,391.1	79.3	18.9	134.5	105.7	640.8	768.2	128.9	167.5	174.0	173.4	—
1960	3,996.5	128.9	24.5	179.4	152.3	1,097.7	1,389.2	189.6	208.7	294.4	321.3	10.7
1965	4,917.6	146.5	27.8	199.9	165.2	1,384.0	1,738.8	222.2	238.3	362.2	420.8	11.9
1970	5,661.3	160.9	30.6	214.9	175.9	1,588.8	2,022.4	246.9	247.3	426.0	527.0	20.5
1975	5,375.8	157.8	27.9	202.6	165.0	1,374.8	1,994.6	228.1	221.0	439.4	542.7	22.1

Note: [a] Total includes Newfoundland for the first time.

Source: Statistics Canada, *Historical Compendium of Education Statistics, From Confederation to 1975* (Catalogue No. 81-568), pp. 31-32.

TABLE 5-2

POPULATION GROWTH, ELEMENTARY-SECONDARY ENROLMENT GROWTH AND ENROLMENT RATES FOR CANADA, 1870-1980

(%)

Period	Average Annual		Enrolment Rates	
	Population Growth[a]	Enrolment Growth[b]	Total Population[c]	Population Aged 5-14 Years[d]
1870-80	1.6	1.2	20.8	77.3
1880-90	1.1	1.0	19.7	79.1
1890-1900	1.1	1.1	19.5	82.3
1900-10	3.0	2.3	19.6	87.6
1910-20	2.0	3.0[e]	18.3	88.8
1920-30	1.7	1.4	20.2	90.4
1930-40	1.0	−0.1	19.6	92.2
1940-50	1.7[e]	1.4	17.4[e]	93.3[e]
1950-60	2.7	5.3	17.1	94.8
1960-70	1.7	3.5	21.9	101.4[f]
1970-80	1.2	−1.3	26.2	123.8[f]

Notes: [a] Between census years (see Table 1-1).

[b] Calculated from Table 5-1.

[c] Total enrolment (Table 5-1) divided by total population (Table 1-1) at the beginning of the period.

[d] Total enrolment (Table 5-1) divided by population aged 5 to 14 years (see Table 1-2) at the beginning of the period.

[e] Excludes Newfoundland up to and including this calculation.

[f] See note 11.

Source: Calculations by the author from Tables 1-1, 1-2 and 5-1.

occurred in different years in different provinces, although in all provinces east of Alberta the peak was reached in the late 1960s or early 1970s. For the western provinces, the peak occurred later, reflecting the westward drift of migration and the fact that younger people have a higher propensity to migrate. These persons often either bring young families with them or start families in their new place of residence, thus contributing to elementary-secondary education enrolments. Note that this has even been the case to some degree in British Columbia, where the fertility rate is relatively low.

150

TABLE 5-3

TOTAL ENROLMENT IN ELEMENTARY AND

SECONDARY SCHOOLS FOR CANADA, 1950-1979

(000's)

Academic Year	Public	Private	Federal	Blind and Deaf	Overseas	Total	Growth Rate[a] (%)
1950-51	2,627.2	121.4	25.5	—	—	2,774.1[b]	—
1955-56	3,124.7	144.5	32.4	—	—	3,301.6[b]	6.0[c]
1960-61	3,989.3	168.2	36.9	2.7	7.3	4,204.3	4.9[c]
1961-62	4,184.3	179.6	37.9	3.0	7.9	4,412.8	5.0
1962-63	4,373.0	191.5	37.8	3.1	7.3	4,612.6	4.5
1963-64	4,554.8	201.1	38.8	3.3	7.4	4,805.3	4.2
1964-65	4,744.6	203.0	38.7	3.5	7.3	4,997.1	4.0
1965-66	4,909.8	203.7	38.3	3.7	7.8	5,163.2	3.3
1966-67	5,075.8	189.0	39.1	3.7	8.4	5,316.0	3.0
1967-68	5,265.9	157.5	39.3	3.8	8.3	5,474.7	3.0
1968-69	5,454.7	145.8	37.6	3.9	8.7	5,650.5	3.2
1969-70	5,579.0	155.6	28.6	4.1	7.9	5,775.3	2.2
1970-71	5,655.4	142.6	28.4	4.1	5.9	5,836.4	1.1
1971-72	5,628.2	139.9	29.2	4.1	4.6	5,806.1	−0.5
1972-73	5,570.3	151.6	29.8	3.9	4.6	5,760.1	−0.8
1973-74	5,491.9	157.9	32.5	3.6	4.6	5,690.5	−1.2
1974-75	5,416.4	175.3	32.9	3.9	4.6	5,633.1	−1.0
1975-76	5,372.0	182.0	32.5	3.8	4.6	5,594.9	−0.7
1976-77	5,284.2	188.3	33.2	3.7	4.4	5,513.8	−1.4
1977-78	5,172.0	189.3	35.1	3.4	4.0	5,403.8	−2.0
1978-79	5,052.9	191.5	34.4	3.4	4.0	5,286.2	−2.2

Notes: [a] Calculated from unrounded data.

[b] Excludes schools for the blind and deaf, and overseas.

[c] Based on public, private and federal enrolments only.

Source: Statistics Canada, *Elementary-Secondary School Enrolment* (Catalogue No. 81-210), various issues.

The 1978-79 enrolment levels are also presented in Table 5-4. They show an enrolment decline from a previous peak in *every* province and territory. The greatest decline is in Quebec (down 21.8 per cent), and the least in Alberta (down 0.9 per cent) and in the territories. Note that the decline in Ontario (4.9 per cent) is well below the Canadian

151

TABLE 5-4
THE PEAK AND 1978-79 ELEMENTARY-SECONDARY ENROLMENT
AND ENROLMENT RATES FOR CANADA AND THE PROVINCES

Province or Territory	Peak Enrolment		1978-79 Enrolment		
	Year	Number (000's)	Number (000's)	Rate[a] (%)	Sex Ratio[b]
Nfld	1971-72	163.7	153.6	92.4	1.05
PEI	1970-71	30.7	27.9	89.8	1.02
NS	1970-71	217.5	196.8	96.6	1.04
NB	1971-72	177.1	160.7	91.8	1.05
PQ	1969-70	1,658.5	1,297.4	92.5	1.08
Ont	1971-72	2,084.0	1,982.0	104.4[c]	1.06
Man	1970-71	261.3	232.5	98.8	1.04
Sask	1968-69	255.7	221.0	97.8	1.04
Alta	1976-77	451.2	447.2	96.1	1.05
BC	1973-74	573.8	545.1	99.6	1.05
Yukon	1977-78	5.4	5.2	96.5	1.12
NWT	1976-77	12.9	12.9	93.6	1.07
Overseas	1968-69	8.7	4.0	—	1.08
Can	1970-71	5,836.4	5,286.2	98.4[d]	1.06[d]

Notes: [a] Total enrolment divided by total population aged 5 to 17 years.
   [b] Ratio of males to females.
   [c] See note 21.
   [d] Includes overseas enrolments.

Sources: Statistics Canada, *Elementary-Secondary School Enrolment* (Catalogue No. 81-210), various issues; and calculations by the author.

average (9.4 per cent), as is the decline in British Columbia (5.0 per cent). These two provinces have the highest participation rates, thus implying that students there remain in the elementary-secondary education systems longer than in other jurisdictions.[12] It is interesting to note that in almost all jurisdictions the enrolment rate, as calculated in Table 5-4, is above 90 per cent.[13] This suggests that further increases in enrolment are not likely to be a result of increases in the enrolment rate. Instead, demographic considerations will be the most important determinant of future elementary-secondary enrolments in Canada. Table 5-4 also shows that the sex ratios of students are consistently above unity; that is, there are more male than female students in all jurisdictions in Canada.

To obtain projections of future enrolments by the enrolment rate method, it is necessary to develop age-sex-specific enrolment rates for each province. Rates for each year of age (from 5 to 20 years) by sex were calculated from Statistics Canada data for all years (for which data were available) since the 1974-75 academic year.[14] These data are almost completely devoid of any trends because of the compulsory nature of elementary-secondary education (thus implying enrolment rates close to 100 per cent). Consequently, average enrolment rates were calculated for the period to remove the impact of any single year's data on the resulting projections. The resulting rates are presented in Tables 5-5 (for males) and 5-6 (for females). Note that as would be expected, rates are generally close to 100 per cent for all provinces for ages 6 through 15 years. Furthermore, rates slightly in excess of 100 per cent are possible because an academic year's enrolment (usually measured in October) is being divided by the relevant population measured the previous June 1. Hence, a net inflow into the province between these two dates could account for increased enrolments without a corresponding increase in the population measure.[15]

By applying these rates to the relevant provincial population futures (see chapter 3), projections of elementary-secondary school enrolment by age, sex, and province are obtained. These can then be aggregated to obtain total enrolments by province, which in turn can be summed to obtain Canada-wide figures. These results are discussed in the following section.

Elementary-Secondary Enrolment Futures

The results of applying the enrolment rates in Tables 5-5 and 5-6 to the first seven alternative population projections described in chapter 3[16] are summarized in Table 5-7 for the entire projection horizon (that is, to the year 2051). A projection of over seventy years permits the differences to accumulate and thus highlights the differences between the alternative projections. Nonetheless, there is a great deal of similarity among the results, with the exception of the alternative fertility scenarios (Projections 3 and 4). The general results would appear to be that enrolments will be below current levels (see Table 5-1) throughout the rest of the century and beyond, and significantly lower than the peak levels of the early 1970s. For example, in the no change scenario (Projection 1), the enrolment projection for the year

TABLE 5-5
AVERAGE ELEMENTARY-SECONDARY ENROLMENT RATES BY AGE BY PROVINCE FOR MALES
(%)

Age (Years)	Nfld[a]	PEI[a]	NS[a]	NB[a]	PQ[b]	Ont[a]	Man[a]	Sask[a]	Alta[c]	BC[a]	Yukon[a]	NWT[a]
5	52.0	12.4	51.2	21.1	54.3	80.4	63.0	59.1	47.6	62.1	62.0[d]	52.3[d]
6	99.7	97.3	99.3	95.9	102.4	100.1	99.2	100.9	98.9	101.5	101.5	97.7
7	99.7	98.8	98.5	98.5	101.2	99.5	99.4	100.2	101.0	101.3	110.0	101.6
8	99.0	98.6	98.6	99.3	99.2	99.4	98.7	100.0	100.4	100.9	105.8	102.3
9	98.6	97.4	98.9	97.7	97.4	99.4	99.1	99.1	100.0	101.3	105.1	104.0
10	98.4	98.0	98.5	99.3	99.8	99.3	98.5	99.2	99.2	100.9	102.4	106.4
11	98.7	96.2	97.7	97.6	102.0	98.8	98.6	99.1	99.4	99.7	103.2	101.6
12	98.6	95.8	98.0	98.9	105.1	99.0	98.7	98.4	100.2	100.2	110.4	101.5
13	99.5	97.0	99.4	100.1	101.7	99.9	98.3	98.6	100.1	100.0	108.8	95.5
14	98.8	94.0	98.0	96.5	93.6	100.6	98.2	98.5	99.5	99.7	115.9	92.4
15	93.9	85.0	93.1	92.3	89.1	99.2	96.2	96.2	96.1	98.6	103.6	82.5
16	80.2	71.4	80.3	81.5	77.9	90.3	86.6	85.4	85.1	90.1	76.7	65.5
17	32.6	51.6	60.2	57.7	47.8	74.3	64.2	60.9	58.5	66.0	48.1	38.7
18	10.1	17.1	21.0	22.2	11.6	39.8	19.1	12.8	15.3	16.7	12.3	15.5
19	1.7	4.8	5.8	6.7	3.7	9.2	5.2	3.1	3.4	3.6	2.9	3.5
20+	0.6	1.5	2.2	2.5	1.9	3.2	2.5	1.4	2.2	1.1	0.2	2.5

Notes: [a] Three-year average based on enrolments from 1974/75 to 1979/80.
  [b] Based on a three-year average data (enrolments 1974/75, 1976/77 and 1977/78) scaled to be consistent with 1979/80 total enrolments.
  [c] Five-year average based on enrolments from 1974/75 to 1978/79.
  [d] Three-year average based on enrolments from 1977/78 to 1979/80.

Sources: Calculations by the author, using Statistics Canada, *Elementary-Secondary School Enrolment* (Catalogue No. 81-210), various issues; and

TABLE 5-6

AVERAGE ELEMENTARY-SECONDARY ENROLMENT RATES BY AGE BY PROVINCE FOR FEMALES[a]

(%)

Age (Years)	Nfld	PEI	NS	NB	PQ	Ont	Man	Sask	Alta	BC	Yukon	NWT
5	51.9	12.5	51.1	21.4	52.8	80.8	63.8	59.7	48.1	62.1	59.4	48.6
6	99.6	100.3	98.3	96.5	98.7	100.5	99.8	100.4	99.9	100.8	92.0	103.6
7	98.7	99.6	98.6	98.7	98.9	99.8	99.5	100.9	100.8	101.3	93.8	106.9
8	100.0	98.0	97.6	99.3	97.7	99.6	98.7	99.9	100.6	100.6	98.5	110.8
9	98.6	99.0	99.0	99.3	92.4	98.8	99.1	99.0	100.3	100.9	96.4	107.0
10	98.9	99.0	98.5	100.9	96.4	99.2	98.6	98.7	99.0	100.8	103.8	106.8
11	99.0	97.0	98.0	98.7	98.3	98.9	98.6	98.8	99.3	100.4	103.7	102.1
12	99.3	97.8	98.7	99.3	101.9	99.2	98.2	98.3	100.2	101.2	105.6	100.2
13	99.6	98.9	99.2	99.7	98.3	100.3	98.7	99.1	99.8	99.9	99.3	94.2
14	98.9	99.1	98.6	98.7	93.6	100.6	98.2	98.2	99.1	100.6	104.7	94.3
15	95.0	96.2	96.3	95.9	89.0	99.3	96.5	96.8	96.4	98.0	100.9	83.4
16	79.3	94.8	86.9	87.4	77.6	90.8	88.1	90.6	88.1	91.0	77.5	62.5
17	29.2	85.9	68.4	58.2	46.3	72.0	64.6	65.6	58.4	62.9	50.7	34.8
18	8.2	16.4	18.2	15.7	9.4	30.5	12.8	9.2	10.3	11.2	12.6	13.4
19	1.3	4.6	4.4	3.9	2.7	4.4	3.4	2.2	2.3	2.2	1.8	3.8
20+	0.5	1.6	2.1	1.9	1.4	3.4	2.8	1.7	5.2	1.6	0.5	3.4

Note: [a] See notes to Table 5-5.

Sources: Calculations by the author, using Statistics Canada, *Elementary-Secondary School Enrolment* (Catalogue No. 81-210), various issues; and post-census population estimates.

155

TABLE 5-7
ALTERNATIVE ELEMENTARY-SECONDARY ENROLMENT PROJECTIONS
FOR CANADA, 1981-2051 [a]
(000's)

Projection Number and Description	Year							
	1981	1991	2001	2011	2021	2031	2041	2051
1 Base (or no change)	4,928.6	4,834.4	4,972.3	4,505.3	4,521.7	4,417.8	4,205.1	4,180.3
2 Increased life expectancy	4,928.6	4,836.1	4,981.1	4,517.5	4,538.0	4,438.7	4,228.7	4,207.7
3 Low fertility	4,928.6	4,736.2	4,568.3	3,984.9	3,842.2	3,581.2	3,290.8	3,146.8
4 High fertility	4,928.6	4,888.5	5,582.3	5,672.1	6,017.5	6,487.0	6,689.6	7,126.3
5 Low immigration	4,912.5	4,729.0	4,763.9	4,218.8	4,155.9	3,974.8	3,696.2	3,605.4
6 Return migration	4,928.7	4,835.7	4,967.9	4,495.1	4,501.0	4,388.1	4,165.8	4,129.0
7 Westward drift	4,928.6	4,833.6	4,972.5	4,506.2	4,526.5	4,424.5	4,215.2	4,194.9

Note: [a] All projections use average enrolment rates (see Tables 5-5 and 5-6).

Source: Projections by the author.

2001 is approximately 15 per cent below the 1970-71 peak. In addition, the sex ratios of the student populations are not projected to change significantly from the current ratios (see Table 5-4).[17]

The time patterns of these projections are, however, very interesting (see Figure 5-1). Not surprisingly, the enrolment pattern follows the time pattern of births (see Figure 3-3) with an approximate lag of a little over a decade. This means that the wave-like pattern of future births that was obtained and examined in chapter 3 will be reflected in the educational system in the years ahead. More specifically, the Baby Boom of the 1950s resulted in the peak elementary-secondary enrolments of the early 1970s; the children of the Baby Boom generation (even assuming no change in fertility — see Projection 1)

FIGURE 5-1
HISTORICAL AND FUTURE TOTAL ELEMENTARY-
SECONDARY SCHOOL ENROLMENTS, CANADA,
1961-2051

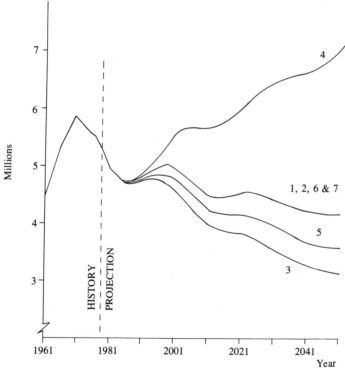

Note: Numbers refer to projection numbers.
Sources: Tables 5-3, 5-7 and projections by the author.

157

will probably be born primarily in the 1980s, resulting in *increasing* enrolments over the last half of the 1980s and the early half of the 1990s. Further projection beyond this time horizon sees the pattern repeat itself twenty-five to thirty years later, although since fertility rates are below replacement levels (in Projection 1), the long-term trend in enrolments is downward.

In the near term, however, these projections show that even under a wide variety of assumptions, elementary-secondary enrolments in Canada can be expected to continue to decline to the mid-1980s, reaching a trough that is approximately 20 per cent below the peak enrolments of the early 1970s. The extent of the subsequent upturn will be largely influenced by fertility behaviour. At unchanged fertility rates, the subsequent increase in enrolments is projected to peak towards the end of the century at a level still well below the previous peak; that is, the 1998 peak in Projection 1 (see Figure 5-1) is still 13.7 per cent below the 1970 peak. Even if fertility was to return to above replacement levels (as in Projection 4), the 1970 peak enrolments are not projected to be achieved until well into the next century. Under these conditions, a plateau of enrolments of around 5.7 million students is reached in the early part of the next century and maintained for approximately a decade. Of course, substantial declines can be expected if the fertility rate continues to decline (Projection 3). Under these conditions, enrolments are over 20 per cent below the previous peak by the turn of the century and declining rapidly (see Figure 5-1). Note that lower immigration (Projection 5) also results in a time pattern of declining enrolments that lies between Projections 1 and 3.

The impact of these general patterns on the provinces is summarized in Table 5-8. These results, of course, also reflect the interprovincial migration assumptions embodied in the population projections. In general, enrolments decline in all provinces and territories, with the notable exceptions of Alberta and British Columbia. Even in these two provinces, enrolments are projected to decline slightly into the 1980s before resuming their upward trend to a peak around the turn of the century. The precipitous decline in enrolments that has already taken place in Quebec (see Table 5-4) — a reflection of low fertility and unfavourable migration patterns — is projected to continue, although a mild respite in the early 1990s can be expected. By the year 2001, enrolments in Quebec are projected to be almost 40 per cent lower than their peak of thirty years earlier.

The projections, again, appear to be remarkably robust under a variety of possible assumptions, excepting — not surprisingly — the

TABLE 5-8

ALTERNATIVE ELEMENTARY-SECONDARY ENROLMENT FUTURES FOR CANADA AND THE PROVINCES, 2001[a]

(000's)

Projection Number	Can	Nfld	PEI	NS	NB	PQ	Ont	Man	Sask	Alta	BC	Yukon	NWT
1	4,972.3	131.9	26.8	173.3	141.2	1,016.7	1,811.8	191.0	233.5	614.0	615.8	4.5	11.7
2	4,981.1	132.0	26.8	173.5	141.5	1,017.5	1,814.4	191.7	234.6	615.7	616.9	4.5	11.8
3	4,568.3	114.4	24.0	159.6	129.9	942.8	1,683.5	173.7	205.2	553.5	567.8	4.0	9.9
4	5,582.3	141.0	29.1	194.7	157.6	1,159.9	2,054.4	211.4	251.0	673.9	692.3	4.9	12.2
5	4,763.9	129.9	26.1	169.3	138.1	984.6	1,715.0	182.9	227.3	588.9	586.1	4.3	11.4
6	4,967.9	131.4	25.7	169.2	136.7	1,074.5	1,886.5	207.6	188.5	519.1	608.1	6.0	14.5
7	4,972.5	124.5	24.7	160.6	131.0	995.9	1,734.0	195.7	233.6	683.7	674.9	3.8	10.1

Note: [a] All projections use average enrolment rates (see Tables 5-5 and 5-6).

Source: Projections by the author.

fertility assumptions. It is interesting to note, for example, that a return to the interprovincial migration patterns of 1966-75 (Projection 7) would *not* improve the enrolments in the Atlantic provinces or in Ontario (compared to Projection 1). Lower immigration (Projection 5) has a relatively greater impact on Ontario, Alberta and British Columbia, while a further westward drift of the population (Projection 6) increases enrolments in the western provinces quite substantially.

Finally, Table 5-9 summarizes the time pattern of these projections. Almost all provinces in all projections experience a trough in enrolments in the 1980s. The trough occurs earlier and is of much smaller relative magnitude in Alberta and British Columbia, and later and of a greater relative magnitude in the eastern provinces. As previously inferred, the decline is greatest in Quebec, where by the late 1980s enrolments over one-third below the previous peak are projected. Generally, from the previous peak of the 1970s enrolment declines in excess of 20 per cent can be expected in all provinces except Ontario, which has the highest enrolment rate of all provinces. The interesting aspect of this conclusion is its robustness — it is true of all projections.

In summary, elementary-secondary school enrolments in Canada can be expected to follow the wave-like pattern of future births, with a lag of approximately a decade. This means continued declines to the mid-1980s, followed by moderate increases in enrolments to the mid-1990s. The trough of the 1980s is projected to be approximately 20 per cent below the peaks of the early 1970s, with greater declines in Quebec and lesser declines in Alberta and British Columbia. The extent of the subsequent increase depends crucially on fertility behaviour, but it does appear very unlikely that the previous enrolment peaks will be obtained in this century, with the possible exceptions of Alberta and British Columbia.

Post-Secondary Enrolments: A Historical Overview[18]

Post-secondary education in Canada is divided between universities and non-university post-secondary institutions, the latter primarily comprising technical and vocational institutions of higher learning.[19] No attempt is made here to survey the historical development of these institutions in each of the provinces. Instead, as for elementary-secondary enrolments, recent (postwar) developments are briefly surveyed as background for the choice of age-sex-province-specific enrolment rate assumptions for each of these two main types of post-secondary institutions. These assumptions are then applied to the

TABLE 5-9

ALTERNATIVE PEAK TO TROUGH ELEMENTARY-SECONDARY ENROLMENT DECREASES FOR CANADA AND THE PROVINCES, 1961-2001[a]

Projection Number	Can	Nfld	PEI	NS	NB	PQ	Ont[b]	Man	Sask	Alta	BC	Yukon	NWT
					YEAR OF TROUGH[b]								
1	1985	1991	1987	1989	1990	1988*	1986	1990*	1984	1980	1983	1988	1988
2	1985	1991	1987	1989	1990	1988*	1986	1990*	1984	1980	1983	1988	1988
3	1986*	N	1990*	1991*	N	1989*	1989*	N	1984	1980	1983	1990*	1990*
4	1985	1990	1987	1988	1989	1987	1986	1989	1984	1980	1983	1988	1988
5	1986	1991	1987	1989	1990	1988*	1989	N	1984	1981	1983	1989	1988
6	1985	1991	1988	1989	1990	1986*	1986	1988	1989*	1981	1983	1983	1984
7	1985	1994*	1989	1990*	1995*	1988*	1989	1989*	1984	1980	1983	1990*	1990*
					PER CENT DECREASE								
1	19.5	20.7	18.5	23.1	22.1	35.5*	16.6	25.2*	20.0	1.6	11.0	20.8	14.9
2	19.3	20.7	18.5	23.1	22.0	35.4*	16.6	25.2*	20.0	1.6	11.0	20.7	14.8
3	19.7*	N	19.0*	24.1*	N	35.9*	17.2*	N	20.0	1.6	11.0	22.3*	17.3*
4	19.5	16.7	18.5	22.9	21.9	35.3	16.5	24.9	20.0	1.6	11.0	20.7	15.1
5	20.5	21.1	19.0	23.7	22.7	36.2*	18.3	N	20.3	1.9	11.8	21.9	15.7
6	19.5	20.6	19.1	23.6	22.9	34.8*	16.0	23.9	22.4*	1.6	11.0	15.4	10.6
7	19.5	22.8*	20.4	25.4*	24.7*	35.8*	17.6	24.5*	20.0	1.6	10.5	27.8*	20.3*

Notes: [a] See Table 5-17 for peak enrolment data. N implies no trough (that is, continued decreases throughout). An asterisk (*) implies that enrolment at the end of the period (2001) is lower than at the trough.

[b] Date of commencement of academic year.

Source: Projections by the author.

161

TABLE 5-10
TOTAL ENROLMENT IN POST-SECONDARY INSTITUTIONS FOR CANADA, 1920-1979
(000's)

Academic Year	Full-Time Undergrad.	Full-Time Graduate	Part-Time Total	Total University		Full-Time Non-University	Total Post-Secondary	
				Enrol-ments	Growth (%)		Enrol-ments	Growth (%)
1920-21	22.8	0.4	—	23.2[a]	—	—	—	—
1930-31	31.6	1.4	—	33.0[a]	3.6[b]	—	—	—
1940-41	34.8	1.6	—	36.4[a]	1.0[b]	—	—	—
1950-51	64.0	4.6	—	68.6[a]	6.5[b]	—	—	—
1960-61	107.2	6.5	—	113.7[a]	5.2[b]	49.4	163.1[a]	—
1961-62	121.3	7.3	—	128.6[a]	13.1[a]	53.4	182.0[a]	11.6[a]
1962-63	132.7	8.4	44.0	185.1	9.7[a]	55.6	240.7	8.1[a]
1963-64	146.8	11.1	56.9	214.9	16.1	62.2	277.1	15.1
1964-65	163.8	13.8	63.7	241.3	12.3	66.0	307.4	10.9
1965-66	187.0	17.2	73.0	277.3	14.9	69.4	346.6	12.8
1966-67	210.6	19.7	84.8	315.1	13.4	80.2	395.3	14.0
1967-68	229.3	24.2	97.9	351.4	11.5	99.4	450.8	14.0

Academic Year	Full-Time Undergrad.	Full-Time Graduate	Part-Time Total	Total University		Full-Time Non-University	Total Post-Secondary	
				Enrolments	Growth (%)		Enrolments	Growth (%)
1968-69	239.7	26.1	101.7	367.5	4.6	129.5	497.0	10.3
1969-70	263.9	30.2	122.0	416.2	13.2	142.7	558.9	12.4
1970-71	276.3	33.2	156.6	466.0	12.0	166.1	632.1	13.1
1971-72	287.1	35.9	155.4	478.4	2.7	173.8	652.2	3.2
1972-73	284.9	37.5	153.0	475.4	−0.6	191.0	666.3	2.2
1973-74	295.0	37.1	161.2	493.3	3.8	201.5	694.7	4.3
1974-75	309.5	37.8	170.2	517.6	4.9	210.8	728.4	4.9
1975-76	327.2	36.0	183.6	546.8	5.7	221.6	768.4	5.5
1976-77	332.7	36.6	188.9	559.2	2.3	227.2	786.4	2.3
1977-78	330.3	36.6	208.0	574.9	2.8	241.7	816.6	3.8
1978-79	323.6	36.6	214.1	574.3	−0.1	248.0	822.3	0.7

Notes: [a]Full-time enrolment only.
[b]Average annual growth.

Sources: Statistics Canada, *Historical Compendium of Education Statistics from Confederation to 1975* (Catalogue No. 81-568), pp. 206, 208 and 240, *Universities: Enrolment and Degrees* (Catalogue No. 81-204), various issues, and *Enrolment in Community Colleges* (Catalogue No. 81-222), various issues.

163

population futures outlined in chapter 3 to obtain post-secondary enrolment projections for Canada and the provinces.

Table 5-10 summarizes post-secondary enrolments in Canada since 1920, and Table 5-11 shows the comparable population growth and implied enrolment rates. From these data it is clear that widespread post-secondary education in Canada is a post-Second World War phenomenon, with growth rates in the 1940s, 1950s and 1960s averaging well in excess of the population growth rates — thus implying rapidly increasing enrolment (or participation) rates over this period. The 1970s has been a decade of reduced but still positive growth, although an overall enrolment decline is no longer an unknown event. Moreover, enrolment rates appear to have stabilized, at least for full-time university enrolments (Table 5-11, note g). Since the mid-1960s, growth has tended to be comparatively stronger in the

TABLE 5-11
POPULATION GROWTH, FULL-TIME UNIVERSITY ENROLMENT GROWTH AND ENROLMENT RATES FOR CANADA, 1920-1980
(%)

	Average Annual		Enrolment Rates	
Period	Population Growth[a]	Enrolment Growth[b]	Total Population[c]	Population 15-24 Years[d]
1920-30	1.7	3.6	0.26	1.53
1930-40	1.0	1.0	0.32	1.69
1940-50	1.7[e]	6.5[e]	0.32	1.69
1950-60	2.7	5.2	0.50[e]	3.27[e]
1960-70	1.7	10.5[f]	0.62	4.36
1970-80	1.2	1.9[f]	1.43[g]	7.71[g]

Notes: [a] Between census years (see Table 1-1).
[b] Calculated from Table 5-10.
[c] Total enrolment (from Table 5-10) divided by total population (Table 1-1) at the beginning of the period.
[d] Total enrolment (Table 5-10) divided by population aged 15 to 24 years (see Table 1-2) at the beginning of the period.
[e] Excludes Newfoundland up to and including this calculation.
[f] Including part-time enrolments would increase these growth rates to 15.4 (1960-70) and 2.7 (1970-80) respectively.
[g] For 1978, the comparable figures are 1.53 and 7.78 respectively.

Sources: Calculations by the author from Tables 1-1, 1-2 and 5-10.

TABLE 5-12
POST-SECONDARY ENROLMENT RATES FOR CANADA,
1961-1978
(%)

Academic Year	Population 18-24 Years (000's)	Full-Time Univ.	Part-Time Univ.	Full-Time Non-Univ.	Total
1961	1,722.6	7.5	—	3.1	10.6[a]
1966	2,191.7	10.5	3.9	3.7	18.0
1971	2,688.8	12.0	5.8	6.5	24.3
1972	2,729.6	11.8	5.6	7.0	24.4
1973	2,799.2	11.9	5.8	7.2	24.8
1974	2,891.7	12.0	5.9	7.3	25.2
1975	2,975.5	12.2	6.2	7.4	25.8
1976	3,046.7	12.1	6.2	7.5	25.8
1977	3,196.0	11.5	6.5	7.6	25.6
1978	3,196.3	11.3	6.7	7.8	25.7

Note: [a] Excludes part-time university.

Sources: Statistics Canada, *Population* (Catalogue No. 91-518); and calculations by the author (using Table 5-10).

non-university sector, as new institutions have been introduced to handle demands for technical and vocational training. Nonetheless, the 1970s witnessed reduced growth for these institutions, as well as the stabilization of enrolment rates (see Table 5-12).

Of total post-secondary enrolments included in Table 5-12, full-time university students currently comprise almost 44 per cent of the total, part-time university students around 26 per cent, and full-time non-university students the remaining 30 per cent.[20] This latter percentage had gradually increased from around 20 per cent in the mid-1960s. Within the university total, full-time undergraduate students currently account for over 60 per cent of the total, down from almost 75 per cent in the early 1960s. Graduate student enrolment has stabilized at approximately 11.5 per cent of total university enrolments since 1975, up from around 7.5 per cent in the early 1960s. The percentage of female students rose from around 30 per cent in the early 1960s to almost 50 per cent by the late 1970s. No comparable information is available for the non-university sector.

The provincial distributions of 1978-79 enrolments are summarized in Table 5-13. Approximately one in four Canadians of age 18 to 24 years attends a post-secondary educational institution. The provincial range is from a low of one in seven in Newfoundland to a high of one in three in Quebec, the latter reflecting the high enrolments in the two-year pre-university CEGEPs in that province (see the non-university columns).[21] Enrolment rates above 20 per cent are recorded for Nova Scotia (which has a high full-time university enrolment rate), Ontario, Manitoba (which has a high part-time university enrolment rate), and Alberta (which has a high full-time non-university rate). The rates for the remaining provinces are below 20 per cent.

To obtain enrolment projections, it is necessary to break down these province-specific enrolment rates by age and sex. Because enrolment rates have tended to stabilize since the mid-1970s, data from 1975-76 to 1979-80 (where available) were combined to calculate average enrolment rates for selected age groups.[22] For university enrolments there is a plethora of data on enrolments, broken down by full-time/part-time and undergraduate/graduate as well as by age and sex. Upon examination of these data, it was decided for projection purposes to aggregate all university enrolments into seven age groups for each sex: less than 20 years, 20 to 24 years, 25 to 29 years, 30 to 34 years, 35 to 39 years, 40 years and over, and a residual group of unknown age. Enrolment rates were calculated by dividing by the appropriate population estimates, with the population aged 18 and 19 years used for the first group and the population 18 years and over used for the "age unknown" group. The resulting enrolment rates, averaged over the period 1975-76 to 1979-80, are presented in Table 5-14.

For non-university enrolments no breakdown by sex is available. In addition, total enrolments in the higher-age groups are sufficiently small that age groups of 30 years and over were combined into a single age group for the enrolment rate calculations. For some provinces, averages from the four academic years 1975-76 through 1978-79 were employed.[23] The resulting enrolment rates are presented in Table 5-15. The impact of the CEGEPs in Quebec is clearly apparent in these results. Almost 40 per cent of the 18- and 19-year-olds in that province enrol in one of these institutions.

By applying these enrolment rates to the relevant population futures (of chapter 3), one obtains projections of post-secondary enrolment by age and sex (for university enrolment) by province. These can then be aggregated to obtain total enrolments by province, which in turn can be

TABLE 5-13
POST-SECONDARY ENROLMENTS AND ENROLMENT RATES
FOR CANADA AND THE PROVINCES, 1978-1979

Province	Population 18-24 Years (000's)	Enrolments (000's)				Enrolment Rates (%)[a]			
		Full-Time Univ.	Part-Time Univ.[a]	Full-Time Non-Univ.	Total	Full-Time Univ.	Part-Time Univ.	Full-Time Non-Univ.	Total
Nfld	77.8	6.2	3.2	2.0	11.3	7.9	4.1	2.5	14.6
PEI	16.1	1.4	0.8	0.8	3.0	8.6	5.1	4.8	18.5
NS	114.8	17.6	6.6	2.8	27.0	15.3	5.8	2.4	23.5
NB	97.7	10.9	4.1	1.7	16.7	11.2	4.2	1.7	17.1
PQ	888.1	82.0	80.9	136.1	299.1	9.2	9.1	15.3	33.7
Ont	1,112.9	150.7	80.0	64.5	295.3	13.5	7.2	5.8	26.5
Man	137.0	16.6	11.1	3.1	30.8	12.1	8.1	2.3	22.4
Sask	126.6	13.9	6.0	2.4	22.3	11.0	4.7	1.9	17.6
Alta	287.4	30.7	9.4	17.3	57.4	10.7	3.3	6.0	20.0
BC	32.8	30.2	11.9	17.4	59.6	9.2	3.6	5.3	18.2
Yukon/NWT	9.8	0	0	0	0	0	0	0	0
Can	3,196.3	360.2	214.1	248.0	822.3	11.3	6.7	7.8	25.7

Note: [a] Calculated from unrounded numbers.

Sources: Statistics Canada, *Universities: Enrolment and Degrees, 1978* (Catalogue No. 81-204), and *Enrolment in Community Colleges, 1978* (Catalogue No. 81-222).

167

TABLE 5-14
AVERAGE UNIVERSITY ENROLMENTS RATES BY AGE BY PROVINCE FOR MALES AND FEMALES[a]
(%)

Age Group (Years)	Nfld	PEI	NS	NB	PQ	Ont	Man	Sask	Alta	BC
MALES										
Less than 20	15.24	12.82	15.15	14.12	3.31	10.76	14.53	11.62	10.84	8.53
20-24	6.20	8.53	13.54	9.89	10.85	16.26	12.95	10.70	10.04	8.60
25-29	3.58	2.09	4.86	3.05	6.16	6.28	5.60	4.74	4.50	3.77
30-34	2.10	1.43	2.52	1.52	3.84	3.41	2.87	2.35	2.24	1.84
35-39	1.25	0.94	1.37	0.94	2.21	2.01	1.53	1.19	1.17	0.94
40+	0.18	0.23	0.31	0.12	0.41	0.37	0.29	0.17	0.26	0.18
Unknown	0.00	0.01	0.34	0.41	0.49	0.06	0.27	0.13	0.02	0.11
FEMALES										
Less than 20	14.50	15.81	18.85	15.72	3.62	12.00	15.58	14.25	11.39	8.82
20-24	4.58	6.86	10.50	7.35	8.37	12.56	10.40	9.11	8.07	6.82
25-29	2.80	2.80	3.29	2.00	4.19	4.39	4.30	3.93	3.10	2.61
30-34	2.55	2.84	2.18	1.60	3.70	3.20	3.18	2.79	2.30	1.69
35-39	2.08	2.73	1.84	1.36	2.99	2.54	2.51	2.24	1.91	1.04
40+	0.45	0.82	0.48	0.31	0.68	0.59	0.63	0.49	0.50	0.35
Unknown	0.00	0.01	1.29	0.65	0.35	0.05	0.43	0.12	0.02	0.11

Note: [a] Average of enrolment rates for academic years 1975/76 through 1979/80.

Source: Calculations by the author using Statistics Canada, *Universities: Enrolments and Degrees* (Catalogue No. 81-204), various issues.

summed to obtain Canada-wide figures. These results are discussed in the following section.

Post-Secondary Enrolment Futures

The results of applying the enrolment rates in Tables 5-14 and 5-15 to the first seven alternative population futures described in chapter 3 are summarized in Table 5-16 and Figure 5-2 for the entire population projection horizon (that is, to the year 2051). Since enrolment rates are held constant over the projection horizon, these results isolate the impacts of population aging on future post-secondary enrolments. Once again the extended projection horizon highlights the differences between the alternative projections.

However, there is considerable similarity among the results, especially within the balance of this century. This arises because the vast majority of potential post-secondary enrolees are already born and resident in Canada. For total university enrolments, the variation is between 555.9 thousand (Projection 5) and 583.5 thousand (Projection 6) by the year 2001 — a variation of only 27.6 thousand students, or less than 5 per cent of the no change scenario (Projection 1). By 2051 the changed fertility alternatives finally dominate the results, and the variation between the alternatives is much greater, with the high fertility projection (Projection 4) providing the highest projected enrolment, 44 per cent above the base projection (Projection 1), and the low fertility projection (Projection 3) providing the lowest projected enrolment, 17 per cent below the base projection.

For full-time non-university enrolments, the variation follows a similar pattern. By 2001, the variation is between 185.5 thousand students (Projection 5) and 195.3 thousand students (Projection 6) — that is, a variation of only 9.8 thousand students country-wide, or about 5 per cent of the no change scenario (Projection 1). At the end of the projection horizon (2051) the variation is, of course, much greater, ranging between the high fertility alternative of 241.0 thousand (Projection 4) and the low fertility alternative of 123.7 thousand (Projection 3), a range of 76 per cent around the base projection.

From these results it is clear that immigration and interprovincial migration patterns are important determinants of post-secondary enrolments over the remainder of this century, and that alternative fertility patterns are not relevant for post-secondary enrolment until the next century. These results suggest some interesting outcomes. A reduction of 40,000 in annual immigration lowers total university enrolments by 23.7 thousand and full-time non-university enrolments

TABLE 5-15
AVERAGE NON-UNIVERSITY POST-SECONDARY ENROLMENT RATES
BY AGE BY PROVINCE

(%)

Age Group (Years)	Nfld[a]	PEI[b]	NS[a]	NB[a]	PQ[b]	Ont[b]	Man[a]	Sask[b]	Alta[b]	BC[b]
Less than 20	6.06	9.09	4.63	3.40	38.57	9.31	3.51	3.76	9.41	8.48
20-24	0.90	2.70	1.37	0.72	3.79	3.36	1.46	0.96	3.43	2.94
25-29	0.11	0.15	0.21	0.10	0.36	0.49	0.28	0.18	0.84	0.66
30+	0.01	0.02	0.01	0.01	0.05	0.06	0.03	0.02	0.14	0.08

Notes: [a] Average of five years' enrolment rates, 1975/76 to 1979-80.
       [b] Average of four years' enrolment rates, 1975/76 to 1978-79.

Source: Calculations by the author using Statistics Canada, *Enrolment in Community Colleges* (Catalogue No. 81-222), various issues.

TABLE 5-16
ALTERNATIVE POST-SECONDARY ENROLMENT FUTURES FOR CANADA, 1981-2051[a]

Projection Number and Description	Year							
	1981	1991	2001	2011	2021	2031	2041	2051
UNIVERSITY								
1 Base (or no change)	622.1	602.4	579.6	600.1	572.0	561.7	552.9	529.7
2 Increased life expectancy	622.1	603.0	581.1	602.5	575.2	565.5	557.5	534.6
3 Low fertility	622.1	602.4	576.5	571.5	527.3	501.7	475.1	440.2
4 High fertility	622.1	602.4	580.4	636.7	665.8	692.4	737.8	764.1
5 Low immigration	619.4	588.5	555.9	565.0	527.1	507.4	489.4	458.0
6 Return migration	622.1	604.5	583.5	605.2	578.0	567.5	558.6	534.7
7 Westward drift	622.1	600.0	575.2	593.5	564.2	553.2	543.8	520.5
NON-UNIVERSITY[b]								
1 Base (or no change)	241.7	186.0	192.6	192.1	169.6	171.5	163.7	153.9
2 Increased life expectancy	241.7	186.1	192.8	192.6	170.3	172.3	164.7	155.0
3 Low fertility	241.7	186.0	189.3	177.4	152.4	148.4	135.7	123.7
4 High fertility	241.7	186.0	193.8	217.3	212.4	225.1	238.3	241.0
5 Low immigration	240.8	182.1	185.5	181.2	156.1	155.0	144.6	132.5
6 Return migration	241.7	187.2	195.3	196.2	174.0	176.6	169.1	159.3
7 Westward drift	241.7	186.0	192.4	191.8	169.5	171.3	163.6	154.0

Notes: [a] All projections use average enrolment rates (see Tables 5-14 and 5-15).
[b] Full-time only.
Source: Projections by the author.

172

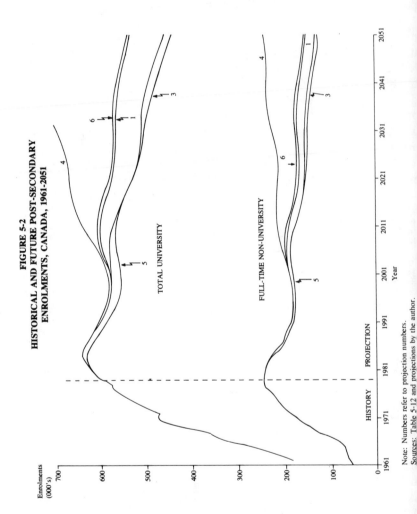

FIGURE 5-2
HISTORICAL AND FUTURE POST-SECONDARY
ENROLMENTS, CANADA, 1961-2051

TOTAL UNIVERSITY

FULL-TIME NON-UNIVERSITY

HISTORY   PROJECTION

Enrolments
(000's)

700

600

500

400

300

200

100

0

1961   1971   1981   1991   2001   2011   2021   2031   2041   2051
Year

Note: Numbers refer to projection numbers.
Sources: Table 5-12 and projections by the author.

by 7.1 thousand by 2001.[24] Perhaps surprisingly, a return to the interprovincial migration patterns of 1966-75 would increase total university enrolments by 3.9 thousand (0.7 per cent) and full-time non-university enrolments by 2.7 thousand (1.4 per cent). Further westward movement of the population is projected to decrease total post-secondary enrolments.

The provincial impacts of these alternative projections are summarized in Table 5-17. It is apparent from this table that reduced immigration reduces enrolments most in Quebec, Ontario and, to a lesser degree, British Columbia. A return to the interprovincial migration patterns of 1966-75 is projected to increase enrolments in the two central provinces of Quebec and Ontario, together with Manitoba, primarily at the expense of Saskatchewan and Alberta; a further westward drift of the population has exactly the opposite effect. Some of the magnitudes involved are quite substantial: for example, a return to the 1966-75 migration patterns would reduce post-secondary enrolments in Alberta by almost 15 per cent by 2001.

Of particular interest is the time pattern of these enrolment projections. The Canada-wide figures are presented in Figure 5-2 for the period 1961-2051. From these data it is apparent that regardless of the scenario, total university enrolments are projected to peak in the early 1980s, that is, in the *very* near future. In the no change scenario (Projection 1), the peak occurs in 1984 at 639.5 thousand students.[25] Thereafter enrolment is projected to decline (almost 10 per cent in Projection 1) to a trough in the late 1990s, after which the children of the peak enrolees of the 1980s can be expected to result in an enrolment "boomlet" around the year 2011. Subsequently, all but the high fertility alternative (Projection 4) show gradual declines in total university enrolments.

Table 5-18 summarizes the provincial implications of this pattern for the base scenario (Projection 1). Total university enrolments are projected to peak in *every* province in the early 1980s. The peak is projected to be reached first in Manitoba in 1982 or 1983, then shortly after in Prince Edward Island, Quebec (in 1983), Nova Scotia and New Brunswick (in 1983 or 1984), Ontario and Saskatchewan (in 1984), and Newfoundland and British Columbia (in 1984 or 1985). Only in Alberta are total university enrolments projected to continue to increase well beyond the 1980s; there a peak is not projected to occur until the year 2014.

The level (as distinct from the timing) of the enrolment peak depends on the enrolment rate assumptions. Since a discontinuity is

173

TABLE 5-17
ALTERNATIVE POST-SECONDARY ENROLMENT FUTURES FOR CANADA AND THE PROVINCES, 2001[a]
(000's)

Projection Number	Can	Nfld	PEI	NS	NB	PQ	Ont	Man	Sask	Alta	BC
UNIVERSITY											
1	579.6	9.8	2.4	26.6	16.0	133.5	235.6	26.1	22.7	57.8	49.2
2	581.1	9.8	2.4	26.7	16.0	133.8	236.1	26.2	22.8	58.0	49.3
3	576.5	9.7	2.4	26.4	15.8	133.2	234.6	25.9	22.4	57.3	48.8
4	580.4	9.8	2.4	26.7	16.0	133.5	236.0	26.1	22.7	57.9	49.2
5	555.9	9.7	2.4	26.1	15.6	129.4	223.3	25.0	22.1	55.5	46.9
6	583.5	9.7	2.3	26.0	15.5	140.3	244.9	28.2	18.4	49.4	48.7
7	575.2	9.3	2.2	24.8	14.9	130.9	226.3	26.7	22.7	63.8	53.5
NON-UNIVERSITY[b]											
1	192.6	1.7	0.7	2.4	1.3	85.8	55.2	2.5	2.4	22.1	18.4
2	192.9	1.7	0.7	2.4	1.3	85.9	55.3	2.6	2.4	22.1	18.5
3	189.3	1.7	0.7	2.4	1.3	84.1	54.5	2.5	2.3	21.7	18.2
4	193.8	1.7	0.7	2.4	1.3	86.6	55.5	2.6	2.4	22.1	18.5
5	185.5	1.7	0.7	2.4	1.3	83.4	52.5	2.4	2.3	21.2	17.6
6	195.3	1.7	0.7	2.4	1.3	90.1	57.4	2.8	1.9	19.0	18.2
7	192.4	1.6	0.6	2.2	1.2	84.2	53.1	2.6	2.4	24.3	20.0

Notes: [a] All projections use average enrolment rates (see Tables 5-14 and 5-15). [b] Full-time only.

TABLE 5-18
PROJECTED PEAK AND TROUGH TOTAL UNIVERSITY ENROLMENTS
FOR CANADA AND THE PROVINCES, PROJECTION 1, 1979-2001

Province	Peak				Trough	
	Year[a]	At 1979 Rates[b]	At Average Rates[c] (000's)	Per Cent Increase[d] (1979 to Peak)	Year[a]	Per Cent Decrease[d] (Peak to Trough)
Nfld	1984	10.6	10.9	6.4	2001	9.6
PEI	1983	2.2	2.5	6.5	1996	6.4
NS	1984	25.3	28.6	5.7	1997	8.2
NB	1984	16.0	17.2	5.4	1998	8.2
PQ	1983	179.6	165.1	3.4	←—— No Trough ——→	
Ont	1984	253.0	262.2	7.3	1998	10.6
Man	1983	27.5	30.1	2.1	2001	13.2
Sask	1984	21.3	23.3	7.9	1994	5.3
Alta	←—— Enrolments Increase Throughout ——→					
BC	1985	48.4	48.3	9.8	1996	2.4
Can	1984	630.3	639.2	6.6	1998	9.8

Notes: [a]Date at which academic year commences.
[b]Calculated using 1979/80 actual enrolment rates to facilitate comparison with recent data.
[c]See Table 5-14.
[d]From the calculation with average enrolment rates.

Source: Projections by the author.

introduced by using average rather than actual enrolment rates beginning in 1979, and since the peak is projected to occur in the very near future, the no change scenario (Projection 1) was also estimated by using 1979 actual enrolment rates. The difference in total enrolments between the two results reflects the impact of moving from average to current (1979) enrolment rates.[26] Both results are included in Table 5-18 to assess the impact of the rate assumptions on the projected peak enrolments: if enrolment rates were to remain at the 1979 levels, the first column measures the peak enrolment; if enrolment rates moved to their five-year average (Table 5-14), the second column measures the peak enrolment. Enrolment rates between these two assumptions will result in a peak between the two column measures. Total university enrolments in Canada are projected to rise 6.6 per cent above the 1979 (actual or hypothetical) levels by 1984; that is, demographic impacts alone are projected to lead to increased university enrolments in Canada of 6.6 per cent in the five years between 1979 and 1984.[27] Thereafter a decline of almost 10 per cent is projected over the period between 1984 and 1998. Although largely influenced by the projected declines in the 18-to-24-year-old age group in the population, the projected enrolment decline is moderated by increasing enrolments in the higher age groups, which are projected to become relatively more important in the population projections (see Table 3-14).

Although these overall trends are projected for almost every province, the quantitative impacts are quite diverse. For example, university enrolments in British Columbia are projected to increase a further 9.8 per cent and then to decrease by a moderate 2.4 per cent, whereas in Manitoba they are projected to increase only 2.1 per cent and then to decrease by a substantial 13.2 per cent. In all of the provinces east of Saskatchewan the percentage increase is more than offset by the subsequent decline.

In summary, as a result of demographic factors alone, total university enrolments in Canada are projected to peak in every province except Alberta around 1984 at around 5 per cent above current levels and thereafter to decline to a trough towards the end of the century at about 10 per cent below the previous peak level. The exact magnitudes, however, depend on the province and on the projection considered.

In regard to full-time non-university enrolments, it is apparent from Figure 5-2 that enrolments are *currently* at their peak, and from this point they are projected to decline, at least into the 1990s. A trough is

176

reached in 1992 approximately 25 per cent below current enrolment levels. Thereafter enrolments gradually increase to approximately 18 per cent below the current peak enrolment levels by 2005. At first glance, this might appear to be a surprising result, but it must be remembered that a substantial part of the total enrolments are students at Quebec's CEGEPs, largely dominated by the 18- and 19-year-old population (see Tables 5-13 and 5-15).[28] Since this population is declining rapidly, it is not surprising to arrive at the above result. When the Quebec data are removed from the full-time non-university total, the total of the remaining nine provinces moves over time in a pattern that is very similar to the university projection. A peak is reached in 1983 that is approximately 5.5 per cent above the 1978-79 enrolment levels. This is followed by a gradual decline to a trough in 1996 that is approximately 15 per cent below the previous peak, with a subsequent modest recovery to a peak in 2009 that is only 3.5 per cent below the previous peak (in Projection 1). Even under alternative population projections there is very little variation in this time pattern of enrolments (see also Table 5-17).

The provincial patterns of these full-time non-university projections are summarized in Table 5-19 (for Projection 1). Again an attempt has been made to assess the impact of moving to average rates, although here data on 1979-80 enrolments were far from complete (see Table 5-19, note b). In all provinces except New Brunswick and Quebec, an increase in enrolments is projected to peak in the early 1980s. The extent of the increases depends on the province under consideration. Thereafter *substantial* declines (in excess of 20 per cent) are projected for most provinces, the exceptions being Alberta and, to a lesser extent, British Columbia. The decline for Canada is 26.4 per cent, but as previously noted, removing the effect of Quebec reduces this figure to approximately 15 per cent.

In summary, as a result of demographic factors alone, full-time non-university enrolments are projected to peak in the early 1980s, followed by a substantial decline (a greater percentage than for universities) to a trough in the mid- to late 1990s that remains well *below* current enrolment levels.

Future Education Policy

The results of this chapter, especially when viewed in the context of the previous chapter, suggest a number of important considerations for policy development for the education sector in Canada in future years. A major finding in the analysis in chapter 4 was the need, with an

TABLE 5-19
PROJECTED PEAK AND TROUGH FULL-TIME NON-UNIVERSITY ENROLMENTS FOR CANADA AND THE PROVINCES, PROJECTION 1, 1979-2001

Province	Year[a]	Peak at 1978 rates[b]	Peak at average rates[c]	Per Cent Increase	Trough Year[a]	Trough Per Cent Decrease
Nfld	1984	2.1	2.1	7.6	1998	21.2
PEI	1983	0.8	0.8	6.9	1994	19.7
NS	1982	2.7	3.0	8.6	1997	23.6
NB	1982	1.8	1.8[e]	—	1998	22.1
PQ	1978	136.4[d]	136.1[e]	—	1998	38.3
Ont	1982	67.5	66.1	2.5	1997	19.8
Man	1981	3.0	3.2	4.1	1998	22.7
Sask	1982	2.5	2.6	9.4	1993	17.0
Alta	1983	19.5	19.8	14.1	1992	3.0
BC	1982	18.7	18.9	8.1	1993	11.3
Can	1978	251.0[d]	248.0[e]	—	1992	26.4

Notes: [a] Date at which academic year commences.

[b] 1979/80 rates for Newfoundland, Nova Scotia, New Brunswick and Manitoba; 1978/79 rates for all other provinces.

[c] See Table 5-15.

[d] Occurs in 1979, the first year of the projection.

[e] Actual.

Source: Projections by the author.

aging population as anticipated in Canadian population futures, to effect the relative gradual transfer of resources away from public programs used primarily by the young to those used primarily by the more senior members of the population. It would appear that one of the major programs used extensively by the younger members of the Canadian population is education, particularly elementary and secondary education.

The analysis of future elementary-secondary enrolments presented in this chapter suggests that these enrolments will continue to decline to the mid-1980s, reaching a trough that is approximately 20 per cent below the peak levels of the early 1970s. Thereafter the subsequent "boomlet" in the 1990s is likely to be well below the historically high enrolment levels of the early 1970s. Consequently, it would appear, on

178

the basis of this analysis, that general public policies towards the elementary-secondary educational system in Canada should be to effect the gradual relative transfer of resources out of this system, so as to meet increasing needs of a growing elderly population. Note, however, that in so doing, recognition should be given to the wave-like pattern of enrolments likely to be experienced to the turn of the century and beyond.

For the post-secondary educational system in Canada the conclusion is not so clear-cut, since both universities and non-university post-secondary institutions serve a broad spectrum of age groups in Canadian society. For example, currently *over 40 per cent* of total university enrolees in Canadian universities are aged 25 years and over.[29] This suggests that even though enrolments in full-time undergraduate programs decreased in the early 1980s, Canadian universities are in an excellent position to benefit from the projected aging of the Canadian population over the remainder of the century and beyond. The net loss in full-time (undergraduate and graduate) enrolments in Canada to the year 2001 is projected to be approximately 12 per cent,[30] while the net loss in total (full-time and part-time) enrolments over the same period is projected to be only a little over 3 per cent (see Table 5-18). The net loss in full-time *equivalent* enrolments would, therefore, be somewhere between these two figures.

This conclusion conveys a dramatically different picture from other studies, which concentrate on the relatively young full-time under-graduate population and suggest declines in university enrolment in the order of 20 per cent or more.[31] Increases in graduate and part-time enrolments, in which students are relatively older,[32] should signifi-cantly compensate for the projected declines in full-time undergraduate enrolments. This poses a clear challenge to future university administrations and government priorities. On the basis of this analysis, the relative transfer of resources out of post-secondary university education, although perhaps warranted by a slight projected decline in total enrolments, should be much more moderate than for the elementary-secondary system and should not occur until *after* the projected peak in the mid-1980s. This would not appear to be in accord with current policy perceptions and practices.

It is tempting to apply this conclusion unaltered to the post-secondary non-university educational system. However, the results of the above analysis would suggest that this might be very unwise. Because *full-time* post-secondary non-university enrolments in Canada

179

are almost exclusively concentrated in the 18-to-20-year age group, the post-secondary non-university educational system is extremely vulnerable to dramatic shifts in the age composition of the population. This system will not benefit (as do universities) from the projected aging of the Canadian population. Moreover, since the currently largest single age group in Canada is now at the upper end of the 18-to-20-year age group, large declines in enrolments are likely in these institutions, at least on the basis of demographic trends. This analysis suggests that this enrolment decline over the 1980s could well exceed 20 per cent; that is, be even *greater* than the preceding declines in elementary-secondary enrolments. This result is likely to appear as yet another of those demographically induced "inevitable surprises" in the years ahead.

Of course, increased enrolment rates and/or increases in part-time enrolments could weaken this impact. However, both of the above would have to be quite significant to offset this underlying trend in full-time enrolments. Currently very little is known about either of these issues in Canada, and hence formal analysis is not possible. However, on the basis of the analysis presented in this chapter, it would appear that the recent rapid growth in post-secondary non-university enrolments in Canada will slow dramatically in the 1980s and may well be reversed quite significantly, since these institutions may not be ready, in terms of appropriate courses, for the future aging of the Canadian population. Thus, relative resource transfers out of this part of the education sector may well be possible in the years ahead. This conclusion is not in harmony with current policy development.

In summary, given the context of the previous chapter, relative resource transfers will need to be made out of the education sector as the Canadian population ages in future years. However, it would appear that such resource transfers should come primarily from the elementary-secondary and perhaps from post-secondary non-university systems, where current programs are oriented towards younger students, and not from the post-secondary university system, which, on the basis of current enrolments, appears to be quite ready to participate in the future aging of Canada's population.

Summary
The education sector in Canada is perhaps the most notable area where public policies can be considerably influenced by the effects of

180

demographic changes. The use of age-sex and province-specific enrolment rates enables educational enrolments by province by type of institution to be consistently derived from projections of future population. By holding enrolment rates constant, the impact of population futures on enrolments is isolated and examined.

Elementary-secondary enrolment in Canada peaked in the 1970-71 academic year and subsequently has been declining. Since enrolment at this level is now compulsory for school-age children in all provinces, the assumption of constant enrolment rates (based on a six-year average) is not only convenient but also realistic." The resulting projections, based on age-sex-province-specific enrolment rates, show a wave-like pattern of future enrolments, which follow births with a lag of approximately a decade. Future enrolment is projected to decline to a trough in the mid-1980s at approximately 20 per cent below the peak enrolments of the early 1970s. The extent of the subsequent upturn will be largely influenced by fertility behaviour, although it is likely that enrolments will peak again towards the end of the century at levels below the previous peaks. In general, this pattern is experienced in all provinces except Alberta and British Columbia. The results remain considerably insensitive to the alternative projections of population futures.

Post-secondary education in Canada is divided between universities and non-university post-secondary institutions. The growth of post-secondary education is a post-Second World War phenomenon, with rapidly rising enrolment rates in the 1950s and 1960s. The 1970s witnessed reduced growth, and since the mid-1970s enrolment rates have stabilized at around 25 per cent of the 18-to-24-year-old population. Based on average age-sex- and province-specific enrolment rates from the past five years, the post-secondary enrolment futures (based on demographic factors alone) generally peak in the early 1980s at levels around 5 per cent above current levels; thereafter they decline to a trough towards the end of the century, at about 10 per cent below the previous peak level for total university enrolments and at over 20 per cent below the previous peak level for full-time non-university enrolments. The exact magnitudes depend on the province; Quebec and Manitoba suffer the largest decreases, and Alberta and British Columbia suffer the least. Enrolment sensitivity to alternative projections of future population is not large, and there is very little variation in the time pattern of enrolments. Enrolment futures at the post-secondary level of education can also be expected to follow a wave-like pattern into the next century.

Relative resource transfers will need to be taken from the education sector as the Canadian population ages. Such transfers should come mainly from the elementary-secondary and perhaps the post-secondary *non*-university systems, where the student body is relatively younger, and not from the university system where the student body is relatively older. This conclusion appear at odds with current policy approaches.

Canada's Labour Force Outlook

6

Introduction

The impacts of demographic trends on labour force growth, although readily apparent, do not appear to be well understood. In Canada the compositional changes associated with the sharp decline in fertility rates since the early 1960s appear to have been masked by the high rates of immigration over the late 1960s and early 1970s, and also by noticeably increasing participation in the labour force by women. Both these factors helped to maintain labour force growth at relatively high levels. However, employers, labour force participants and policy makers appear to have been unprepared for the demographically inevitable surprise of high youth unemployment over the latter half of the 1970s. What is in store for the 1980s and beyond? This chapter explores the likely impacts of Canada's population futures (developed in chapter 3), especially the aging of the population, on future labour force growth in Canada and the provinces. These impacts will be quite diverse, affecting not only labour force growth but also its age and sex composition and the regional distribution of its growth.

The growth of the labour force in Canada and in the provinces is an important determinant of the potential growth of real economic activity in the region. High rates of economic growth may be constrained by lack of available labour resources, whereas low rates of economic growth can result in unemployed labour resources. Successful utilization of the available labour resources also requires information on the characteristics of these resources — the age and sex composition, the educational achievements, the occupational and regional distribution, and so on. Canada's future labour force, therefore, will be a crucial determinant of the growth potential in the country, and the effective utilization of the available labour resources will depend on knowledge of its composition. A concluding section to this chapter briefly explores the issue of whether or not a general shortage or surplus is likely to characterize Canada's labour markets in the years ahead.

It should be noted briefly that the growth of this working-age, non-dependent population in Canada is crucial to the general conclusions concerning numerical and expenditure dependency outlined in chapter 4. In fact, if it can be established that the labour force is likely to grow more than proportionately to the working-age (15 to 64 years) population, then the relative "responsibility or burden" on the working-age population with regard to the support of the non-working-age population is likely to be reduced even further. This can have important implications for the distribution of the tax burden resulting from the growth of demographically induced government expenditures.

The basic relationship between labour force and population is the labour force participation rate, which is defined, for any age-sex group (in a province), as the ratio of the labour force to the relevant source population.[1] In Canada the relevant source population includes the civilian, non-institutionalized population aged 15 years and over. An adjustment is made to the relevant total population measure to remove members of the armed forces and those persons in institutions (jails, reformatories, homes for the mentally retarded, and so on) who are not available to the labour force.[2] This definition follows the principle, outlined in chapter 3, that the relevant population measure in the denominator should represent the population "at risk"; that is, potential entrants to the labour force.

Projections of future labour force that are linked to population futures can be obtained by rewriting the labour force participation rate definition so that the size of the labour force is the product of the participation rate and the adjusted future population in each age-sex group and aggregating across all groups. In this way, future labour force participation rates become the parameters of the model in much the same way as, for example, the out-migration rates are in the generation of population futures (see chapter 3).

The specification of future age-sex-specific participation rates remains a contentious issue. Numerous theories of labour force participation have been developed and tested in the literature,[3] and this remains a fertile field for research. Nonetheless, since the primary objective of this study is to examine the impact of population futures on labour force growth, the analysis will be first developed with *constant* labour force participation rates. This will be followed by a

184

brief review of likely trends in future participation rates and the implications for labour force growth in Canada and the provinces.

In summary, labour force participation rates for age-sex-specific groups[4] in each province are calculated and, initially, held constant throughout the projection horizon. These are applied to adjusted population futures (derived from chapter 3) to isolate the labour force implications of alternative future demographic developments. Participation rates are then permitted to change to develop a "likely" labour force outlook for Canada and the provinces, which also would recognize the impacts of the previously examined demographic developments. The implications for potential output and unemployment growth are then briefly examined in a concluding section.

It should be emphasized that this methodology permits the transition over time of population cohorts through different age groups, where the labour force participation rates may well be quite different. Consequently, the age-sex composition, as well as the sizes of the provincial populations, is an important determinant of the provincial labour forces. This is particularly important with regard to the impact of the Baby Boom of the late 1950s and early 1960s on labour force growth in Canada. Persons born during this period are currently entering the labour force and can be expected to have an effect on the labour force for some period as they move over time through ages that have traditionally had different rates of attachment to (or participation in) the labour force.[5]

Labour Force Growth: A Historical Overview

Estimates of the labour force in Canada have been obtained in the census since 1911. This information is summarized in Table 6-1 for Canada over the period 1921-71. As previously noted, the population aged 15 years and over is *defined* to be the labour force source population. Consequently, the growth of this source population is relevant in determining labour force growth. If the source population grows slower than the labour force, the labour force participation rate increases, and vice versa.

This inverse relationship is readily apparent from the information presented in Table 6-1.[6] In the 1910s, source population growth exceeded labour force growth, so the participation rate fell. The opposite occurred in the 1920s, whereas the 1930s repeated the pattern of the 1910s. During the 1940s, source population and labour force growth were equal, so there was no change in the participation rate.

TABLE 6-1
POPULATION, LABOUR FORCE AND LABOUR FORCE PARTICIPATION RATES FOR CANADA, 1911-1971

Census Year	Population[a] Total (000's)	Population[a] 15 + Years	Growth[b] (%)	Labour Force Total (000's)	Labour Force Growth[b] (%)	Participation Rates Percentage of Total Population	Participation Rates Percentage of Population 15 + Years
1911	7,191.6	4,818.6	—	2,698.5	—	37.5	56.0
1921	8,775.2	5,755.8	1.8	3,143.6	1.5	35.8	54.6
1931	10,363.2	7,086.1	2.1	3,908.1	2.2	37.7	55.2
1941	11,489.7	8,296.7	1.6	4,498.1[c]	1.4	39.1	54.2
1951	13,984.3[d]	9,742.1[d]	1.4	5,276.6[d]	1.4	37.7[d]	54.2[d]
1961	18,200.6	12,023.2	2.1[d]	6,458.2	2.0[d]	35.5	53.7
1971	21,515.1	15,157.6	2.3	8,688.5	3.0	40.4	57.3

Notes: [a] Excludes the Yukon and Northwest Territories.
      [b] Average annual per cent growth over previous decade.
      [c] Includes persons on active service on June 2, 1941.
      [d] Includes Newfoundland for the first time.

Source: Statistics Canada, *Historical Labour Force* (Catalogue No. 94-702), pp. I-1, 2.

The 1950s displayed a slight reduction in the participation rate, but during the 1960s labour force growth substantially exceeded source population growth, thereby implying the largest (upward) movement in the participation rate recorded in any decade over the previous fifty years. Even so, it would be difficult to conclude from these data that the aggregate participation rate in Canada has been increasing over time. The average rate over the sixty-year period was 55 per cent, with the lowest rate of 53.7 per cent recorded in 1961 and the highest rate of 57.3 per cent recorded in 1971.

However, these data do mask some important underlying trends, which can be best illustrated by disaggregating these data by sex (see Table 6-2). From these results it is clear that the relative constancy in the aggregate participation rate is the result of a gradually declining male participation rate and an increasing female participation rate over the period. Since historically there have been considerably more males than females in the labour force, even substantial increases in the female participation rate can be more than offset by quantitatively smaller reductions in the male participation rate (see, for example, 1941 to 1951). However, over the 1960s the female participation rate rose almost ten percentage points, and this more than offset the reduction of two percentage points in the male participation rate, resulting in a substantial increase in the overall participation rate (see Table 6-1). Note, however, that the female participation rate in Canada in 1971 was only about one-half of the male participation rate.

These trends are apparent in all provinces (see Table 6-3). In general, the western provinces have displayed higher labour force participation rates than the eastern provinces. In 1971 the highest participation rates for both males and females were recorded in Alberta and the lowest rates in Newfoundland. Moreover, this interprovincial variation is quite substantial. It is also clear from these data that in 1971 the intersexual difference existed in all provinces, with female rates approximately one-half of male rates across the country.

An examination of the data broken down by age (see Table 6-4) helps to explain the trends experienced in all provinces. The declining male rates are apparent over *all* ages, but especially in the 65 years and over group and, to a lesser extent, in the youngest age group. This could be explained by earlier retirement and more schooling respectively. For females, there are increasing participation rates in all age groups, except in the oldest and, perhaps the youngest age groups.[7] The increasing rates are especially apparent in the 25 to 34 years age group and, to a slightly lesser degree, in the 35 to 64 years age group.

187

TABLE 6-2
POPULATION, LABOUR FORCE AND LABOUR FORCE PARTICIPATION RATES
FOR MALES AND FEMALES IN CANADA, 1911-1971[a]

Census Year	Population			Labour Force		Participation Rates Percentage of	
	Total (000's)	15+ years (000's)	Growth (%)	Total (000's)	Growth (%)	Total Population	Population 15+ Years
MALES							
1911	3,812.1	2,611.8	—	2,341.4	—	61.4	89.6
1921	4,522.1	2,998.7	1.4	2,658.5	1.3	58.8	88.7
1931	5,366.7	3,710.1	2.2	3,244.8	2.0	60.5	87.5
1941	5,890.7	4,274.2	1.4	3,665.9	1.2	62.3	85.8
1951	7,074.4	4,910.6	1.2	4,114.4	0.9	58.2	83.8
1961	9,197.9	6,039.2	2.1	4,694.3	1.3	51.0	77.7
1971	10,775.9	7,523.2	2.2	5,698.3	2.0	52.9	75.7
FEMALES							
1911	3,379.5	2,206.8	—	357.0	—	10.6	16.2
1921	4,253.0	2,757.2	2.3	485.1	3.1	11.4	17.6
1931	4,996.5	3,376.0	2.0	663.3	3.2	13.3	19.6
1941	5,599.0	4,022.5	1.8	832.3	2.3	14.9	20.7
1951	6,910.0	4,831.5	1.6	1,162.2	3.2	16.8	24.1
1961	9,002.7	5,984.0	2.2	1,763.9	4.3	19.6	29.5
1971	10,739.2	7,634.4	2.5	2,990.2	5.4	27.8	39.2

Note: [a] See notes to Table 5-19.

Source: Statistics Canada, Historical Labour Force (Catalogue No. 94-702), pp. 1-1, 2

TABLE 6-3

LABOUR FORCE PARTICIPATION RATES[a] BY SEX FOR CANADA AND THE PROVINCES, 1911-1971

(%)

Census Year	Can	Nfld	PEI	NS	NB	PQ	Ont	Man	Sask	Alta	BC
TOTAL											
1911	56.0	—	50.3	52.7	52.3	52.3	54.9	58.4	63.9	63.5	68.1
1931	55.2	—	53.3	52.2	52.7	54.8	54.3	56.0	56.8	58.0	58.5
1951[b]	54.2	48.4	51.9	50.9	50.9	54.6	56.1	53.8	52.3	54.2	51.6
1971	57.3	45.7	56.6	52.6	52.2	51.8	61.5	59.4	57.8	62.2	58.4
MALES											
1911	89.6	—	88.8	88.7	88.1	87.3	89.6	89.8	94.4	92.2	91.9
1931	87.5	—	88.7	85.5	86.5	87.1	86.7	87.5	89.9	90.3	87.8
1951[b]	83.8	78.9	84.0	81.5	81.4	85.0	85.6	82.6	82.4	84.0	78.3
1971	75.7	65.0	75.0	71.9	70.8	70.4	79.8	77.2	76.5	80.1	76.9
FEMALES											
1911	16.2	—	12.3	15.0	14.7	16.2	17.6	16.7	10.9	12.7	17.1
1931	19.6	—	15.0	16.6	17.1	21.9	20.6	20.0	14.3	15.7	19.5
1951[b]	24.1	16.0	18.5	19.9	20.5	25.0	26.5	24.2	18.7	20.4	23.4
1971	39.2	25.7	38.1	33.4	33.6	33.9	43.7	41.7	38.6	43.8	39.8

Notes: [a] Percentages of the population 15 years and over. [b] Includes Newfoundland for the first time.

Source: Statistics Canada, *Historical Labour Force* (Catalogue No. 94-702), pp. 1-1, 4.

TABLE 6-4
LABOUR FORCE PARTICIPATION RATES BY AGE
AND SEX FOR CANADA, 1921-1971
(%)

Census Year	Age Group (Years)				
	15-19[a]	20-24	25-34	35-64	65+
MALES					
1921	65.4	92.3	96.2	94.3	71.0
1931	57.3	92.6	97.7	95.8	69.0
1941	55.4	91.5	97.9	95.2	58.9
1951	58.6[b]	92.4	96.4	93.2	38.6
1961	41.4	87.2	94.1	90.6	28.4
1971	46.6	86.5	92.6	88.6	23.6
FEMALES					
1921	29.5	38.3	19.9	11.8	19.0
1931	29.1	47.0	21.7	13.5	22.8
1941	30.1	46.5	27.5	15.2	19.9
1951	37.8[b]	46.9	24.2	19.6	5.1
1961	34.2	49.5	29.6	30.3	6.7
1971	37.0	62.8	44.5	41.5	8.3

Notes: [a] 14 to 19 years for 1921 to 1941.

[b] The comparable 14-to-19-year figures are 48.8 for males and 31.4 for females.

Sources: M. C. Urquhart, *Historical Statistics of Canada* (Toronto: Macmillan, 1965), p. 63 (1921-41); Statistics Canada, *Historical Labour Force* (Catalogue No. 94-702) pp. 2-1, 2; and calculations by the author.

In summary, Canada's labour force growth has historically closely matched the growth in the source population. The implied relative constancy in labour force participation rates does, however, reflect offsetting trends in male and female participation rates. Historically, male rates have been declining in all age groups but especially in the retirement and schooling ages, whereas female rates have been increasing, especially in the mid-career ages. The pattern has been the same in every province, although the western provinces generally have higher labour force participation rates than the eastern provinces.

190

Labour force data in Canada are currently collected on a much more frequent basis than census data, using a monthly survey of 55,000 households. The current survey was revised in 1975, and consistent data back to 1966 have been published. These data are presented in Table 6-5.[8] By 1979 the Canadian labour force had grown to over 11.2 million persons, which represented an average annual growth rate of 3.1 per cent since 1966, or 3.3 per cent over the 1970s. Comparison with Table 6-1 shows that the 1970s produced the fastest growing labour force of any decade, at least since the early 1900s. This growth has not been uniform across the country. Newfoundland, Prince Edward Island and Alberta had average annual growth rates in excess of 4 per cent. In Alberta the pattern is one of an accelerating rate in the late 1970s, while the rate in the two Atlantic provinces generally has been slowing down. Above-average annual labour force growth was also experienced in New Brunswick and British Columbia. The slowest labour force growth over the period was in the Prairie provinces of Manitoba and Saskatchewan, although the rate in the latter has been increasing since the mid-1970s. The relatively slow growth in Quebec is also apparent from these results.

These data clearly reflect the demographic changes previously outlined in chapter 2. For example, the impacts of the changing interprovincial migration patterns, which are reflected in the growth of the source population, can be found in these data. The remaining growth in the labour force can be attributed to increases in the labour force participation rates. Table 6-6 summarizes the movements in participation rates from 1966 to 1979.[9] After a period of relative constancy in the late 1960s, the decade of the 1970s witnessed gradually increasing participation rates and thus continued the overall trend of the 1960s. This is apparent in all provinces and reflects a continuation of the previously noted trends of rapidly increasing female participation rates, especially in the middle age groups, offsetting slightly decreasing male participation rates in all provinces (see Table 6-7).

The relative importance of the components of labour force growth is summarized in Table 6-8. Over the 1966-79 period, the growth of the source population accounted for approximately three-quarters of labour force growth, and the participation rate growth for the remaining one-quarter.[10] Source population growth was relatively less important in Newfoundland, Prince Edward Island, Manitoba and, especially, Saskatchewan. Consequently, even in recent years when increases in participation rates have been substantial (see Table 6-6), the

TABLE 6-5
LABOUR FORCE AND GROWTH FOR CANADA AND THE PROVINCES, 1966-1979

Year/Period	Can[a]	Nfld	PEI	NS	NB	PQ	Ont	Man	Sask	Alta	BC
						LABOUR FORCE (000's)[b]					
1966	7,493	131	37	251	196	2,113	2,787	361	332	569	716
1967	7,747	134	37	257	197	2,184	2,891	365	335	586	759
1968	7,951	136	37	261	201	2,205	2,980	382	345	615	789
1969	8,194	137	39	267	204	2,264	3,077	383	350	643	830
1970	8,395	139	37	271	205	2,288	3,177	392	347	667	871
1971	8,639	147	40	276	210	2,347	3,290	402	346	682	899
1972	8,897	154	41	280	220	2,383	3,410	408	351	711	938
1973	9,276	168	42	295	232	2,499	3,532	421	355	746	987
1974	9,639	171	44	313	239	2,570	3,686	435	360	781	1,040
1975	9,974	176	46	317	248	2,647	3,818	437	376	822	1,087
1976	10,206	182	47	323	254	2,689	3,885	447	394	871	1,116
1977	10,498	191	48	329	261	2,756	3,994	456	410	909	1,144
1978	10,882	198	50	342	273	2,827	4,147	471	421	960	1,192
1979	11,207	207	53	352	280	2,878	4,289	478	433	1,015	1,223
						GROWTH (%)[c]					
1966-70	2.9	1.5	0.0	1.9	1.1	2.0	3.3	2.1	1.1	4.1	5.0
1970-75	3.5	4.8	4.5	3.2	3.9	3.0	3.7	2.2	1.6	4.3	4.5
1975-79	3.0	4.1	3.6	2.7	3.1	2.1	3.0	2.3	3.6	5.4	3.0

Notes: [a] Excluding Yukon and Northwest Territories.
[b] A new labour force survey was introduced in 1975, and consistent results have been calculated back to 1966.
[c] Average annual labour force growth over the period.
Sources: Statistics Canada, *Historical Labour Force Statistics, 1979* (Catalogue No. 71-201), pp. 25 and 39-46; and

TABLE 6-6

LABOUR FORCE PARTICIPATION RATES FOR CANADA AND THE PROVINCES, 1966-1979

(%)

Year	Can	Nfld	PEI	NS	NB	PQ	Ont	Man	Sask	Alta	BC
1966	57.3	44.8	54.3	52.5	51.3	56.0	59.8	57.4	54.0	61.7	56.7
1967	57.6	45.0	53.6	52.9	50.6	56.4	60.2	57.4	53.9	61.8	57.5
1968	57.6	44.3	52.5	52.7	50.6	55.6	60.3	59.0	55.0	62.7	57.6
1969	57.9	43.7	54.4	52.8	50.3	55.9	60.5	58.1	55.4	63.4	58.2
1970	57.8	43.4	51.5	52.3	49.9	55.4	60.5	58.7	55.3	63.6	58.7
1971	58.1	45.0	54.3	52.2	49.8	56.0	60.9	59.3	55.3	63.0	58.3
1972	58.6	46.2	54.1	52.1	51.2	55.9	61.7	59.6	56.5	63.8	58.8
1973	59.7	49.2	54.6	53.7	52.8	57.6	62.4	60.7	57.3	64.8	59.6
1974	60.5	49.2	55.4	55.8	53.3	58.0	63.4	61.5	57.9	65.6	60.3
1975	61.1	49.4	56.5	55.3	53.8	58.5	64.1	60.9	59.2	66.1	61.1
1976	61.1	49.4	56.7	55.2	53.6	58.3	63.9	61.2	60.5	66.9	61.3
1977	61.5	50.7	57.0	55.2	53.7	58.9	64.3	61.7	61.5	67.0	61.5
1978	62.6	51.7	57.8	56.4	55.0	59.7	65.5	63.1	61.9	68.2	62.6
1979	63.3	52.7	59.3	56.9	55.3	60.1	66.6	63.7	62.6	69.4	62.7

Source: Statistics Canada, *Historical Labour Force Statistics, 1979* (Catalogue No. 71-201), pp. 146 and 161-167.

TABLE 6-7
LABOUR FORCE PARTICIPATION RATES BY AGE AND
SEX FOR CANADA, 1971-1979
(%)

Year	Age Group (Years)				
	15-19	20-24	25-44	45-64	65 +
MALES					
1971	43.7	83.5	96.7	90.0	20.0
1973	49.6	85.3	96.8	88.9	18.1
1975[a]	52.8	85.5	96.7	87.8	17.3
1975[b]	54.6	85.0	95.6	87.0	18.5
1977	54.0	85.2	95.5	85.4	15.6
1979	57.2	86.4	96.0	85.5	15.3
FEMALES					
1971	35.9	60.2	40.8	36.7	5.1
1973	40.0	62.7	44.5	37.7	4.4
1975[a]	42.3	64.8	49.3	37.1	4.5
1975[b]	47.4	67.0	52.3	39.4	4.9
1977	46.6	68.9	55.4	41.5	4.4
1979	50.8	71.3	60.0	43.7	4.2

Notes: [a] Old labour force survey.
        [b] New labour force survey.

Sources: Statistics Canada, *Historical Labour Force Statistics, 1979* (Catalogue No. 71-201), and unpublished information.

demographically induced source population growth has been the most important determinant of labour force growth. Holding participation rates constant over the 1966-79 period would have reduced average annual labour force growth from 3.1 per cent to 2.3 per cent (that is, 0.8 percentage points or a difference of only 25.8 per cent). This has important implications for Canada's labour force futures, and they are examined in the following section.

Labour Force Futures
An examination of future labour force growth for Canada and the provinces requires an analysis both of the growth in the labour force

TABLE 6-8
THE DECOMPOSITION OF LABOUR FORCE GROWTH
BY PROVINCE, 1966-1979
(Average Annual Per Cent)

Province	Labour Force Growth	Components		
		Participation Rate Growth	Adjustment[a] Growth	Source Population Growth
Nfld	3.6	1.3	0.0	2.3
PEI	2.8	0.7	0.1	1.9
NS	2.6	0.6	0.1	1.9
NB	2.8	0.6	0.1	2.1
PQ	2.4	0.5	0.1	1.8
Ont	3.4	0.8	0.1	2.5
Man	2.2	0.8	0.0	1.4
Sask	2.1	1.1	0.0	1.0
Alta	4.6	0.9	0.1	3.6
BC	4.2	0.8	0.0	3.4
Can	3.1	0.8	0.0	2.3

Note: [a] See text for further details.

Source: Calculations by the author.

source population and of the trends in labour force participation rates. Over recent years, even when participation rates have increased substantially, source population growth has been by far the more important determinant of labour force growth in Canada and in most of the provinces. This suggests that an analysis of the impacts of future population on labour force growth over the 1980s and beyond can account for a substantial part of the future labour force growth. However, as population growth declines, participation trends could make a relatively greater contribution and hence cannot be ignored. Consequently, the first part of this section is devoted to an analysis of the impacts of Canada's population futures on labour force growth in the absence of further participation rate changes. In this way, the impacts of population aging on future labour force growth can be isolated and examined. This analysis is then followed by a brief review of alternative labour force futures for Canada and the provinces, which

195

incorporate both the impacts of future population *and* the impacts of changing participation rates. Policy and economic challenges posed by these results are reviewed in the subsequent section.

Future labour force projections have as their starting point the population futures outlined in chapter 3, especially the population futures for ages 15 years and over. With appropriate minor· adjustment,[11] this group forms the labour force source population in each province. The application of participation rates to this source population yields estimates of labour force futures. Because of the different underlying trends and participation rates, it is important to consider each of the sexes separately and to separate the population into various age groups in each province. Tables 6-9 and 6-10 set out the adjustment and participation rate assumptions (respectively) that are used to examine the impacts of the population futures (of chapter 3) on labour force futures. In both cases the assumed values are based on the averages for the recent 1975-79 period. The age groups represented in these tables were selected to provide sufficient but not cumbersome detail and were chosen on the basis of similarity within each selected grouping. Holding the assumed values constant throughout the projection horizon results in the projected labour force reflecting purely demographic developments. A continuation of past trends of further increasing female participation rates would mean that these projections will understate female labour force growth, and the opposite could well apply to male labour force growth. However, it is clear that the major determinant of labour force growth is source population growth — a fact that the results capture.

Table 6-11 summarizes the results for the first seven population futures outlined in chapter 3.[12] A labour force of around 13.5 million persons by 2001 is projected in most scenarios. Recall (see Table 6-5) that the average annual growth rate of the labour force in Canada over the 1970s was in excess of 3 per cent, the dominant part of which was attributable to demographic factors alone. All of these future projections under constant participation rates show labour force growth to average around 1 per cent per annum in the 1980s and around 0.7 per cent per annum in the 1990s — both substantial declines from the 3.1 per cent of the 1966-79 period (see Table 6-8).[13]

This decline in labour force growth over the next two decades and beyond is a very robust result — it is insensitive to the alternative assumptions of the scenarios. It reflects the slowing in population growth outlined in chapter 3 and the changing age (and sex) composition of the population. Over this period the increasing median

196

TABLE 6-9
AVERAGE ADJUSTMENT FACTORS RELATING POPULATION TO LABOUR FORCE SOURCE POPULATION FOR MALES AND FEMALES BY AGE BY PROVINCE, 1975-1979[a]

(%)

Age Group (Years)	Nfld	PEI	NS	NB	PQ	Ont	Man	Sask	Alta	BC
MALES										
15-19	100.81	99.06	95.92	97.81	98.32	98.48	95.19	96.60	96.62	97.06
20-24	102.10	98.71	94.72	97.29	97.85	98.27	95.11	97.08	97.82	95.02
25-44	98.92	93.01	92.38	96.20	98.68	98.47	96.09	95.41	97.27	96.65
45-64	98.66	98.11	97.29	97.69	99.05	98.79	96.79	97.72	98.32	98.89
65+	96.58	95.83	96.25	95.89	95.76	94.82	93.40	94.46	91.09	95.93
FEMALES										
15-19	101.01	100.33	98.55	98.88	99.15	99.16	95.96	96.95	98.00	97.57
20-24	101.94	101.06	99.09	99.44	99.05	99.23	96.58	97.97	100.80	96.71
25-44	99.47	99.79	99.80	100.01	99.68	99.75	98.04	97.55	99.29	98.77
45-64	98.74	98.73	98.65	98.36	99.31	99.30	97.95	98.31	98.81	99.58
65+	94.52	92.19	94.41	93.07	92.75	91.84	91.63	91.95	88.27	93.43

Note: [a] Based on the average ratio of labour force source population (labour force survey) to population, 15 years and over (census and post-census estimates), 1975 to 1979 inclusive.

Source: Calculations by the author.

TABLE 6-10
AVERAGE LABOUR FORCE PARTICIPATION RATES FOR MALES AND FEMALES BY AGE BY PROVINCE, 1975-1979[a]
(%)

Age Group (Years)	Can	Nfld	PEI	NS	NB	PQ	Ont	Man	Sask	Alta	BC
MALES											
15-19	54.6	40.5	57.6	50.0	46.1	46.9	56.9	62.2	64.8	66.7	58.9
20-24	85.5	79.1	83.7	85.0	81.3	83.9	85.5	87.6	89.5	89.8	87.0
25-44	95.7	88.0	92.0	93.4	90.4	94.7	96.9	96.4	96.7	97.2	96.4
45-64	85.9	70.6	79.2	77.6	75.6	84.2	88.7	86.9	87.8	89.8	84.5
65+	16.1	6.5	18.6	12.7	11.6	14.3	17.8	17.5	24.1	20.5	12.1
FEMALES											
15-19	48.0	34.9	45.3	41.2	38.2	40.8	52.6	50.6	46.9	56.4	53.6
20-24	69.0	55.0	66.6	64.9	60.6	68.9	71.4	70.0	64.7	69.3	69.1
25-44	56.0	40.6	54.5	50.4	48.1	50.8	61.4	55.9	53.7	58.0	57.7
45-64	41.7	22.8	41.0	35.6	35.6	34.2	47.1	46.3	43.5	48.1	41.5
65+	4.4	2.3	4.1	3.7	3.0	4.9	4.7	4.1	4.8	5.0	3.5

Note: [a] Averages of rates for 1975 to 1979 inclusive.

Source: Calculations by the author using Statistics Canada, *Historical Labour Force Statistics, 1979* (Catalogue No. 71-201).

LABOUR FORCE FUTURES AND GROWTH UNDER ALTERNATIVE POPULATION PROJECTIONS FOR CANADA, 1981-2051[a]

Projection Number and Description	Year							
	1981	1991	2001	2011	2021	2031	2041	2051
LABOUR FORCE (000's)								
1 Base (or no change)	11,346.3	12,647.9	13,570.0	14,218.7	14,030.2	13,511.2	13,324.3	12,932.1
2 Increased life expectancy	11,346.3	12,658.4	13,598.4	14,266.5	14,094.2	13,588.5	13,393.6	13,035.8
3 Low fertility	11,346.3	12,647.9	13,521.5	13,938.5	13,454.5	12,563.1	11,927.5	11,158.0
4 High fertility	11,346.3	12,647.9	13,593.0	14,582.6	15,061.7	15,377.6	16,262.9	17,121.8
5 Low immigration	11,304.9	12,387.0	13,066.9	13,450.7	13,010.4	12,263.4	11,833.1	11,257.0
6 Return migration	11,346.1	12,640.1	13,553.8	14,189.2	13,987.1	13,448.5	13,216.2	12,821.6
7 Westward drift	11,346.5	12,655.6	13,586.5	14,244.4	14,062.4	13,550.8	13,349.3	12,988.4
GROWTH (%)[b]								
1 Base (or no change)	—	1.1	0.7	0.5	-0.1	-0.4	-0.1	-0.3
2 Increased life expectancy	—	1.1	0.7	0.5	-0.1	-0.4	-0.1	-0.3
3 Low fertility	—	1.1	0.7	0.3	-0.4	-0.7	-0.5	-0.7
4 High fertility	—	1.1	0.7	0.7	0.3	0.2	0.6	0.5
5 Low immigration	—	0.9	0.5	0.3	-0.3	-0.6	-0.4	-0.5
6 Return migration	—	1.1	0.7	0.5	-0.1	-0.4	-0.2	-0.3
7 Westward drift	—	1.1	0.7	0.5	-0.1	-0.4	-0.1	-0.3

Notes: [a] All projections use average 1975-79 rates (see Tables 6-9 and 6-10). [b] Average annual growth over the preceding decade.

Source: Projections by the author.

199

age favours labour force growth as current large age groups (see Figures 3-1 and 3-2) gradually move into higher labour force participation rate ages (see Table 6-10). For this reason labour force growth remains *above* population growth for the remainder of the century, even under constant participation rates. Note, however, that the increasing female dominance *retards* labour force growth, since female participation rates are below male participation rates for all ages. These results show the combined impact of these opposing effects of population aging on future labour force growth.

Negative labour force growth characterizes almost all of the results after 2011. This reflects the gradual retirement of the Baby Boom generation. The time pattern of these projections is of considerable interest: it, like births and enrolments, reflects the wave-like effects resulting from the movement of the Baby Boom generation, and their children and grandchildren, through the labour force. However, unlike births and enrolments, the effects are not so substantial for labour force futures, since people stay in the labour force for a much longer period of time. Figure 6-1 summarizes the time profile of these labour force futures.[14] In the no change scenario, the peak of 14.2 million persons occurs in 2011; thereafter the labour force gradually declines to 12.0 million by 2051. The greatest decline is under the low fertility scenario (Projection 3), whereas the high fertility scenario (Projection 4) is the *only* projection to display positive growth throughout the projection horizon. Most of the other projections are approximately contained within these two bounds, with the exception of the low immigration alternative (Projection 5), which is generally the lowest labour force projection through most of the projection horizon (see Figure 6-1). This occurs because most immigrants are of working age (see the Appendix), and consequently, a reduction in immigration reduces the number of potential entrants to the labour force.[15]

Table 6-12 summarizes the regional implications of these labour force futures for the remainder of the century. With a few exceptions, the most notable feature of the results in the table is their robustness. For example, Canadian labour force growth is projected to average 0.9 per cent per annum for the rest of the twentieth century almost regardless of the assumptions adopted, the sole exception being the low immigration scenario (Projection 5), where an average annual growth rate of 0.7 per cent is recorded.[16] Moreover, this robustness generally applies in every province. In general, labour force growth is projected to be lowest in Quebec and Manitoba, and highest in Alberta and British Columbia. Changed fertility assumptions (Projections 3

200

FIGURE 6-1
HISTORICAL AND ALTERNATIVE LABOUR
FORCE FUTURES, CANADA, 1966-2051

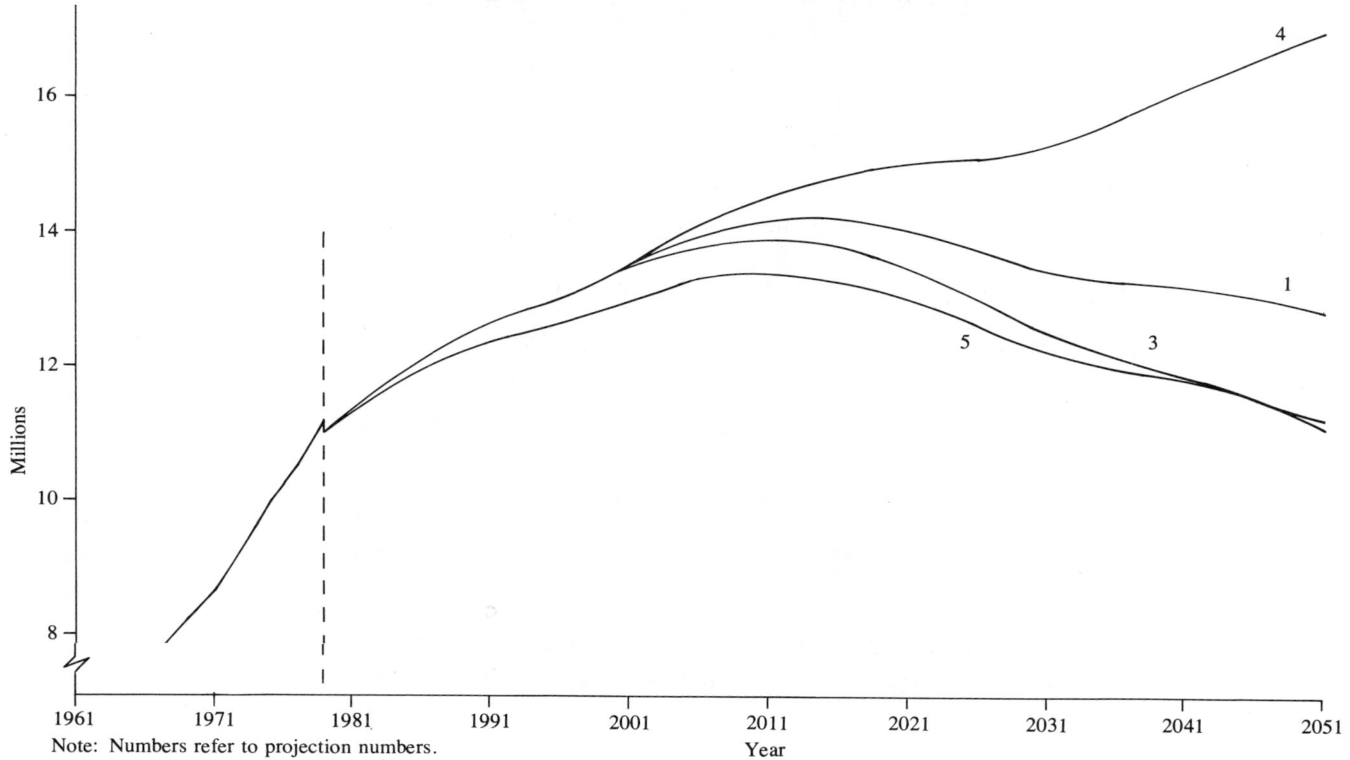

Note: Numbers refer to projection numbers.
Sources: Table 6-4 and projections by the author.

201

TABLE 6-12

PROJECTED ALTERNATIVE LABOUR FORCE IN 2001 AND GROWTH, 1981-2001, FOR CANADA AND THE PROVINCES[a]

Projection Number	Can	Nfld	PEI	NS	NB	PQ	Ont	Man	Sask	Alta	BC
	LABOUR FORCE IN 2001 (000's)										
1	13,570.0	254.1	68.5	433.2	360.8	2,879.8	5,105.5	506.7	566.7	1,682.9	1,711.8
2	13,598.4	254.6	68.6	434.0	362.0	2,884.9	5,113.3	508.1	569.3	1,688.0	1,715.7
3	13,521.5	252.7	68.1	431.6	359.6	2,871.8	5,090.2	504.5	563.3	1,674.3	1,705.4
4	13,593.0	254.3	68.6	433.9	361.4	2,885.1	5,115.2	507.4	567.3	1,685.3	1,714.6
5	13,066.9	250.6	67.0	424.5	353.8	2,802.5	4,868.4	487.6	553.1	1,620.2	1,639.2
6	13,553.8	253.4	65.9	423.6	349.5	3,020.2	5,292.8	547.4	468.2	1,437.8	1,695.1
7	13,586.5	239.9	63.4	403.9	336.7	2,826.9	4,911.5	518.0	566.8	1,861.8	1,857.5
	GROWTH, 1981-2001 (Average Annual Per Cent)										
1	0.9	1.0	1.3	1.0	1.1	−0.0	0.8	0.3	1.3	2.3	1.5
2	0.9	1.0	1.3	1.0	1.2	−0.0	0.9	0.4	1.3	2.3	1.6
3	0.9	1.0	1.2	0.9	1.1	−0.0	0.8	0.3	1.2	2.3	1.5
4	0.9	1.0	1.3	1.0	1.1	0.0	0.9	0.4	1.3	2.3	1.6
5	0.7	0.9	1.2	0.9	1.0	−0.1	0.6	0.2	1.2	2.1	1.3
6	0.9	1.0	1.1	0.8	1.0	0.2	1.0	0.7	0.3	1.5	1.5
7	0.9	0.7	0.9	0.6	0.8	−0.1	0.7	0.5	1.3	2.8	2.0

Note: [a] All projections use constant average rates (see Tables 6-9 and 6-10) and exclude the Yukon and Northwest Territories.

Source: Projections by the author.

and 4) have almost no impact over this period, since a newborn must reach the age of 15 years before any impact on the labour force is registered.

Perhaps of most interest are the impacts of alternative interprovincial migration assumptions (Projections 6 and 7). Under a return to the interprovincial migration patterns of 1966-75, the main beneficiaries are Quebec, Ontario and Manitoba, and the main losers are Nova Scotia, Saskatchewan and Alberta. Nevertheless, Alberta *still* has the highest projected labour force growth rate (now equal to British Columbia), which is a reflection of a favourable age-sex distribution of the Alberta population and the relatively high labour force participation rates in that province. In addition, Quebec still has the lowest projected labour force growth, a reflection of a somewhat unfavourable age-sex distribution, the relatively low labour force participation rates, and the fact that even under this scenario Quebec continues to be in a relatively unfavourable position regarding international and interregional migration.

It is clear that even if the interprovincial migration patterns of the late 1970s were reversed to those of the previous decade, Alberta would still have the highest projected labour force growth rate and Quebec the lowest. Needless to say, when the patterns of the late 1970s are intensified (Projection 7) the discrepancy widens considerably. Both Alberta and British Columbia gain one-half of one percentage point in average annual labour force growth at the expense of all other provinces, especially the Atlantic provinces (since it is the people of labour force age who are moving). Note that Ontario loses under this scenario, but not by as much as under the reduced immigration scenario. Even in spite of these interesting interprovincial differences between the alternative scenarios, it is important not to lose sight of the basic conclusion that regardless of the alternative examined, a substantial decline in labour force growth is projected for every province as a result of demographic developments over the next two decades and beyond. Since demographic developments accounted for approximately three-quarters of Canadian labour force growth since 1966 (see Table 6-8)[17] even though participation rates were increasing at historically high rates, it seems very unlikely that these basic conclusions on provincial labour force growth will be significantly affected by changing participation rates. In this sense, the conclusions are inevitable.

The composition of the labour force will also be changing in the future. As a result of the demographic developments outlined in chapter 3, it might be expected that the future labour force will reflect the general aging and the gradually increasing female dominance of the source population. It will also reflect the different labour force participation rates at different ages and for the different sexes. Table 6-13 summarizes the changing composition of the labour force over the projection horizon. The general aging of the labour force is reflected in the reduced percentages of the young and the increased percentages of the elderly throughout the projection period. In 1981 those aged under 25 years comprise 26.0 per cent of the labour force; by 2001 their share is 18.1 per cent; and by 2051, 16.6 per cent. Note that the largest decrease in this percentage is projected to occur over the remainder of this century. On the other hand, those aged 65 years and over represent 1.8 per cent of the labour force in 1981, increase to 2.2 per cent in 2001, and 3.9 per cent in 2051 under the assumed conditions of constant labour force participation rates. These trends are apparent in all provinces (results not presented). The implication of these results is that the Canadian labour force is projected to age significantly. Since labour force experience is, on average, directly related to age, the Canadian labour force of the future can be expected to be, on average, a more experienced labour force. Whether or not these qualifications will closely match the occupational demand of the future remains a concern of those responsible for labour market policy.[18]

Of special interest are the somewhat counterintuitive results on the bottom line of Table 6-13. As noted in earlier chapters (especially chapter 3), the Canadian population has become, and is projected to continue to become more, female-dominant (see Tables 3-9 and 3-11). Yet the sex ratio for the future labour force under the assumed conditions of constant participation rates is projected to *increase* slightly over the projection horizon and stabilize at around 1.7 by the turn of the century.[19] This result reflects the assumptions used and the future age-sex composition of the population. The projections hold participation rates constant at their average 1975-79 levels (see Table 6-10) to isolate the demographic impact of labour force futures in Canada.[20] This removes one of the important determinants of the historically increased proportion of females in the labour force and hence of the decreased labour force sex ratio. Although this does account for why the labour force sex ratio in the future projections may not continue on its historical downward trend, it does *not* account for the projected turnaround to the slight increase contained in Table 6-13.

To understand this projected turnaround, it is necessary to explore the changing age-sex composition of the projected population. In

Table 6-13
THE CHANGING AGE-SEX COMPOSITION OF THE PROJECTED LABOUR FORCE IN CANADA UNDER CONSTANT PARTICIPATION RATES, PROJECTION 1, 1981-2051
(%)[a]

Age Group (Years)	Year							
	1981	1991	2001	2011	2021	2031	2041	2051
MALES								
15-19	5.5	3.9	4.1	3.7	3.5	3.7	3.6	3.6
20-24	8.8	6.6	5.9	6.1	5.5	5.7	5.7	5.6
25-44	29.4	33.6	30.6	26.8	27.7	27.5	26.9	27.5
45-64	16.8	16.9	20.5	24.7	24.3	23.3	24.1	23.7
65+	1.3	1.5	1.6	1.7	2.3	2.9	2.8	2.8
Total	61.9	62.5	62.7	63.0	63.2	63.2	63.2	63.1
FEMALES								
15-19	4.7	3.3	3.4	3.1	2.9	3.1	3.0	3.0
20-24	7.0	5.2	4.7	4.8	4.3	4.5	4.5	4.4
25-44	17.4	19.8	17.9	15.6	16.2	16.1	15.7	16.1
45-64	8.6	8.6	10.6	12.8	12.5	12.0	12.4	12.3
65+	0.5	0.6	0.6	0.7	0.9	1.1	1.1	1.1
Total	38.1	37.5	37.3	37.0	36.8	36.8	36.8	36.9
Sex ratio[b]	1.62	1.67	1.68	1.70	1.72	1.71	1.71	1.71

Notes: [a] Per cent of total labour force.
   [b] Ratio of males to females.

Source: Projections by the author.

particular, it was noted in chapter 3 that the median age of the population is projected to increase quite rapidly, especially up to the end of this century. For Canada (see Table 3-9), the median age is projected to increase from 29.5 years in 1981, to almost 37 years by 2001, and over 40 years by 2021 — a result which was shown to be insensitive to alternative assumptions (Table 3-10) and to be applicable to all provinces (Table 3-12). An examination of the participation rate assumptions in Table 6-10 shows that for males the highest participation rate is for the 25 to 44 years age group in every province, whereas for females it is the 20 to 24 years age group. Consequently, a median-aged male is moving into a traditionally higher participation age group in the early 1980s, whereas a median-aged female is moving into a traditionally *lower* participation age group. As a result, the ratio of males to females in the labour force can be expected to increase over this period under the assumption of unchanged participation rates. Hence population aging alone is likely to *reduce* the percentage of females in the labour force into the twenty-first century.

There is an additional consideration that reinforces this trend. Much of the reason for the continuing decline of the *population* sex ratio is the projected increase in the number of elderly women (see Figure 3-4). However, since this age group has an especially low labour force participation rate in all provinces, its increasing numbers have a relatively minor impact on the *labour force* sex ratio. In other words, the increasing proportion of elderly women, although contributing to an increased proportion of women in the population at large, provides only a relatively minor impact on the proportion of women in the labour force.

Finally, it has been noted that under most alternatives the size of the future labour force actually peaks around the year 2011 (see Table 6-11 and Figure 6-1), at approximately 20 to 25 per cent above the current labour force.[21] The most notable exception is the high fertility alternative, where there is a pause in growth in the 2020s at a little in excess of 15 million persons, or approximately 35 per cent above the current labour force. *All* provincial labour forces reach a maximum within the projection horizon in Projection 1, the earliest being Quebec in 1986 and the latest, Alberta in 2044. After Quebec, in chronological order, maximum labour forces are reached in Newfoundland and Manitoba (2011), Nova Scotia and Ontario (2014), New Brunswick (2015), Prince Edward Island (2018), Saskatchewan (2019), British Columbia (2022 and 2044) and Alberta (2044). These peaks are relatively high in Saskatchewan, Alberta and British Columbia and relatively low in Quebec and Manitoba.[22] Although hypothetical, these calculations do show the implications of the chosen assumptions when extended over longer time periods.

All of the above results isolate the impacts of future population growth and aging on future labour force growth in Canada and the provinces by keeping labour force participation rates unchanged over the projection horizon. However, additional labour force growth can result from continued increases in overall participation rates in the years ahead. To assess the likely effects from this source, the above results were reestimated, assuming a continuation of the trends in age-sex-specific participation rates over the 1980s.[23] In total, three alternative scenarios were considered, based on two recent studies (which do not include any provincial detail).[24] The Department of Finance Canada "low" scenario embodies higher (comparing Table 6-14 to Table 6-10) but constant rates for males aged 15 to 19 years, increasing rates for males aged 20 to 24 years, slightly declining rates for males aged 25 to 44 years, declining rates for older males, and increasing rates for *all* female age groups. The department's "high" scenario incorporates all of the previous trends but with even higher rates for all female groups aged 25 years and over. A third alternative, which was derived from the "medium" projections of Denton, Feaver and Spencer, incorporates declining rates for males in all age groups and for females in the young (15 to 19 years) and elderly (65 years and over) age groups and increasing rates for all females aged 20 to 64 years. The numerical assumptions are summarized in Table 6-14.

These three alternatives result in average labour force growth rates of 2.0, 2.1 and 1.2 per cent per annum, respectively, over the 1980s, all *well* below the historical experience of the 1970s. Note that the assumptions of the third alternative essentially offset one another, so the resulting labour force growth is very close to the growth previously estimated from source population alone. All display a noticeable decrease in the percentage of the young (15 to 24 years) in the labour force, from current levels of around 26 per cent to approximately 19 per cent by 1991. All alternatives show as well an *increase* in the proportion of females in the labour force, from the current level of around 40 per cent to between 41.5 per cent (Denton, Feaver and Spencer medium scenario) and 45 per cent (Department of Finance Canada high scenario). Therefore, it appears likely that the effects of the increased participation rates of career-aged females will be sufficient to offset the downward pressures of population aging on the proportion of females in the Canadian labour force during the 1980s.

Table 6-15 shows the Canadian labour force's future distribution over the provinces by 1991 and the growth over the preceding decade.[25] In general, the Atlantic provinces show above-average labour force growth; the central provinces of Quebec, Ontario and Manitoba, below-average growth; and the western provinces of Saskatchewan, Alberta and British Columbia, above-average growth. In all cases, however, the growth rates are well below those of the 1970s.

TABLE 6-14
ALTERNATIVE PARTICIPATION RATES
BY AGE AND SEX FOR CANADA, 1991
(%)

Participation Rate Scenario[a]	Age Group (Years)				
	15-19	20-24	25-44	45-64	65+
MALE					
Finance, low[b]	60.0	90.0	95.4	83.3	11.7
Finance, high[b]	60.0	90.0	95.4	83.3	11.7
DFS, medium[c]	50.0	85.2	95.5	82.4	9.3
FEMALE					
Finance, low[b]	58.5	77.0	76.1	58.5	4.6
Finance, high[b]	58.5	77.0	77.8	61.3	6.0
DFS, medium[c]	45.0	78.0	68.9	45.5	2.5

Notes: [a] See text for a description of the scenarios.

[b] Derived from Department of Finance, pp. 43, 45, 47.

[c] Derived from Denton, Feaver and Spencer, p. 26.

Sources: Derived from Department of Finance Canada, *Participation and Labour Force Growth in Canada* (Ottawa: Department of Finance Canada, 1980); and F. Denton, C. Feaver and B. Spencer, *The Future Population of Labour Force of Canada: Projections to the Year 2051* (Ottawa: Economic Council of Canada, 1980).

The sensitivity to alternative demographic assumptions can now be "grafted" on to these results. For example, the low immigration alternative, which reduced labour force growth by an average 0.2 per cent per annum, would reduce the average growth under the Department of Finance Canada high scenario from 2.1 to 1.9 per cent per annum. Similar calculations can be made for all provinces. These calculations can also be extended beyond 1991, and many of the other characteristics discussed above again become apparent. However, so much controversy surrounds the future projection of labour force participation rates, even into the near future, that such an exercise would be conjectural at best. Instead, the economic and policy implications of these results for the 1980s are examined in the following section.

TABLE 6-15

ALTERNATIVE LABOUR FORCE FUTURES BY PROVINCE, 1991

Participation Rate Scenario[a]	Can	Nfld	PEI	NS	NB	PQ	Ont	Man	Sask	Alta	BC
						LABOUR FORCE (000's)					
Finance, low	14,085	272	68	450	375	3,286	5,303	545	559	1,555	1,673
Finance, high	14,257	275	69	456	380	3,329	5,366	552	565	1,572	1,693
DFS, medium	13,102	249	63	401	361	3,044	4,943	506	520	1,458	1,557
						GROWTH[b] (%)					
Finance, low	1.7	2.2	2.1	1.9	2.1	0.8	1.7	1.0	2.0	3.4	2.4
Finance, high	1.9	2.3	2.2	2.0	2.3	1.0	1.8	1.1	2.1	3.5	2.6
DFS, medium	1.1	1.4	1.4	1.4	1.2	0.2	1.1	0.4	1.4	2.8	1.8

Notes: [a] See text for a description of the scenarios.
       [b] Average annual growth, 1981 to 1991.

Source: Projections by the author.

Future Labour Force and Macroeconomic Policy

Even allowing for increases in overall participation rates, future labour force growth in Canada is projected to decline dramatically from in excess of 3 per cent per annum over the 1970s to around 2 per cent per annum over the 1980s. Of this reduced growth, 1.1 per cent per annum (or slightly over half of the growth) is attributable to source population growth, and the remainder to changes in participation rates. Consequently, with no changes in participation rates, average labour force growth in Canada would decline to 1.1 per cent per annum.

The impact of labour force growth on the unemployment rate is, apparently, well understood. The higher the labour force growth, the more likely that the unemployment rate will increase, other things being equal, and vice versa. Hence, it is tempting to conclude that reduced future labour force growth will lead to declining future unemployment rates and perhaps to future labour market shortages. However, it would be extremely foolhardy to make these conclusions without first examining the demand side of the future labour market.

A cursory examination of the results of this chapter and chapter 3 reveals that future labour force growth can be expected to exceed future population growth even with *no* increases in labour force participation rates. To the extent that the former represents a capacity to supply and the latter represents a capacity to demand, this observation, although by no means conclusive, might suggest that it is very unlikely that the future Canadian labour market will be characterized by general labour market shortages as a result of reduced labour force growth.

Further tentative evidence can be gleaned by calculating the potential real growth rate that must be maintained if future increases in unemployment rates are to be avoided. In general, a substantial decline in future labour force growth in Canada implies a substantial decline in future growth potential of the Canadian economy. No longer should average real growth rates in excess of 5 per cent per annum (the record of the 1950s and 1960s) be considered the potential or target growth rate for the Canadian macroeconomy. The record of the 1970s, when real output (GNP) growth in Canada averaged 3.9 per cent per annum, has by now been indelibly imprinted on the minds of most macroeconomic policy analysts. However, over the 1970s the unemployment rate rose from 5.7 per cent (1970) to 7.5 per cent (1980). Consequently, given productivity developments[26] and capital stock growth over the 1970s, real output growth was insufficient to prevent an increase in the unemployment rate over the decade. The

210

relationship between real output growth and the unemployment rate is often referred to as Okun's Law. In its simple terms, Okun's calculations for the United States showed that because of changes in productivity and in average hours worked over the business cycle, an approximately 3 per cent increase in real output (GNP) was needed to bring the unemployment rate down one percentage point.

A recent estimate for Canada implies that a 3.2 per cent increase in real output is necessary to obtain a 1 per cent decrease in the unemployment rate.[27] This result suggests that to have maintained the unemployment rate constant over the 1970s, real output growth in Canada would have had to average approximately 4.5 per cent per annum, or 0.6 per cent per annum above the actual growth rate. Applying this result to the findings of this study, and noting that approximately two-thirds of labour force growth is translated into real output growth,[28] suggests that a reduction of annual labour force growth from 3.2 per cent over the 1970s to around 2.0 per cent over the 1980s (a reduction of 1.2 per cent) might be expected to reduce the potential output growth of the Canadian economy to around 3.7 per cent per annum.[29] This implies that an annual real output growth averaging 3.7 per cent during the 1980s will be necessary in order to avoid increases in the unemployment rate, given capital and productivity growth conditions similar to those in the 1970s. Under these conditions a larger reduction in labour force growth (say to 1.1 per cent per annum as suggested by the source population calculations) will require a lower real output growth (of around 3.1 per cent per annum) over the 1980s to maintain an unchanged unemployment rate, and vice versa.

In addition, improved productivity performance in the 1980s relative to the 1970s would require a higher real output growth rate in the 1980s to maintain an unchanged unemployment rate. Increased capital stock (real investment) growth would result in higher real output and hence employment growth over the 1980s and a lower unemployment rate, and vice versa. Of course, any desired reduction in the unemployment rate from the currently relatively high levels will also require higher rates of real output growth.

What are the real growth prospects for the Canadian economy over the 1980s? Although real growth averaged 3.9 per cent per annum over the 1970s, it is unlikely that a similar *average* annual growth will be obtained in the 1980s. One reason is the declining future population growth that underlies much of the real demand in the macroeconomy. Yet Okun-type calculations for Canada suggest that a 3.7 per cent per

211

annum average output (GNP) growth rate is necessary to stop the unemployment rate from increasing above the current relatively high levels. Failure to achieve this target will contribute to increasing unemployment rates. For example, if real output growth averages 3 per cent per annum, these calculations would suggest unemployment rates approaching 10 per cent by the end of the decade.

From these approximate calculations it seems unlikely that there will be a *general* labour market shortage in the 1980s. Rather, it appears likely that the Canadian macroeconomy over the 1980s will continue to be characterized by general excess supply (unemployment) in the labour market, even though shortages may appear in selected occupations. By 1990, at approximately 2 per cent average annual growth, the Canadian labour force is likely to be around 14 million persons. To maintain the 1980 unemployment rate of 7.5 per cent, almost 13 million persons will have to be employed in 1990; that is, nearly 2.3 million new jobs will have to be generated in the 1980s just to maintain the unemployment rate. Although not an impossible task given the record of the 1970s when almost 2.75 million new jobs were created, it presents a clear challenge for macroeconomic policy, especially since much of the employment creation of the 1970s resulted from decreased productivity performance.[30] Furthermore, as outlined above, there will be downward pressures on employment creation in the 1980s relative to the 1970s.

In summary, it appears that a challenge of the 1980s will be the creation of over 2.25 million new jobs for future new labour market entrants over the decade. This is likely to require a real output growth rate averaging 3.7 per cent per annum. Failure to achieve these goals, a distinct possibility, is likely to result in increasing unemployment rates. Consequently, a *general* labour market shortage is unlikely in the 1980s. As before, this conclusion appears contrary to current policy views and practices.

Summary
Canada's labour force growth has historically closely matched the growth in source population. The implied relative constancy in labour force participation rates does, however, reflect offsetting trends in male and female participation rates. Historically, male rates have been declining in all age groups, but especially in the retirement and schooling ages, whereas female rates have been increasing, especially in the mid-career ages. The pattern has been the same in every

province, although the western provinces generally have higher labour force participation rates than the eastern provinces.

The 1970s witnessed historically high rates of labour force growth in Canada, averaging in excess of 3 per cent per annum, with Alberta and British Columbia at the high end of the growth spectrum and Manitoba and Saskatchewan at the low end. Of this growth, approximately three-quarters is attributable to the demographic component, with participation rate growth accounting for the remaining one-quarter. The demographic component was relatively more important in Alberta and British Columbia and relatively less so in Newfoundland, Prince Edward Island, Manitoba and, especially, Saskatchewan.

The labour force is related to the source population (aged 15 years and over) by labour force participation rates. The source population for the sample-based labour force survey is the non-institutionalized population of the Canadian provinces; hence a minor adjustment is necessary to convert total population to labour force source population. The use of age-sex-specific adjustment factors and participation rates enables labour force futures to be derived from population futures. The historical change in the labour force can be broken down into a participation rate component, an adjustment component, and a demographic component. By holding the participation rates and adjustment factors constant, the impact of the demographic component can be isolated and examined in connection with the population futures.

Using the average participation rates and adjustment factors from the 1975-79 period, annual future labour force growth in Canada is projected to decline to below 1 per cent per annum over the remainder of the century and beyond. In general, labour force growth is projected to be lowest in Quebec and Manitoba, and highest in Alberta and British Columbia. These results are very robust, being relatively insensitive to alternative population assumptions. For the rest of this century, labour force growth is somewhat sensitive to immigration, insensitive to fertility, and influenced slightly by alternative interprovincial migration patterns. One interesting result is that even if the interprovincial migration patterns of 1966-75 were reestablished, Alberta would still have the highest provincial labour force growth because of a favourable age-sex composition and relatively high participation rates.

The future labour force is aging. Because participation rates for mid-career males are higher than for young males, while the opposite is the case for females, the *demographic* pressures on the labour force will be for a *decreased* proportion of females.

Of course, higher female participation rates over the projection period may offset this trend. Such calculations show that future average labour force growth in Canada may be as high as 2.1 per cent per annum over the 1980s. Hence, a challenge of the 1980s may be the creation of over 2.25 million new jobs for future labour market entrants. This is likely to require a real output growth rate averaging 3.7 per cent per annum over the decade. Failure to achieve these goals is likely to result in increasing unemployment rates over the decade. Consequently, it is unlikely that a *general* labour market shortage will appear in the 1980s in Canada. Once again this finding apparently conflicts with current policy perceptions and practices.

Further Challenges of Future Populations   7

Introduction

The detailed analyses of the previous two chapters have demonstrated the impacts of future population and population aging on future education enrolments and labour force growth in Canada and the provinces. The economic challenges posed by these results have been outlined, and in a number of cases, the apparent implications for public policies run counter to current ideas and practices. The applications of the methodology provide clear examples of the potential uses of a consistent demographic framework in developing current and future policies. Moreover, the dependency analyses of chapter 4 provide a general context in which to place the more specific conclusions generated in these detailed applications.

In general, in an aging population such as Canada's, resources must be gradually transferred from the young to the elderly if the increasing needs of the aged (because of their growing numbers) are to be met without increasing the tax burden on the employed (or productive) members of the population. The future for educational enrolments in Canada would appear to be consistent with such an overall policy, although its application should take account of the future waves in enrolments and be selective by educational type. The labour force futures suggest that the tax burden, at least for the remainder of this and into the next century, is not likely to be excessive by historical standards, providing the challenge of maintaining or improving the unemployment rate can successfully be faced.

However, although extremely important, these two detailed applications only demonstrate a methodology that has much wider scope for potential use in Canada and elsewhere. The purpose of this chapter is to outline some further possible applications and suggest some of the challenges that they could pose for current and future policies. The topics covered in this chapter are intended to be illustrative only, and by no means represent an exhaustive list of possible applications. Further research in these and other related areas is necessary if the full implications of Canada's population futures on current and future policies are to be fully understood.

Future Populations and Income Support for the Elderly

The impacts of Canada's population futures on pension obligations have recently received considerable attention.[1] Consequently, no attempt to survey all of the issues will be attempted here. Rather, the implications of the population futures developed in this study will be briefly outlined so that these results can be integrated with the observations and recommendations on current policies that can be found elsewhere.

In the life-cycle models of economists, retirement is described as normally being a period of the decumulation of financial assets accumulated during the working-age years. It is on the income generated from the investment or decumulation of these assets that the retired person is expected to live. However, not all consumption is private consumption, and not all consumption is paid for out of current private income. In Canada many public services are provided, especially to the elderly, and these are paid out of public revenues. To be sure, some of these public revenues have themselves been generated from previous investments (such as the Canada and Quebec Pension Plans), but in most cases they are generated by taxation on the current population. To the extent that a society has required or encouraged (either voluntarily or through public schemes such as the CPP/QPP) persons to accumulate assets during their working-age lifetimes for "consumption" during their retirement years, there is a relatively smaller burden placed on the current, usually working-age, population to finance public services for the elderly. But to the extent that this has not occurred, the current population can be expected to experience a relatively greater tax burden to maintain a given real level of services — otherwise the real level of services will decline.

This tendency is exacerbated by population aging. Population aging generally places an ever-increasing *proportion* of the population in the senior age groups, and consequently, the maintenance of the real level of public services to these people can place an ever-increasing tax burden on the current population (which may also include the elderly). If this does not occur, then either the real level of public services must decline along with the standard of living of the elderly, or the elderly must maintain their standard of living by obtaining the difference in the level of services from their private resources. This latter approach would imply a more rapid decumulation of private financial assets than would otherwise take place.

Even if real output growth in the economy is sufficient to maintain the existing real level of public services to the elderly, thus removing the need to increase the tax burden on the current population, the implication is that much of the growth in real output will be necessary to support the elderly and that, as a consequence, they will share disproportionately in the current income generated by that real growth.[2]

One of the most important public and private services provided to the elderly is the provision of income upon retirement. In Canada the public component of this income is provided by the Old Age Security (OAS), Guaranteed Income Supplement (GIS) and Canada and Quebec Pension Plans. In addition, a number of provinces also have their own programs of supplementary assistance to the elderly, which, like the OAS and GIS, are financed from the general revenues of the governments concerned. The resources required by this combination of income floor and income replacement programs[3] are directly related to the number of the elderly in the Canadian population, and hence the future costs of these programs can be anticipated to reflect the future numbers of the elderly in the population. With population aging, this group can be expected to grow considerably more rapidly than the Canadian population at large.

As shown in the population futures of chapter 3 (see Table 3-9), the percentage of the Canadian population aged 65 years and over is projected to more than double in the next fifty years, rising from current levels of around 10 per cent to levels above 20 per cent by 2031 and beyond (see Figure 4-2). This increase will be substantial over the 1980s, will proceed at a slower rate over the 1990s because of the increasing births coming from the children of the Baby Boom cohort, and then will be followed by another period of substantial increase between 2011 and 2031 as the Baby Boom generation reaches retirement ages. Subsequently, the proportion stabilizes as the Baby Boom generation passes away. The lingering effects of this particular generation are very apparent in these results.

Newfoundland, Quebec, Alberta and the territories currently have percentages of their populations aged 65 years and over that are below the Canada-wide figure. Prince Edward Island, Nova Scotia, Manitoba, Saskatchewan and British Columbia are above the Canada-wide figure (see Table 1-8). In 1981 the percentages in

Saskatchewan, Manitoba and Prince Edward Island all exceed 11 per cent, while the province with the lowest percentage is Newfoundland at 7.4 per cent. The interprovincial differences are clearly quite substantial. The future projections (see Table 3-15) generally show that by 2001 Alberta (at 9.1 per cent) has replaced Newfoundland at the low end of the spectrum, and Manitoba (at 13.7 per cent) has replaced Saskatchewan at the high end of the spectrum; thus, the interprovincial differences are, if anything, widening over the projection horizon to 2001. Beyond that year, however, all provinces follow a similar pattern, rising to levels around 20 per cent by 2031 and then stabilizing. As previously noted, this pattern is relatively insensitive to alternative population futures.

In analyses of pension costs, it is common to define the pension ratio as the number (or percentage) of the elderly (usually aged 65 years and over) divided by the number (or percentage) of the working-age population (usually aged 15 to 64 years). This measure indicates the number of persons aged 65 years and over as a proportion of the number of persons in the working-age population. In the case of a program for the elderly that is financed on a pay-as-you-go basis by a payroll tax primarily collected from the working-age population, this ratio can indicate the pressures on the tax rates solely as a result of demographic changes. On a more general basis, its inverse shows the relative number of persons available to ''support'' the elderly at any point in time.

These data (see Table 7-1 and Figure 7-1) show a ratio that increases two and a half times between 1851 and 1951 and then increases another two and a half times between 1951 and 2051. By the end of the projection horizon there is one person of pensionable age for every three persons in the working-age population.[4] Currently there are approximately seven working-age persons for every pensionable person in Canada. These results alone would suggest a substantial increase in the tax burden on the working-age population to support the senior members of the population in future years. For example, the projected pension ratio increases 26.6 per cent between 1981 and 2001. This would be a measure of the increased per capita burden on the working-age population *if* all costs of supporting the elderly were pay-as-you-go costs, labour force participation rates and unemployment rates remained unchanged, real incomes remained unchanged, the costs of supporting the elderly increased in direct proportion to their numbers, and no new resources were available elsewhere in society.

218

TABLE 7-1
HISTORICAL AND FUTURE PENSION RATIO AND INVERSE
RATIO FOR CANADA, 1851-2051

Census Year	Pension Ratio[a]	Inverse Pension Ratio[b]	Census Year	Pension Ratio[a]	Inverse Pension Ratio[b]
History			*Projection[c]*		
1851	0.051	19.6	1981	0.143	7.0
1861	0.056	18.0	1991	0.170	5.9
1871	0.067	14.9	2001	0.181	5.5
1881	0.072	13.9	2011	0.195	5.1
1891	0.077	13.0	2021	0.259	3.9
1901	0.083	12.0	2031	0.332	3.0
1911	0.075	13.4	2041	0.329	3.0
1921	0.079	12.7	2051	0.329	3.0
1931	0.088	11.3			
1941	0.102	9.8			
1951	0.125	8.0			
1961	0.131	7.7			
1971	0.130	7.7			

Notes: [a] Number of persons aged 65 years and over divided by the number of persons aged 15 to 64 years.

     [b] Inverse of [a].

     [c] Projection 1.

Sources: Tables 1-2 and 3-9.

It would be well to consider each of these assumptions in turn. Although many of the programs oriented towards the elderly (including medical and hospital care) are funded out of current tax revenues, not all are. In particular, the Canada/Quebec Pension Plans are partially funded by an investment fund and partially on a pay-as-you-go basis.[5] This places some downward pressures on the increased future burden on the working-age population.

As noted in chapter 6, labour force participation rates have been approximately constant in Canada over this century, with the increasing female rates being largely offset by declining male rates. However, during the 1960s and 1970s, increasing female rates have dominated, with the result that overall labour force participation rates have increased. Should this trend continue, a greater percentage of the

FIGURE 7-1
HISTORICAL AND FUTURE PENSION RATIO
AND INVERSE PENSION RATIO, CANADA,
1851-2051

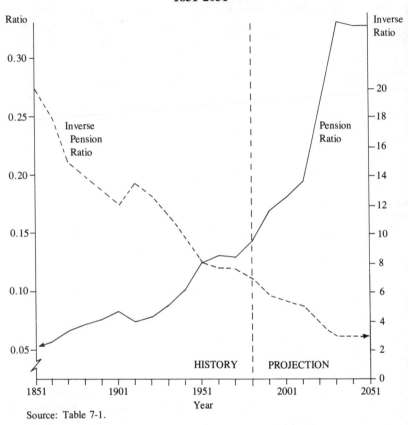

Source: Table 7-1.

working-age population would be available to work and, under approximately constant unemployment rates, available to support the elderly. This would also ease the future per capita burden on the working-age population. Of course, if these people were not gainfully employed (implying increased unemployment rates), the opposite would be the case.[6]

Increases in productivity result in increases in output and income, even without increases in the number of working-age persons. Hence, if the projected labour force is more productive (as *might* be expected

220

in an aging population, since experience is positively related to age and, furthermore, educational levels have been rising), additional incomes will be generated that could be used to support the elderly. This would also lighten the future per capita burden on the working-age population indicated by the above measures of pension costs.

Turning to the proportionality assumption, one notes that if the provision of services to the elderly can be accomplished at lower average costs as the size of the program expands (a situation economists call increasing returns to scale), then once again the increased future per capita burden will not be in direct proportion to the above measures.

Finally, the analysis so far has concentrated on the two upper age groups and has not considered the youngest age group. As is apparent from the previous chapters, the number of the young, and especially their percentage, in the population is projected to decline noticeably. Since these ages are the dominant consumers of publicly financed education services, it might be expected that public resources could be transferred from servicing the young to servicing the elderly over the projection horizon. If this were possible, the increased future per capita burden of population aging on the working-age population could be further reduced.

In summary, there is a potentially substantial impact of future populations on Canadian income support programs for the elderly, including both public and private pensions. Whether or not the increasing tax burden on the working-age population implied by these population futures will, in fact, be necessary depends on a variety of future conditions, such as labour force participation, unemployment, productivity performance, economies and diseconomies of scale in the provision of these services, and the ability to effect the relative transfer of resources from the young to the elderly.

Future Populations and Health Care

The impacts of future populations on health care programs have also received some attention in Canada in recent years.[7] The future for these programs can be obtained based on the observation that the per capita cost of providing these services to the public varies with the age and sex of the recipient. The calculation of age-sex- (and possibly province-) specific per capita costs can then be related to the future size and aging of the Canadian population (reviewed in chapter 3) to obtain the demographic impacts of future populations on these public programs. The implications and challenges posed by these trends for current and future policies can then be ascertained.

The relationship between the per capita cost of health services[8] and age can be described by an asymmetric U-shaped curve for both males and females.[9] In general, this cost rises dramatically with age after about 60 years, with the female cost being above the male cost over ages 15 through 55 years approximately and below at other ages.[10] Consequently, the future aging of the Canadian population, which results in rapidly increasing numbers of people in the senior age groups, can be expected to place upward pressures on the real cost of public health care programs in the years ahead — given that care is maintained at current standards. Moreover, the changing age composition will necessitate a relative transfer of resources within this sector from the young (maternity services) to the elderly (geriatric services).

Conclusions reached to date suggest an increase in real per capita costs of 5.6 per cent in physicians' services and 15.9 per cent in hospital services to the turn of the century,[11] and a further increase of 7.5 and 30.9 per cent respectively between 2001 and 2031, when the percentage of the elderly in the population stabilizes.[12] In other words, since the elderly are relatively much heavier users of hospital services, the ratio of physician to hospital costs will decline and the percentage of hospital services attributable to persons aged 65 years and over will increase.[13] These future projections can be placed in perspective when one notes that if current participation rates persist, by the second decade of the twenty-first century all of current hospital capacity will be required just to take care of the elderly.

In the context of chapter 4, these conclusions clearly point to the health care sector, and the hospital system in particular, as a likely recipient of the gradual relative transfer of society's resources from the young to the elderly in an aging population such as Canada's. However, they also inexorably lead to questions regarding the viability of current policies regarding the provision of health services, especially to the elderly. The demographically induced trends in this sector appear to be unambiguous — it can only be hoped that the policy responses will be just as unambiguous.

Future Populations and Housing

Household formation and the requirements of the population for various types of housing units vary systematically with the age of the individuals comprising the population. Individuals typically form

222

separate household units some time in their early twenties, and by age 30 most live in family units in households separate from their parents. The size of the household may increase over the subsequent twenty to thirty years as children are added to the unit. In later years these family units are reduced in size as the young leave the household and the elderly members die. In addition, family separations contribute to the formation of new households, whereas remarriages and other forms of cohabitive living arrangements have the opposite impacts. This typical life-cycle process is reflected in the housing needs of the individuals comprising the population. In the early ages of household formation the individual typically demands an apartment or some other form of multiple-unit residential accommodation. As families are formed, the transition to a relatively small single-family home or townhouse appears to be the goal of most Canadian families. Later, in the middle age groups as the family size grows, the family housing will be upgraded, probably to relatively large, detached single-family dwellings. Then, as the young leave the family unit and partners die, there is a relocation to a smaller house, apartment or, perhaps, retirement home.

These impacts of demographic change on housing demand in Canada have been recognized for some time. In the context of most macroeconometric models, for example, the need for housing is usually related to some measure of household or family formation (along with other determinants, such as replacement needs), which is in turn related to the age-sex composition of the Canadian population.[14] In this way, Canada's population futures have an impact on the need for housing and, therefore, influence the formation of public policies towards this sector.[15]

Relating household or family formation to population is not a simple task.[16] It requires the definition of a household or family and the identification of single-person and multiple-person units. This in turn requires the specification of formation (for example, marriage) and separation (for example, divorce) rates by age and sex or, alternatively, the determination of household headship rates — that is, the proportion of designated household heads in the population aged 15 years and over — by age and sex and, perhaps, by marital status (and province). General household headship rates in Canada have been gradually increasing over the postwar period and are currently around 40 per cent. The historical gradual upward trend might be expected to continue in future years, as a greater percentage of the population enters the middle age groups of a typical life span. These headship rates vary by marital status and tend to increase with age until the 55-to-64-year age group, after which they decline slightly. Consequently, the impact of an aging population can be expected to be reflected in the formation of households and families in the years ahead.

To assess the likely impacts of these future demographic trends on housing needs in Canada, first note that the average age of marriage in Canada is currently around 22 years for females and 24 years for males. Since the population in these age groups will peak in the early to mid-1980s (see Figures 3-1 and 3-3), the contribution of the young to household and family formation in Canada can be expected to peak at this time. Moreover, the subsequent cohorts that can be expected to enter young adulthood during the 1980s and 1990s are much smaller, so the future growth in the number of households and families can be expected to slow. Estimates of household growth in Canada over this period suggest a slowing from rates approximately averaging 2.5 per cent per annum over the 1970s, to rates averaging around 1.6 per cent per annum over the 1980s, and perhaps to around 1.0 per cent per annum over the 1990s.[17] Note, however, that although declining, these growth rates remain *above* population growth over the remainder of the twentieth century because of the changing demographic composition of future populations.

Consequently, by the mid-1980s it is expected that there will be little net new housing requirements from the lower end of the age spectrum and significantly lower net new requirements for homes from first-time home buyers. The net new demand at the other end of the age spectrum will, however, be gradually increasing. Of course, although related primarily to future populations, the long-run housing demand depends on several other factors, such as the number of vacant housing units, the demolition of existing housing units or their conversion to other uses, together with traditional economic factors of income, price and financing costs.

By the 1990s there may well be a marked shift in housing demand towards the single-family dwellings required by a predominantly middle-aged population.[18] Because of decreased average family size, however, it might be expected that the average house size may not need to be as large as in the 1960s and 1970s when the Baby Boom generation was being reared. Moreover, since the proportion of home ownership peaks in the 45-to-54-year age bracket and declines at an accelerating rate beyond approximately age 60 years, it is likely that the strength in *new* housing demand in this period will be from the

224

elderly and will be for multiple-unit type dwellings oriented to their specific needs. Note, however, that at the same time, this will release single-family housing, which can be used to satisfy some of the (decreased) net demand for homeownership.

In summary, the impacts of future populations on household and family formation and, hence, on future housing needs in Canada appears to be relatively clear. Although declining, these needs can be expected to remain somewhat buoyant during the early 1980s as the Baby Boom generation forms households and families. Thereafter the needs can be expected to decline substantially, with most net new requirements being in the type of housing oriented to the specific needs of the elderly.[19] In the context of the general overview presented in chapter 4, therefore, it would appear that housing is a sector from which relative resource transfers can be made in future years, although the changing needs of future populations on the type of housing should not be ignored.

Future Populations and Justice

One area in which the impacts of demography and future demographic change have received very little attention in Canada to date is the justice system — on the courts of law and on the institutions of detainment. Since these are important instruments of public policy, the impacts of future Canadian populations in this area may have profound implications for the future structure and fabric of Canadian society. Overcrowding in the courts and prisons can lead to an inappropriate administration of justice. Consequently, it should be useful to attempt to assess the impacts, if any, of future populations on the justice system and to plan the training of personnel and the construction of appropriate facilities accordingly.

While much remains to be understood about the determinants of criminal activity, there has been a growing recognition in recent years that crime rates are strongly related to the demographic composition of the population.[20] This research suggests that during the late 1960s and 1970s the Baby Boom generation was moving through the high crime ages of 15 to 25 years, and hence the number of crimes increased over this period. However, at least in the U.S., the prison population *declined* over the 1960s and did not start to increase until the 1970s. This suggests that even though the Baby Boom generation was moving through the high crime ages in the 1960s, they were still juveniles or first-time offenders and, if caught, not likely to go to prison for their crimes. However, over the 1970s a sufficient proportion of these Baby

225

Boom offenders became old enough to have developed an adult criminal record, resulting in an increase in the prison population.

The relationships between future populations and criminal activity can be assessed by calculating crime rates by age and sex (and perhaps by province) for different types of crime. Similarly, the relationship between future court activity and future populations can be obtained by applying age-sex- (and perhaps province-) specific arrest rates to these future crimes by type of crime. These in turn can form the basis for institutional commitments by the application of commitment rates to each group and, when combined with estimates of the average length of commitment, can form the basis for future projections of institutional populations by province.

Application of this methodology to the population of Pennsylvania suggests that arrests should peak in 1980, prison commitments in 1985, and the prison population in 1990. The subsequent decline reflects the maturation of the Baby Boom generation — first out of the high crime ages, then out of the commitment-prone ages, and, finally, out of the prison-prone ages. Whether or not the same future time profile would apply in Canada remains an open question,[21] but it would appear to be highly likely that a similar demographically induced process would have an impact on the justice sector in the years ahead. If this is the case, it should be reflected in current public policies with regard to training and institutional construction if a deterioration in the administration of justice is to be avoided in future years. In the context of the relative resource transfer issue outlined in chapter 4, it would appear, on the basis of the fragmentary evidence outlined above, that the justice sector in Canada might well be a worthy recipient of resources (from education?) at least over the decade of the 1980s (after which the health sector becomes a prime candidate).

Future Populations and Consumption and Savings Patterns

The impacts of future populations on the changing nature of household consumption patterns should be apparent from previous discussions. Private, as well as public, expenditures on medical care can be expected to increase in relative importance, whereas those on education and housing (shelter) and related items can be expected to decline. Household necessities (food, energy and perhaps clothing) can also be expected to decline in relative importance, partly because of the declining household size. A corollary of these observations is the increasing proportion of the consumer budget that is likely to be devoted to discretionary-type expenditures, such as recreational durables (for example, sporting and electronic products) and enter-tainment (such as sporting and cultural events). The movement to single-family dwellings, even if relatively smaller in size, over the remainder of the twentieth century could result in the relative importance of expenditures on household operations (telephone, water, and so on) and on home appliances and furnishings remaining stronger than might be anticipated on the basis of new housing information alone.

Conclusions such as these can be derived from Canada's population futures by breaking down family expenditures[22] by sex and age of purchaser and applying these constant expenditure proportions to Canadian population futures. This approach would isolate the demographic impacts on changing consumption patterns in much the same way as the constant participation rate analyses of chapters 5 and 6 isolated the impacts on future enrolments and labour force respec-tively. These results are essential to planning in the private sector and to policies developed in the public sector. They can assist in the determination of relatively more profitable investments for both private and public sector capital. In addition, since consumption taxes are an important source of government revenue, changing consumption patterns in the future can be expected to have impacts on future government revenue generation prospects. To date almost all the attention in regard to population aging has been devoted to the expenditure side of government budgets (see chapter 4) and very little to the revenue side. This would appear to be an unfortunate omission.

A related but separate topic that has received some attention in the literature is the impact of future populations on private savings. Besides the somewhat indirect effects through wealth accumulation in the form of pensions and housing,[23] there is a further substantive concern with the direct effect of changing demographic composition on the national savings rate. Recent analyses[24] have produced ambiguous results. Using a simple life-cycle model in which savings are related to age, are accumulated over working years and are consumed in the retirement years, suggests an increase in the savings rate in Canada of around two percentage points over the late 1980s and 1990s as the Baby Boom generation moves into the high savings rate age groups. However, exploratory analysis with a more complex model that permits decumulation in the middle-age years associated with the education of children and other family responsibilities, produces opposite results. Under these conditions the savings rate could well decline over the 1980s and early 1990s by perhaps as much as two

227

percentage points, after which it increases. Consequently, simulations of the impacts of future populations on the national savings rate appear to produce contradictory results and further research is required to ascertain the likely outcome.

The impact of aging on national savings may be an important consequence of population aging in Canada. It has implications for taxation policies with respect to private savings and for the capital markets and the financing of future investment projects in Canada. It is unfortunate that current results appear to be so ambiguous.

Future Populations and Voting Behaviour

Public policies in future years may also be influenced by the possible impacts of demography on the voting behaviour of the Canadian electorate. The number of young voters increased dramatically over the decade of the 1970s, with the peak when the Baby Boom reached voting age (18 years) in the late 1970s. Canada's population futures show this youngest age group becoming relatively less important, with relative importance gradually shifting to the working ages over the remainder of the twentieth century and to the retirement ages in the twenty-first century. Whether or not this changing composition of the voting population will affect future voting behaviour, political outcomes and public policies is purely conjectural.[25] If voting behaviour is related to age and sex, then significant impacts can be expected. In particular, if voting patterns tend to become ideologically more conservative (and perhaps Conservative) with age, then the future aging of the Canadian population could lead to more conservative outcomes and policies. However, if voting behaviour is more related to the time of birth, then future voting patterns will reflect the current voting behaviour more closely, at least until the new cohorts reach voting age in the twenty-first century.

The demographics of politics is a largely uncharted field in Canadian political science. This may reflect the paucity of information or, perhaps, the conjecture that demography is a relatively unimportant determinant of voting behaviour, political outcomes and public policies. Nonetheless, it remains a topic ripe for research and suggests the arena where the challenges of Canada's population futures must be ultimately addressed.

Conclusions

The analysis of the impacts of future populations on the economy and society, and the interaction between population and public policy, is

228

not a new field of economic enquiry. It extends back at least to the seminal work of Malthus almost two centuries ago and remains a cornerstone of much of the literature in development economics, labour economics, and other areas of the discipline. Yet it appears to have been relatively neglected in the mainstream of contemporary economics. Perhaps this is a reflection of the success of many modern societies in eradicating or postponing the dreaded "Malthusian checks," as they came to be known; perhaps it is a reflection of the shorter-term fine-tuning orientation of much of recent economic science; or perhaps it just reflects the specialization of disciplines of recent times. This is not to say that advances have not been made, but generally they have tended to be sporadic and relatively neglected in contemporary mainstream economics.

Yet much of the historical and future Canadian economic developments are dominated by demographic developments. The immigration waves of the early part of this century and the postwar period, and the Baby Boom of the 1950s are notable examples. Moreover, regional development has been dramatically influenced by the westward drift of the Canadian population. The impacts on certain sectors and public policies (for example, education and health) are now well defined, while those in other areas do not seem to be nearly so well understood (for example, crime and savings). What does seem clear, however, is that the development of economic policy in Canada and elsewhere requires a cognizance of current and future demographic developments, and of the possible interactions between these important components of future economic development.

In this study, the methodology (in most cases) has been (explicitly or implicitly) to apply constant rates (for enrolment, labour force participation, per capita health cost, household formation, savings, et cetera) to *isolate* the challenges of Canada's population futures on areas of current and future policy concern. The orientation has been not only towards consistency, but also towards sensitivity. Many, if not most, of the conclusions are clearly shown to be relatively insensitive to the chosen assumptions. In this sense, they are "inevitable," and the policy maker can proceed in relative confidence. For example, population growth in Canada is slowing, and as a consequence, the Canadian population is aging and, not surprisingly, becoming more female-dominant. Numerous other conclusions have been made with similar confidence throughout the study.

But what of the policy challenges of those future trends? A primary purpose of this study has been to provide to those concerned with the formulation, development and implementation of economic (especially public) policy in Canada a framework in which to prepare their contributions. In the previous chapters a number of implications of the trends and their associated challenges have been explored. In a number of cases the conclusions do not appear to agree with current policy perceptions and practices. Policy makers undoubtedly will be interested and concerned with many additional issues that are related to those outlined in this study. Some of these have been described in this last chapter, but numerous others also deserve attention.[26]

A major conclusion arising from these analyses is that there is a necessity, in any aging population such as Canada's, to gradually effect a relative transfer of society's resources from those programs oriented primarily to the young (such as education) to those programs oriented primarily to the elderly (such as pensions and medical care). The implied tax burden resulting from the increasing per capita costs of supporting the latter group can be made less severe by such relative resource transfers. In the foregoing pages a number of areas have been identified as possible "winners" and "losers" in this resource transfer exercise.

But whatever the area, it is clear from this demographic analysis that the early 1980s provide a unique period for policy formulation and development in Canada. Over this period the demographic pressures from the elderly population are still being offset by declining pressures from the young population. This will come to an end by the mid-1980s as the higher relative per capita costs of servicing the elderly start to dominate the declining pressures from the young. One method of delaying or overcoming these increased pressures on public programs would be a reduction in the per capita costs of providing services to the elderly (perhaps through a restructuring of the health care system). However, it is likely that however advantageous this might be, it would only postpone the inevitable. Sooner or later the increased tax burden for support of the elderly will become apparent. What is comforting is the knowledge (from the results in chapter 4) that this burden is unlikely to be as great, at least within the next thirty years, as was the burden associated with supporting the Baby Boom generation of the late 1950s.

The future demographic trends in Canada are clear and the time for appropriate policy formulation and implementation is now. But it is comforting to realize that even though posing a new challenge, the overall economic impact of these population futures, at least throughout the remainder of this century, is unlikely to be greater than those already faced in relatively recent Canadian history.

Appendix

Projection Assumptions

The population futures presented in this study were developed with the Statistics Canada population projection model. As noted in the text (chapter 3), this model is based on the standard population identities, which have been parametrized for simplification of use and modified to include the age-sex compositional details of the provincial populations. The national population is a sum of the provincial and territorial populations. A rate approach is applied to fertility and mortality and to interprovincial migration, while a level approach is applied to international migration (both immigration and emigration). These meet with the general principle of relating population change to the population "at risk," with the exception of emigration, where insufficient information is available to adopt a rate approach. Note also that the use of out-migration rates and in-migration *proportions* ensures internal consistency with respect to the treatment of interprovincial migration. To develop projections of future population, it is necessary to develop assumptions regarding these rates and levels for future time periods. To test the sensitivity of the results to the assumptions, a small set of alternative assumptions are used in this study. It is to a review of these assumptions that this appendix is devoted.

By way of background, Table A-1 summarizes the main assumptions used by Statistics Canada in each of its series of published population projections. In both series of Statistics Canada population projections, four primary scenarios were considered, together with three supplementary scenarios.[1]

In the first series of projections, effectively three alternative total fertility rates were considered — a high (2.60), medium (2.20) and low

TABLE A-1
SUMMARY OF ASSUMPTIONS UNDERLYING STATISTICS CANADA POPULATION PROJECTIONS FOR CANADA AND THE PROVINCES

Projection Designation	Total Fertility Rate for Canada	Net Internat'l Immigration to Canada	Interprov. Migration Pattern
FIRST SERIES: 1972-2001			
Primary:			
A	2.60	100,000	450,000[a]
B	2.20	60,000	435,000[a]
C	1.80	60,000	435,000[a]
D	1.80	60,000	218,000[a]
Supplementary:			
E	2.19	0	0[a]
F	2.19	100,000	450,000[a]
G	2.20	100,000	218,000[a]
SECOND SERIES: 1976-2001			
Primary:			
1	2.06	100,000	B[b]
2	2.06	75,000	D[c]
3	1.71	75,000	C[d]
4	1.71	50,000	A[e]
Supplementary:			
5	1.71	25,000	C
6	2.06	0	0[f]
7	1.71	0	0

Notes: [a] Gross Migration—sum of net gains and net losses—per year.
[b] A return to the "long term" pattern observed during the 1960s by 1981-82.
[c] A partial reversal to the "long term" pattern by 1986-87.
[d] A partial reversal to the "long term" patterns with further westward shift.
[e] Continuation of the 1975-78 patterns.
[f] Net interprovincial migration is assumed to be zero in all areas.

Sources: Statistics Canada, *Population Projections for Canada and the Provinces, 1972-20* (Catalogue No. 91-514), pp. 59 and 79, and *Population Projections for Canada and t Provinces, 1976-2001* (Catalogue No. 91-520), pp. 29-46.

234

(1.80); these were held constant throughout the projection horizon. In the second series two alternative rates were considered — increasing to 2.06 by 1991 and decreasing to 1.71 by 1991. Two points are worth noting: first, that over the period between these two series of projections the fertility assumptions generally were revised downward; and second, that given the recent observations on fertility (see Table 2-2), the assumed values would still appear to be on the high side.

In the first series of Statistics Canada projections, age-sex-specific mortality rates for 1975-79 and for 1985-89 were projected from the trends in disease-specific mortality and accidents in the 1950s and 1960s. These rates, which reflected continued improvements in life expectancy, were gradually attained over the projection period and held constant after 1990. A similar approach was adopted for the second series of population projections.[2] This resulted in a projected life expectancy of 70.2 years for males and 78.6 years for females by 1985-87.[3] A comparison of these figures with recent data (see Table 2-6) shows that the male life expectancy had already been achieved by 1975-77 and that the female life expectancy had already moved half way (since 1970-72) to this projected figure by 1975-77. As previously noted (in chapter 2), these new data are relatively surprising, but they do suggest that the Statistics Canada mortality projections are in need of modification for use in this study.

Assumptions regarding net international migration have also been revised downward slightly between the two series of projections, primarily as a result of upward revisions in emigration estimates. In the first series of projections, emigration was set at 60,000 persons annually, while for the second series it was set at 75,000 persons.[4] This revision would appear to be consistent with recent data. Alternative immigration levels of 160,000, 120,000 and 60,000 persons per year were used in the former series and of 175,000, 125,000 and 75,000 in the latter series.[5] Alternative immigration assumptions permit an analysis of the sensitivity of the results to different *levels* of immigration. This is an appropriate approach, since a relatively new Canadian immigration act requires the minister, after appropriate consultations, to specify "the number of immigrants that the Government of Canada deems it appropriate to admit during any specified period of time."

As previously noted, the methodology for incorporating net interprovincial migration was changed between the first and the second series of Statistics Canada population projections. In the first series a gross migration[6] *level* was chosen, based on historical observations. In

235

the second series, provincial age-sex-specific out-migration *rates* were used to obtain a pool of interprovincial migrants that was then allocated back to the provinces, using provincial age-sex-specific in-migration proportions. Since the methodology is quite different between the two series, it is difficult to compare them, but it should be reemphasized that the latter methodology more closely follows the principle of relating the population movements to the population at risk.

A general conclusion that emerges from this brief summary of the assumptions employed by Statistics Canada in developing their population projections is that over time new information is constantly becoming available and that, as a consequence, it may be necessary to periodically update any series of population projections to incorporate recent theoretical advances and empirical observations. It is with this important consideration in mind that the following review of the assumptions employed in this study is presented. Table 3-1 contains an overview of these assumptions.

Three alternative fertility patterns are considered: current (1.75 throughout), low (1.55 by 2001) and high (2.25 by 2001). The low fertility assumption is much lower than anything previously published by Statistics Canada.

Two alternative mortality assumptions are considered, reflecting the need to take account of the recent (1975-77) life expectancy data. One (A) combines these data with the previous Statistics Canada projections, while the other (B) extends life expectancy even further by continuing recent improvements over the next decade.

Similar to the methods of Statistics Canada, three alternative net immigration assumptions are considered, all reflecting differences in immigration. Emigration is assumed to be 75,000 persons throughout; while the immigration assumptions are for 140,000, 100,000 and 75,000 persons per year, the latter only being included to generate a hypothetical zero net immigration scenario for study purposes.

Finally, three interprovincial migration patterns are considered: continuation of the 1976-79 patterns (I), a partial return to the more "traditional" patterns (II) and further movement towards western Canadian destinations (III). In two scenarios the different combinations of out-migration rates and in-migration proportions are examined to explore the sensitivity to assumptions *within* the interprovincial migration patterns. In addition, somewhat slightly different age-sex compositions of immigrants, emigrants and interprovincial migrants as based on the most recently available data are used in this study.

In summary, although adopting the methodology and framework of

236

the Statistics Canada projections, this study takes into consideration the data of the late 1970s and reports on some different alternative future population projections for Canada and the provinces. The remainder of the Appendix is devoted to a detailed outline and evaluation of the chosen assumptions.

The three alternative fertility assumptions used in the study are outlined in Table A-2. The 1979 values are estimates based on the best information available at the time the projections were undertaken and are the same for all projections. In many of the alternative projections these are held constant throughout the projection horizon in an attempt to explore the implications of continuing at current levels and to abstract from the conflicting theories regarding fertility determination. For example, Easterlin predicts a turnaround based on the increasing scarcity of young people, which will raise their relative wages and thus provide the opportunity for women to relinquish income-earning responsibilities in favour of raising children.[7] On the basis of a projected relative scarcity in the 1980s, Easterlin argues for a turnaround in fertility behaviour. On the other hand, Butz and Ward argue for a continued decline in fertility rates on the basis that rising female wage rates will increase the foregone income of raising children.[8] In the Butz and Ward thesis, male earnings capture the (Easterlin) income effect and female wages the price effect. Butz and Ward argue that since the early 1960s, when wage differentials between the sexes have been narrowing, the price effect has dominated the income effect and that this is likely to continue. The data in Table A-2 (top half) could be considered to represent the Butz and Ward hypothesis: total fertility rates decline to 1.5 children per woman in the two most populous provinces of Ontario and Quebec, and the rates in the remaining provinces show a narrowing of the gap between the fertility rates.[9] The data in the bottom half of Table A-2 are consistent with the Easterlin hypothesis, with total fertility rates gradually rising to above replacement levels in the low fertility provinces of Ontario and Quebec. Again a narrowing of the differences between the provincial rates is incorporated into these data.

Note that these assumed fertility rates are province-specific. In the first series of population projections, Statistics Canada set a national fertility rate, and rates for the provinces were derived based on projected province-to-Canada ratios. In the second series of projections, rates for each province were specified, with the national rate being determined from an aggregation of the provinces. This is the approach used in this study.

237

TABLE A-2
PERIOD TOTAL FERTILITY RATE ASSUMPTIONS[a] FOR CANADA AND THE PROVINCES, 1979-2001

Year	Can[b]	Nfld	PEI	NS	NB	PQ	Ont	Man	Sask	Alta	BC	Yukon	NWT
1979	1.75	2.15	1.95	1.71	1.73	1.67	1.67	1.83	2.10	1.90	1.71	2.12	3.10
LOW FERTILITY ASSUMPTIONS													
1981	1.71	2.08	1.89	1.67	1.70	1.64	1.64	1.78	2.03	1.84	1.67	2.05	2.88
1986	1.64	1.92	1.77	1.61	1.62	1.58	1.58	1.69	1.88	1.73	1.61	1.90	2.53
1991	1.58	1.82	1.70	1.56	1.57	1.53	1.53	1.63	1.78	1.67	1.56	1.80	2.35
1996	1.56	1.76	1.66	1.53	1.55	1.51	1.51	1.60	1.74	1.64	1.53	1.75	2.26
2001	1.55	1.74	1.64	1.52	1.53	1.50	1.50	1.58	1.72	1.62	1.52	1.73	2.22
HIGH FERTILITY ASSUMPTIONS													
1981	1.76	2.15	2.96	1.72	1.74	1.68	1.68	1.84	2.10	1.91	1.72	2.12	3.06
1986	1.85	2.18	2.01	1.81	1.83	1.78	1.78	1.91	2.14	1.96	1.81	2.16	2.99
1991	2.02	2.31	2.16	1.98	2.00	1.96	1.96	2.07	2.27	2.12	1.98	2.29	2.99
1996	2.19	2.41	2.30	2.15	2.16	2.13	2.13	2.22	2.38	2.27	2.15	2.39	2.98
2001	2.25	2.44	2.34	2.22	2.23	2.20	2.20	2.28	2.42	2.32	2.22	2.43	2.92

Notes: [a] Annual data, which are used in the projection, are obtained by smoothed interpolation.
[b] Calculated from an aggregate of the province-specific rates.

Source: Projections by the author.

However, the Statistics Canada population projection model does require single-year age-specific fertility rates. Since the projection of this number of rates can be a rather cumbersome, and, in some cases, an inappropriate exercise, a three-parameter mathematical function is used to translate a total fertility rate projection into single-year age-specific rates.[10] The three parameters required as inputs (or assumptions) are the total fertility rate, and the mean and modal ages of childbearing. By far the most important input from a projection viewpoint is the total fertility rate, since it determines the *level* of fertility (or average number of children per woman). The assumptions for this parameter have been described above. The *timing* of fertility is determined by the remaining two parameters. As has been noted previously, the 1970s have seen an apparent reversal of the historical downward trend in the modal age of fertility in Canada (see Tables 2-3 and 2-4). In retrospect, the first series of Statistics Canada projections overestimated the mean age and underestimated the modal age because of an actual decrease in the difference between the two, with the mean stabilizing at around 26 years and the mode increasing to around 25 years in the mid-1970s. Although this "new" trend continued into the late 1970s, it was decided that the Statistics Canada second series province-specific mean and modal ages be adopted for this study.[11] These were held constant throughout the projection horizon for all projections.

As previously noted, the most commonly used summary measure of mortality is life expectancy at birth. These data for the 1970s (see Table 2-6) show that it is probably unsatisfactory to leave mortality rates unchanged as Statistics Canada did when it produced its second series of projections. Since it was not possible to reexamine the trends in disease-specific mortality and accidents and develop new projections along the same lines,[12] an alternative procedure was used for this study. The actual (1975-77) age-sex-specific survival rates were compared to the Statistics Canada projected survival rates for 1976, 1981 and 1986, and whenever the actual rate exceeded the projected rate, the actual rate was inserted in its place. This procedure was used for 1976, 1981, 1986 and 1991.[13] Age-sex-specific survival rates for intervening years were calculated by interpolation. The resulting figures were 70.8 years for males and 80.3 years for females. These were held constant after 1991. In the alternative mortality scenario, the survival rates for 1981 were calculated by applying one-half of the actual increase between 1971 and 1976 to the periods 1976-81 and 1981-86.[14] Since the change between 1971 and 1976 was rather

TABLE A-3
ASSUMED DISTRIBUTION OF IMMIGRANTS BY PROVINCE OF DESTINATION

	Statistics Canada		This Study		
Prov.	Series 1[a] (%)	Series 2[b] (%)	Distribution (%)	Level 1[c] (000's)	Level 2[c] (000's)
Nfld	0.51	0.52	0.50	700	500
PEI	0.11	0.15	0.20	275	200
NS	1.32	1.29	1.20	1,700	1,200
NB	0.72	1.10	1.00	1,400	1,000
PQ	17.34	17.32	17.00	23,800	1,700
Ont	53.27	49.47	47.50	66,500	47,500
Man	4.15	4.03	4.30	6,000	4,300
Sask	1.54	1.72	2.20	3,050	2,200
Alta	7.12	10.19	11.40	16,000	11,400
BC	13.79	14.04	14.50	20,300	14,500
Yukon	0.04	0.05	0.06	85	60
NWT	0.09	0.11	0.14	190	140
Can	100.0	100.0	100.0	140,000	100,000

Notes: [a] Average of 1968-71 data.
  [b] Average of 1975-78 data.
  [c] Rounded.

Sources: Calculated from Statistics Canada, *Population Projections for Canada and the Provinces, 1972-2001* (Catalogue No. 91-514), p. 48, *Population Projections for Canada and the Provinces, 1976-2001* (Catalogue No. 91-520), p. 25; and assumptions by the author.

substantial (see Table 2-6), this procedure implies higher life expectancy for both males and females than arrived at through the previous method.

Immigration to Canada has averaged 140.4 thousand persons over the 1950s, 1960s and 1970s. There has been a slight decadal downward trend over this period,[15] and immigration has been well below this level during the late 1970s. However, past immigration history has been quite volatile, attributable to many factors, including domestic economic conditions and refugee resettlements, and it would appear unlikely that the most recent data signal a permanent reduction in Canadian immigration inflow. Improved average economic conditions in Canada relative to other countries over the 1980s and beyond, together with a continued humanitarian position regarding refugee intake, would suggest that recent immigrant levels could well be on the low side from a long-run historical perspective. Therefore, the basic assumption adopted for this study is for an average annual immigration level of 140,000 persons (the average of the 1950s, 1960s and 1970s), with an alternative assumption of 100,000 persons annually, a little below the annual average of the 1976-79 period.[16] This permits an evaluation of the impacts of continued low levels of immigration, together with assessment of the sensitivity of population growth to this component of growth.

The assumed provincial distribution of immigrant destinations was based on the data of the 1970s (see Table 2-7), and incorporates the westward drift of destinations previously noted. In particular, it is assumed that the Prairie provinces will receive a slightly higher proportion of immigrants than they have in recent years, largely at the expense of Ontario. The assumed distribution is summarized in Table A-3, along with the numerical consequences for the two levels of immigration mentioned above. The assumptions used by Statistics Canada are also included for comparison purposes.

The age-sex composition of immigration inflows has been tending to become more "dependent" and somewhat female-dominant (see Tables 2-8 and 2-9); that is, relatively more immigrants of non-working ages (0 to 14 years and 65 years and over) and relatively more women have been coming to Canada in recent years. Since this appears to be a long-term trend, reflecting in part the aging of the immigrant source populations, the age-sex composition of immigrants is based on the most recent data published by Statistics Canada.[17] Separate distributions are assumed for males and females (see Table A-4), with a slightly higher proportion of immigrants being female (a sex ratio of 0.90 is assumed). Again the Statistics Canada assumptions are included for comparison purposes, where the assumed aging of immigrant inflows relative to the earlier assumptions is apparent. These distributions are applied to all provinces and are held constant throughout the projection horizon.

Emigration from Canada, although somewhat volatile, has been gradually increasing, at least since the 1930s (see Table 1-1). This might be expected in a population that has been increasing in size. Estimates for the five years following the 1971 census averaged 71.4 thousand persons annually and for the subsequent three years have

241

TABLE A-4
ASSUMED AGE-SEX COMPOSITION OF IMMIGRANTS
(%)

| Age Group (Years) | Statistics Canada | | | | This Study | |
| | Series 1 | | Series 2 | | | |
	Male	Female	Male	Female	Male	Female
0-4	4.88	4.61	5.09	4.78	3.40	3.30
5-9	4.18	3.90	4.90	4.63	4.20	3.95
10-14	2.95	2.81	3.82	3.69	3.80	3.60
15-19	3.76	4.10	3.93	4.94	4.50	4.85
20-24	8.97	10.47	7.51	9.05	6.75	8.85
25-29	9.15	8.05	8.47	7.75	7.60	7.85
30-34	5.73	4.84	5.20	4.72	5.10	4.60
35-39	3.70	3.12	3.25	2.51	2.95	2.60
40-44	2.19	1.93	1.82	1.56	1.75	1.60
45-49	1.32	1.37	1.16	1.31	1.20	1.55
50-54	0.93	1.23	0.84	1.40	1.00	1.95
55-59	0.69	1.16	0.68	1.42	1.10	2.25
60-64	0.53	1.01	1.17	1.45	1.75	2.10
65-69	0.47	0.76	0.75	0.97	1.20	1.55
70+	0.43	0.80	0.65	1.06	1.20	1.90
All Ages[a]	49.86	50.14	49.22	50.78	47.50	52.50

Note: [a] Column totals may be subject to rounding error.

Sources: Statistics Canada, *Technical Report on Population Projections for Canada and the Provinces, 1972-2001* (Catalogue No. 91-516), p. 217; D.A. Norris and J. Perreault, "Migration Projections for Canada and the Provinces, 1976-1991," Background paper (Ottawa: Statistics Canada, 1979), p. 58; and assumptions by the author.

averaged 75.3 thousand persons annually. Consequently, although these flows are also probably influenced by relative international economic conditions, there appears to be little reason to depart from the latest Statistics Canada emigration assumption of 75,000 persons annually in any long-run evaluation of population futures, so this figure is incorporated into the projections in this study as well. From the limited data available, it appears that a slightly larger proportion of emigrants are coming from the older provinces of Ontario and British Columbia and, in the later 1970s, from Quebec, apparently signifying

242

TABLE A-5
ASSUMED DISTRIBUTION OF EMIGRANTS
BY PROVINCE OF ORIGIN

| Province | Statistics Canada | | This Study | |
	Series 1 (%)	Series 2 (%)	Distribution (%)	Levels[a] (000's)
Nfld	2.85	1.80	1.20	925
PEI	0.53	0.38	0.30	200
NS	3.12	2.80	1.80	1,375
NB	4.18	2.25	1.50	1,125
PQ	28.58	26.09	28.80	2,160
Ont	40.21	43.79	43.90	32,900
Man	3.01	3.10	2.10	1,575
Sask	3.13	2.36	1.90	1,425
Alta	5.00	5.66	4.80	3,600
BC	9.20	11.53	13.50	10,125
Yukon	0.07	0.08	0.10	75
NWT	0.13	0.16	0.10	75
Can[b]	100.0	100.0	100.0	75,000

Notes: [a] Rounded to the nearest 25 persons.
[b] Totals may not equal due to rounding.

Sources: Statistics Canada, *Population Projections for Canada and the Provinces, 1972-2001* (Catalogue No. 91-514), pp. 59 and 79, and *Population Projections for Canada and the Provinces, 1976-2001* (Catalogue No. 91-520), pp. 29-46.

a return to its relative contribution of the 1960s. These trends are incorporated into the assumed distribution of emigrants by province (see Table A-5), which is held constant throughout the projection horizon. The Statistics Canada assumptions are also included for comparison purposes.

The age-sex composition of emigrants is based on the most recent (1977) data on emigration to the U.S. It displays some slight aging relative to the Statistics Canada assumptions (see Table A-6). As with the Statistics Canada projections, these distributions are held constant for all provinces throughout the projection horizon.[18]

The changing pattern of interprovincial migration in Canada poses some difficult problems for population projections. In the absence of

TABLE A-6
ASSUMED AGE-SEX COMPOSITION OF EMIGRANTS
(%)

| Age Group (Years) | Statistics Canada | | | | This Study | |
| | Series 1 | | Series 2 | | | |
	Male	Female	Male	Female	Male	Female
0-4	6.37	5.99	3.34	3.21	4.00	4.00
5-9	5.05	5.07	3.76	4.00	4.50	4.50
10-14	3.53	3.45	3.78	3.52	4.00	4.00
15-19	2.69	3.60	2.91	3.75	3.75	4.00
20-24	3.60	8.88	4.23	9.06	3.75	6.50
25-29	6.44	7.24	7.99	8.81	6.50	8.50
30-34	6.10	5.11	6.35	6.09	6.00	5.75
35-39	4.86	3.83	4.03	4.13	4.00	3.75
40-44	3.20	2.76	2.90	2.60	3.00	2.50
45-49	2.14	1.85	2.07	2.01	2.00	2.00
50-54	1.40	1.48	1.54	1.82	1.75	2.00
55-59	0.94	1.07	1.03	1.47	1.25	1.75
60-64	0.54	0.72	0.88	1.35	1.25	1.50
65-69	0.43	0.52	0.84	0.95	1.00	1.00
70+	0.50	0.68	0.65	0.96	0.75	0.75
All Ages[a]	47.78	52.22	46.29	53.71	47.50	52.50

Note: [a] Column totals may be subject to rounding error.

Sources: Statistics Canada, *Technical Report on Population Projections for Canada and the Provinces, 1972-2001* (Catalogue No. 91-516), p. 218; D.A. Norris and J. Perreault, "Migration Projections for Canada and the Provinces, 1976-1991," Background paper (Ottawa: Statistics Canada, 1979), p. 60; and assumptions by the author.

an explanatory model of interprovincial migration, it is not easy to assess whether the patterns of the late 1970s represent a temporary phenomenon or the emergence of new trends. It is likely that interprovincial migration flows strongly reflect differences in economic factors, such as wage rates and employment (or unemployment) rates. Government programs, such as those of the Department of Regional Economic Expansion, also undoubtedly have some impact on interprovincial migration.[19] The relative future movements of such factors are extremely difficult to ascertain. Consequently, the Statistics

Canada approach of developing a number of alternative, often quite divergent, assumptions regarding interprovincial migration patterns is adopted in this study. Since the methodology of using out-migration rates and in-migration proportions was not developed until the second series of Statistics Canada projections, only these will be reviewed here.[20] Pattern A assumes that the 1975-76 to 1977-78 averages are maintained for the duration of the projection period. Pattern B assumes a return to the more traditional migration patterns observed during the 1960s. An intermediate pattern between A and B (or partial return pattern) is the basis underlying pattern C. Pattern D assumes a further westward shift, with an increase in the percentage of interprovincial migrants going to Alberta and British Columbia at the expense of Ontario.[21] With the publication of recent data (see Tables 3-5 and 3-6), pattern B looks more and more remote. Consequently, three alternative interprovincial migration patterns are considered in this study. These are motivated by the Statistics Canada patterns A, C and D.

Pattern I in this study assumes a continuation of the trends of the late 1970s. The chosen out-migration rates and in-migration proportions are based on the averages of the 1976-79 data modified slightly for the noticeable trends over the period. These rates and proportions are held constant throughout the projection horizon. Pattern II postulates that a partial reversal to the patterns of 1966-75 will occur gradually by 1986-87, after which the patterns will remain unchanged. This pattern is relatively more favourable to Quebec and Ontario and less favourable to Saskatchewan and Alberta. Finally, pattern III postulates that a continued westward shift will occur in interprovincial patterns by generally decreasing the out-migration rates except in Ontario and the territories, and by increasing the in-migration proportions in Saskatchewan, Alberta and British Columbia at the expense of all other provinces, especially Ontario and, to a lesser extent, Quebec. The relevant assumptions are summarized in Table A-7, along with the Statistics Canada assumptions for comparison purposes. Note that, unlike the Statistics Canada westward drift alternative (compare C and D in Table A-7), *both* out-migration rates and in-migration proportions are changed in the westward drift scenario developed in this study (compare II and III in Table A-7). Note also that in the case of scenarios D (Statistics Canada) and III (this study), the new rates are assumed to be gradually achieved by 1986-87 and held constant thereafter.

For projection purposes these provincial aggregate rates and proportions must be broken down by age and sex. For the Statistics

245

TABLE A-7

ASSUMED OUT-MIGRATION RATES AND IN-MIGRATION PROPORTIONS BY PROVINCE[a]

(%)

Projection Designation	Can[b]	Nfld	PEI	NS	NB	PQ	Ont	Man	Sask	Alta	BC	Yukon	NWT
						OUT-MIGRATION RATES[c]							
Statistics Canada:													
A	—	2.25	3.05	2.69	2.70	0.92	1.19	3.03	2.70	3.10	2.42	8.59	8.59
B	—	2.45	4.06	3.43	3.69	0.79	1.11	3.65	3.92	3.48	2.16	6.51	6.51
C	—	2.35	3.55	3.06	3.19	0.85	1.15	3.34	3.31	3.29	2.29	7.55	7.55
D	—	2.35	3.55	3.06	3.19	0.85	1.15	3.34	3.31	3.29	2.29	7.55	7.55
This Study:													
I	—	2.15	3.40	2.60	2.60	0.95	1.20	3.25	2.60	3.20	2.05	12.50	11.20
II	—	2.40	3.70	3.15	3.30	1.00	1.25	3.60	3.90	3.40	2.45	10.00	9.40
III	—	2.30	3.60	2.75	2.75	1.00	1.30	3.15	2.60	2.85	1.80	13.30	11.90

Projection Designation	Can	Nfld	PEI	NS	NB	PQ	Ont	Man	Sask	Alta	BC	Yukon	NWT
						IN-MIGRATION PROPORTIONS[d]							
Statistics Canada:													
A	100.0	2.80	1.18	6.13	5.46	7.77	23.80	6.76	7.29	21.21	15.98	0.55	1.06
B	100.0	1.99	0.95	5.68	4.93	10.47	26.82	6.93	5.94	16.49	18.19	0.55	1.06
C	100.0	2.39	1.07	5.91	5.19	9.13	25.31	6.84	6.61	18.84	17.10	0.55	1.06
D	100.0	2.39	1.07	5.91	5.19	9.13	17.95	6.84	6.61	24.31	19.00	0.55	1.06
This Study:													
I	100.0	2.55	1.15	5.85	4.85	6.40	23.75	5.90	6.65	23.40	18.00	0.55	0.95
II	100.0	2.60	1.05	6.05	5.15	9.55	26.35	7.20	6.05	16.10	18.40	0.55	0.95
III	100.0	2.30	1.05	5.25	4.35	5.75	21.30	6.00	6.65	26.00	20.00	0.50	0.85

Notes: [a] Assumed to be reached by 1986-87. See text for a description of the scenarios.

[b] Canada figures for out-migration rates are not relevant, while the row totals of in-migration proportions may not equal 100.0 due to rounding.

[c] Rate per 100 of source population.

[d] Percentage of total interprovincial migrants.

Sources: D.A. Norris and J. Perreault, "Migration Projections for Canada and the Provinces, 1976-1991," Background paper (Ottawa: Statistics Canada, 1979), p. 47; and assumptions by the author.

Canada projections, census data for 1956-61 and 1966-71 were examined for both out-rates and in-proportions; it was concluded that the age structures were very similar for males and females. Consequently, the same age structure was used for both sexes and the value assigned to the middle age of the five-year group. These data were then adjusted to yield the required provincial aggregates (see Table A-7). This is a complicated procedure because the provincial age-specific out-rates determine the age structure of the pool of interprovincial migrants, which in turn determines the size and age composition of the in-migrant population. For this study an easier procedure was adopted. An estimated age-sex composition of in- and out-migrants by province for 1978-79 has recently been published by Statistics Canada. This composition is based on the most recent census-derived (1971-76) interprovincial migration flows, and hence incorporates long-run trend information. A detailed examination of this composition reveals that: (1) the assumptions of uniformity in age structures between males and females may no longer be warranted, and (2) considerable similarity existed in each province's in-migration proportions over all age groups (see Table 2-15). Consequently, the Statistics Canada approach was extended by considering separate out-migration rates for *each* sex, and restricted by imposing the provincial average in-migration proportion across *all* ages. This procedure circumvents the cumbersome interactive procedure required by Statistics Canada to obtain consistency with the province-wide totals (Table A-7), since the age-sex-specific out-migration rates can all be scaled' to yield the desired province-specific total out-migration rate, and since the constant in-migration proportion over all ages guarantees that the province-specific total in-migration proportion will be obtained and will sum to 100 per cent.

Finally, because these migration values are assigned to the median age in the group, the Statistics Canada population projection model does *not* contain the same age groups for which the published information is provided. Access to the single-year-of-age data underlying these numbers was kindly provided by Statistics Canada so that age-sex typologies could be developed in the age groups required by the population projection model. Given the assumption of constant (over all ages and both sexes) in-migration proportions at the provincial average (Table 2-15), it is only necessary to develop these typologies for out-migration rates for each scenario. However, a separate typology was developed for each sex, thus resulting in six different typologies (three scenarios by two sexes). Because of the considerable detail involved, these assumptions are not presented here.[22] Note that all out-migration rates and in-migration proportions are assumed to be independent of the *level* of interprovincial migration flows.

The assumptions for each of the six components of provincial population change — births, deaths, immigration, emigration, in-migration and out-migration — have now been reviewed. In the case of births, deaths and interprovincial migration, province-specific values were chosen, with Canada-wide implications resulting from a summation of the province-specific assumptions. In the case of international migration — immigration and emigration — totals for the country were assumed and then distributed back over the provinces. In all cases a province-specific age-sex composition must be developed for projection purposes.

In the last analysis the reader must choose the combination of the above assumptions that best incorporates his or her prior judgement according to the purpose for which they are to be used. Not all combinations could be covered in this study, but a representative selection has been included and reviewed. In this way the sensitivity of the results to the various assumptions can be evaluated. Unfortunately, the concern of much analysis is with *the* population future rather than with *a* population future. For these purposes, it is often useful if a guide to selection of alternatives can be supplied. The no change alternative posits a continuation of the characteristics of the late 1970s, with the exception of immigration, which is presumed to return to postwar historical levels. The low immigration alternative actually provides a closer approximation to the late 1970s characteristics. However, to many the assumption of a constant total fertility rate in this scenario may appear unrealistic. For those who give considerable weight to past trends and opt for continued declines in fertility, the low fertility alternative might be preferred. The importance of interprovincial migration to provincial population futures is apparent from these results. Here there appears to be considerably more uncertainty with respect to the choice of assumptions. The westward drift of the population appears likely to continue, but whether or not it will accelerate is unknown. It may continue not only at the expense of Ontario and Quebec (the pattern of the late 1970s), but also at the expense of the remaining eastern provinces (the pattern of 1966-75). Regrettably, this alternative is not included in the historically based scenarios of this study — but that only goes to underscore the difficulty in making a selection from the three interprovincial migration patterns offered in this study. The final selection should be on the basis of a careful analysis of the alternative out-migration rates and in-migration proportions presented in Table A-7.

Notes

Introduction

[1] See T. R. Malthus, *An Essay on the Principle of Population* (London: Johnson, 1798).

[2] The potato famine in Ireland in 1846 provides one such example and was important to the growth of population in Canada.

[3] See, for example, the works of Keynes (1937), Reddaway (1939) and Robinson (1951) evaluating post-Depression prospects for the United Kingdom.

[4] A summary international comparison available in the *1980 World Population Data Sheet* (Washington: Population Reference Bureau, 1980) shows East Germany (16 per cent), Austria, West Germany and Sweden (all 15 per cent) with the highest percentages of population aged 65 years and over.

[5] J. Overbeek, *Population and Canadian Society* (Toronto: Butterworths, 1980), pp. 11-12. See also chapter 2.

[6] See, for example, D. K. Foot, "Demognomics and the 'Inevitable Surprises,'" *Economic Policy Review*, vol.1, no.2 (1979), pp. 1-29; idem, "The Economic Impact of Aging in Canada—Some Macroeconomic Indicators," Paper presented to the Sixth Annual Meetings of the Eastern Economics Association, Montreal, 1980; idem, *Public Policy and Future Population in Ontario* (Toronto: Ontario Economic Council, 1979); and idem, "Population Aging in Ontario: Economic and Policy Issues," in B. T. Wigdor and L. Ford, eds., *Housing for an Aging Population: Alternatives* (Toronto: University of Toronto Press, 1981), pp. 11-22.

[7] This will be documented in the subsequent chapter.

[8] Of course, this is not to say that demographic developments are the *most* important determinant of economic policy in these areas—only that they are *one* of the most important and probably one of the most predictable determinants.

[9] See V. W. Marshall, *Aging in Canada: Social Perspectives* (Don Mills: Fitzhenry & Whiteside, 1980) for a useful compendium of papers.

[10] Consistency is used in this study in both a logical and a multiregional context. A quantitative population projection model is used to ensure that the outcomes are consistent with the assumptions in both a qualitative and quantitative sense. For example, if fertility rates decline, so do the number of births, other things being equal. Consistency in a multiregional context ensures that, with regard to interprovincial migration, all "emigrants" from one province become "immigrants" to some other province, and that all provinces are treated similarly with regard to the basic assumptions.

251

[11] Realism is, of course, person-and time-specific.

[12] See, for example, D. C. Dallimore and B. Lampert, "Demographic Trends in Ontario: Some Policy Considerations," *Ontario Economic Review*, vol.11 (November-December 1973), pp. 8-9.

[13] Some of these issues are discussed in L. O. Stone and C. Marceau, *Canadian Population Trends and Public Policy through the 1980s* (Montreal: McGill-Queen's University Press for the Institute for Research on Public Policy [IRPP], 1977).

[14] For a review of such models see D. K. Foot, *Labour Market Analysis with Canadian Macroeconometric Models: A Review* (Toronto: University of Toronto, Centre for Industrial Relations and Ontario Manpower Commission, 1980).

Chapter 1

[1] In 1851 and 1861 separate censuses were taken for each of the provinces, with the first nation-wide census being taken in 1871.

[2] For the 1981 census, one in five Canadians filled out a "long" form of forty-six questions and the remainder filled out a "short" form of twelve questions. The reduction in the proportion of full coverage and number of questions is attributable to budgetary considerations.

[3] However, it is interesting to note that immigration over the 1951-61 period was not as high as that over the 1901-11 period. For annual immigration totals since 1851, see J. Overbeek, *Population and Canadian Society* (Toronto: Butterworths, 1980), p. 100.

[4] From this brief history it is tempting, but probably unwise, to predict another increase in fertility one hundred years from the 1951-61 decade (that is, in 2051-61), and another period of rapid population growth fifty years from this same decade (that is, in 2001-11)!

[5] Previous waves occurred during the latter part of the seventeenth century, the Loyalists from the American War of Independence (1783), the English as a result of the depressed economic conditions in England (1830s), and Europeans, particularly the Irish, because of the Irish potato famine (1846). See L. O. Stone, *Migration in Canada: Regional Aspects* (Ottawa: Dominion Bureau of Statistics, 1969), p. 23.

[6] For an excellent recent review of intergovernmental transfers in Canada, see R. W. Boadway, *Intergovernmental Transfers in Canada* (Toronto: Canadian Tax Foundation, 1980).

[7] For a review of the historical and projected trends in other characteristics, see L. O. Stone and C. Marceau, *Canadian Population Trends and Public Policy through the 1980s* (Montreal: McGill-Queen's University Press for the IRPP, 1977).

[8] That is, there were 1,129 males for every 1,000 females in the Canadian population in 1911.

[9] The median is the most easily measured and is unique. The mean cannot be calculated from grouped data without making some assumption about the average age in the open-ended highest-age group (for example, 70 years and over), while it is difficult to calculate the mode if the peak is in the age group at either extreme of the distribution (for example, 0 to 4 years).

[10] A third measure of central tendency of a distribution, the mode, which measures the age at which there is a maximum number of persons, has been predominantly in the youngest age group (0 to 4 years) throughout the period, but an examination of this measure (not presented) does highlight the two periods of noticeable aging when this was not the case. The first was over the 1920s and 1930s and the second was the 1970s, thus confirming the previous observations.

[11] See, for example, Overbeek, *Population and Canadian Society*, p. 140.

[12] In fact it had expanded to 2.1 per cent by the 1891 census and was already contracting by 1901.

[13] The 1976 quinquennial census showed the following ranking of Canadian urban areas: Toronto (Ontario) 2,803,101, Montreal (Quebec) 2,802,485, Vancouver (B.C.) 1,166,348, Ottawa-Hull (Ontario-Quebec) 693,288, Winnipeg (Manitoba) 578,217, Hamilton (Ontario) 529,371, Edmonton (Alberta) 554,228, Quebec (Quebec) 542,158 and Calgary (Alberta) 469,917.

[14] The same could also be said for Winnipeg, Manitoba.

[15] Statistics Canada, *Vital Statistics*, vol.1, Catalogue No. 84-204, and vol.3, Catalogue No. 84-206. Data in these volumes are compiled from provincial registry data.

[16] For further information see M. V. George, *Population Growth in Canada* (Ottawa: Dominion Bureau of Statistics, 1970).

[17] They had been on the decline since the 1870s. See ibid., p. 9.

[18] By 1979 Nova Scotia (6.5) had surpassed British Columbia (6.7) as the province with the lowest crude rate of natural increase.

[19] See also J. A. Norland, *The Age-Sex Composition of Canada's Population*, 1971 Census Profile Study (Ottawa: Statistics Canada, 1976), especially Table 2.

[20] This age distribution can be explained by the out-migration of persons of working age.

[21] For further information see L. O. Stone, *Migration in Canada, Regional Aspects*, 1961 Census Monograph (Ottawa: Dominion Bureau of Statistics, 1969); M. V. George, *Internal Migration in Canada, Demographic Aspects*, 1961 Census Monograph (Ottawa: Statistics Canada, 1970); and L. O. Stone and S. Fletcher, *Migration in Canada*, 1971 Census Profile Study (Ottawa: Statistics Canada, 1976).

[22] No census information is available, since emigrants no longer reside in Canada and hence do not fill out Canadian census forms.

[23] This involves rewriting the equation on page 5 so that $E(t)$ is on the left-hand side and can be calculated from all the known values on the right-hand side, namely, births, deaths, immigration and the intercensal change in population. This is not possible on a provincial basis unless information on the additional unknown—interprovincial migration—is available (see the equation on page 16).

[24] See Statistics Canada, *International and Interprovincial Migration in Canada, 1978-79* (Ottawa: Statistics Canada, 1980), p. 11, for a detailed explanation.

[25] Approximately one-half of movers relocated in the same municipality. If short-distance moves across municipal boundaries were added, the vast majority of movement in Canada would be accounted for. For a survey of these data see, for example, L. O. Stone and S. Fletcher, *Migration in Canada*, 1971 Census Profile Study (Ottawa: Statistics Canada, 1976).

[26] See George, *Internal Migration in Canada,* p. 18.

[27] As a percentage of Canadian-born population, however, it was at its lowest in 1941. See Ibid., p. 94.

[28] In all cases emigration is treated as the residual item. See note 23 above.

[29] The relevant percentages for natural increase are 94 (1961-66), 73 (1966-71), 66 (1971-76) and 85 (1976-79). Over the entire 1961-79 period the natural increase accounted for 80 per cent of total population growth in Canada.

[30] It occurred in four of forty-four cases—Prince Edward Island in 1971-76, Saskatchewan in 1966-71 and 1971-76, and Alberta in 1976-79.

[31] In fact, in thirty-one of the forty-four cases, but four of these cases involve zero, so that the "effective" percentage is actually closer to 77.5 per cent.

[32] Prince Edward Island and New Brunswick in 1976-79 fall in neither category. See note 30 above.

Chapter 2

[1] The main exceptions were Quebec and Manitoba during the 1966-71 period.

[2] With the annual contribution from net immigration held at its average annual level throughout the decade, growth in the 1970-75 period averaged 1.21 per cent, while growth in the later 1975-79 period averaged 1.14 per cent.

[3] It might be useful to remind readers that Canada experienced similar trends in the 1920s and early 1930s and that it is only in the 1970s that the rate of natural increase fell below the trough of 1937.

[4] See, for example, J. Overbeek, *Population and Canadian Society* (Toronto: Butterworths, 1980), pp. 70-74 and 37-39 respectively.

[5] Note that there is a distinction between fertility, which denotes the *actual* reproductive performance, and fecundity, which implies a physiological *capacity* to reproduce.

[6] Consequently, the total fertility rate (T.F.R.) for a Canadian provincial population is calculated as:

$$\text{T.F.R.} = 5 \sum_{i=1}^{7} \frac{B_i}{W_i}$$

where B_i denotes the number of births to women in age interval i (for example, 15 to 19 years) in any time period, and W_i denotes the number of women in the same age interval during the same time period. In general the formula is $\text{T.F.R.} = w \sum (B_i/W_i)k$, where w is the width of the class interval and k is the rate constant (that is, per 1, per 100, per 1,000, et cetera). Usually, a year is taken as the time period relevant to the flow B_i, and the mid-point of the year is used to measure the stock W_i.

[7] Population total fertility rate replacement levels are around 2.1 children per woman, since every child-bearing couple must replace themselves and some proportion of the childless couples.

[8] These percentages are calculated from unrounded data.

[9] That is, an increase from 1.757 to 2.093, which is still below replacement levels.

[10] Unfortunately, no calculation is available for Newfoundland, since the mother's age is not stated on the birth registration form, although hospital statistics do provide a breakdown of deliveries by age of mother.

[11] Note that this is in standardized terms; that is, when the effects of the different provincial age structures are taken into account.

[12] This is the opposite of the fertility pattern (see Table 1-11), which is an inverted U-shaped distribution.

[13] A useful meaning can be attached to the total fertility rate (see pages 45-46) but no useful meaning could be attached to a comparable mortality measure.

[14] The following discussion is a summary of Overbeek, *Population and Canadian Society*, pp. 41-43. See also Statistics Canada, *Life Tables Canada and the Provinces*, Catalogue No. 24-532, various issues.

[15] Data on deaths for three years centred on the census year are used to construct the tables.

[16] M. V. George, *Population Growth in Canada* (Ottawa: Dominion Bureau of Statistics, 1970), pp. 14-15. See also K. S. Gnanasekaran, "Revised Mortality

Projections for Canada and the Provinces, 1971-86,'' Background paper for the 1976 Statistics Canada Population Projections, March 1979, p. 16.

[17] See, for example, D. M. Keith, ''Mortality Projections Based on Population Data,'' Paper read to the Canadian Institute of Actuaries, March 1980, pp. 13-15.

[18] The female proportion for the period 1971-79 is 50.6 per cent, which implies a sex ratio of 0.98.

[19] The relevant sex ratio for the 1971-79 period is 1.06.

[20] See Canada House of Commons, *Bill C-24, An Act Respecting Immigration to Canada*, passed 25 July 1977.

[21] The relevant sex ratio is a low 0.66.

[22] The relevant sex ratio is 0.97.

[23] Which was 62.4 per cent in 1971 and is expected to be around 67.8 per cent in 1981 (see Table 1-3).

[24] Over the 1970s, the sex ratio was below unity in 1973 (0.91), 1975 (0.97), 1977 (0.63) and 1978 (0.69).

[25] The relevant percentage declined from 54 per cent over 1961-66 to 19 per cent over 1971-76. See D. A. Norris and J. Perreault, ''Migration Projections for Canada and the Provinces, 1976-1991,''· Background paper for the 1976 Statistics Canada Population Projections, March 1979, p. 36.

[26] Ibid., p. 40.

[27] These two periods represent times of considerable political uncertainty in Quebec: the October Crisis in 1970 and the election of the separatist Parti Québécois government in November 1976.

[28] This allocation or distribution of interprovincial migrants may or may not be independent of the rates of outflow.

[29] In essence, for each province and territory a specific rate for each of the remaining potential destinations is required. This involves $12 \times 11 = 132$ rates for each year!

[30] Of course, the same approach could be taken with respect to international migration. For a further evaluation of this method, see chapter 4.

[31] See George, *Internal Migration in Canada*, chap. 7,· and L. O. Stone and S. Fletcher, *Migration in Canada*, 1971 Census Profile Study (Ottawa: Statistics Canada, 1976), chap. 3. Note that these patterns reflect family migration in that both partners migrate together and take their young children with them.

[32] For the provinces, the coefficients of variation are generally around 5 per cent, with Prince Edward Island, a very small province, being the only exception.

[33] Note, however, that the fertility rate was declining long before the average age of childbearing began to increase.

[34] See, for example, Employment and Immigration Canada, *Annual Report to Parliament on Immigration Levels, 1981*, Catalogue No. WH-5-005, p. 6.

Chapter 3

[1] Hence t-1 represents the immediately preceding time period.

[2] To demonstrate this proposition, note that, for the first year:

$$P(1) \equiv P(0) + B(1) - D(1) + I(1) - E(1) \, ,$$

which then becomes an input into the calculation for the second year:

$$P(2) \equiv P(1) + B(2) - D(2) + I(2) - E(2) \, ,$$

and the calculation can be repeated for every successive year over the calculation horizon.

[3] See, for example, Statistics Canada, *Population Projections for Canada and the Provinces, 1976-2001*, Catalogue No. 91-520 (Ottawa: 1979).

[4] See Figure 1-1 for representative values.

[5] Note that in this notation the difference between β and δ is the crude rate of natural increase (as shown in Figure 1-1).

[6] Although introduced here for expository convenience, it is more usual to specify international migration in level rather than in rate terms. This approach is discussed in some detail in this chapter and in the Appendix.

[7] Using successive substitutions, or the theory of linear difference equations, the general solution of the equation can be written as:

$$P(t) = \frac{-K}{(\beta-\delta)} + \left\{ P(0) + \frac{K}{(\beta-\delta)} \right\} (1+\beta-\delta)^t.$$

By way of an illustrative example, consider the Canadian population in 1871 as the starting population $(P(0) = 3,689.3)$, let the crude rate of natural increase be 1.6 per cent $(\beta\text{-}\delta = 0.016)$, and set net international migration at its historical average over the subsequent 100 years, namely 18.4 thousand persons per year $(K = 18.4)$. Substitution into the above formula yields:

$$P(t) = \frac{-18.4}{0.016} + \left\{ 3,689.3 + \frac{18.4}{0.016} \right\} (1.016)^t$$
$$= -1,150 + 4,389.3 \, (1.016)^t.$$

Hence a population projection for 1971, 100 years later, would be obtained as:

$$P(100) = -1,150 + 4,839.3(1.016)^{100} = 22,517.6 \text{ (thousand persons)},$$

which is reasonably close to the actual value of 21,568.2 (see Table 1-1).

[8] Note that since the sum of all out-migration must equal the sum of all in-migration in the country, these rates are not independent. See Tables 2-11 and 2-12 for representative values.

[9] Using the same approach as in note 7 above, consider starting with the 1871 population of Ontario $(P(0) = 1,620.9$. See Table 1-3). Assume, for convenience, that the average contribution of net international migration to Ontario was half the national contribution $(K = 9.2)$ and that the rate of net interprovincial migration was 0.1 per cent. Using a crude rate of natural increase of 1.2 per cent, the projection for the 1971 population $(t=100)$ becomes:

$$P(100) = \frac{-9.2}{0.013} + \left\{ 1,620.9 + \frac{9.2}{0.013} \right\} (1.013)^{100}$$
$$= 7,765.3 \, ,$$

which is slightly on the high side (see Table 1-3).

[10] However, a high rate of out-migration (ϕ) could reduce this magnitude to less than unity, in which case the population would gradually (or asymptotically) tend to a maximum value.

[11] Note that over a long period of time, birth rates (β) may not be independent of the sex composition of the population.

[12] It is assumed that there are N age groups in both the male and the female population. For example, the calculations might be based on 20 five-year age groups, in which case $N = 20$.

[13] That is:

$$P(t) = \sum_{j=1}^{N} PM^j(t) + \sum_{j=1}^{N} PF^j(t),$$

where $PM^j(t)$ represents male age groups and $PF^j(t)$ represents female age groups and Σ is a summation symbol.

256

[14] For further details see the Appendix.

[15] For example, see notes 7 and 9 above.

[16] Another important issue is whether or not the main components should be considered separately or in net terms; for example, net interprovincial migration, or out-migration and in-migration separately.

[17] This is an often-used term to describe the source of the population change.

[18] This avoids the task of collecting and perhaps combining the compositions of all potential source country populations.

[19] Either as specific source-destination rates or as a proportion of the total "pool" of interprovincial migrants.

[20] See Statistics Canada, *Population Projections for Canada and the Provinces, 1972-2001*, Catalogue No. 91-514 (Ottawa: Information Canada, 1974); and idem, *Population Projections for Canada and the Provinces, 1976-2001*, Catalogue No. 91-520 (Ottawa: 1979).

[21] D. A. Norris and J. Perreault, "Migration Projections for Canada and the Provinces, 1976-1991," Background paper for the 1976 Statistics Canada Population Projections, March 1979, p. 20.

[22] See Statistics Canada, *Technical Report on Population Projections for Canada and the Provinces, 1972-2001*, Catalogue No. 91-516 (Ottawa: Information Canada, 1975), pp. 212-13. Assumption A was based on the 1968-71 period, assumption B was based on the 1965-71 period, assumption C was based on half the movement over the 1965-71 period, and assumption D was based on three "good" years for losing provinces and three "bad" years for gaining provinces chosen from the 1961-71 decade, appropriately adjusted to ensure consistency.

[23] There are 132 (12 × 11) required rates for *each* age-sex group, even if the rates are held constant over the entire projection horizon.

[24] See D. A. Norris and J. Perrault, "Migration Projections," p. 21.

[25] See Appendix.

[26] This model is described in some detail in Statistics Canada, *Technical Report on Population Projections for Canada and the Provinces, 1972-2001*.

[27] Forty thousand persons per year for twenty-two years equals 880,000 persons plus their children.

[28] All subsequent comparisons are relative to the no change alternative (Projection 1).

[29] An increase from 1.75 to 2.25 by 2001 (29.5 per cent) increases average annual population growth from 0.82 to 1.00 (or 22 per cent), while a decrease from 1.75 to 1.55 by 2001 (11.5 per cent) decreases average annual population growth from 0.82 to 0.71 (or 13 per cent).

[30] The percentage drops approximately 0.1 per cent for every 20,000 reduction in immigration (compare Projections 1, 5 and 14).

[31] Recall, from Table 3-9, that this process can be expected to be reversed in the early part of the twenty-first century.

[32] The exception is Prince Edward Island, which shows an increase in the sex ratio (of males to females) in all projections. This reflects the combination of a high out-migration rate which is female-dominant and a relatively high (to population) in-migration proportion which is male-dominant (see the Appendix).

[33] The dramatic projected decline in the sex ratio of the Northwest Territories also reflects combinations of relatively extreme interprovincial migration assumptions. Here, a very high out-migration rate is extremely male-dominant, and a relatively high (to population) in-migration proportion is only slightly male-dominant.

257

[34] The territories, of course, remain younger than Newfoundland.

[35] Recall that the age composition of international migration is held constant over all provinces.

[36] From Figure 2-3 it is possible to calculate the median age of interprovincial migrants for 1978-79, which turns out to be 23.7 years. This is lower than the population median of 28.8 years (see Table 3-12).

[37] To some degree this is a distortion caused by one of the simplifying assumptions applied in this study. Since the age distribution of in-migrants is held constant over all provinces (see the Appendix), relatively more older in-migrants are not "permitted" to settle (retire?) in British Columbia. However, since they also cannot settle in southern Ontario, the Ontario results are biased in the same direction.

Chapter 4

[1] For a similar viewpoint see Howe Research Institute, *Anticipating the Unexpected: Policy Review and Outlook, 1979* (Montreal: C. D. Howe Research Institute, 1979), chap. 6.

[2] This issue will be addressed in greater detail in chapter 7.

[3] See D. K. Foot, "Demognomics and the Inevitable Surprises," *Economic Policy Review*, vol. 1 no. 2 (1979), pp. 1-29.

[4] The increase in the median age from 1851 to 1981 was 12.3 years (Table 1-2), while the projected increase from 1981 to 2051 is 12.5 years (Table 3-9).

[5] The actual maximum is 42.5 years, which occurs in the year 2040. The range of the maximum median age is from 36.9 years in the year 2032 in the high population scenario (Projection 8) to 46.5 years in the year 2042 in the low population scenario (Projection 9).

[6] See, for example, D. K. Foot, *Public Policy and Future Population in Ontario* (Toronto: Ontario Economic Council, 1979); or idem, "Population Aging in Ontario: Economic and Policy Issues," in B.T. Wigdor and L. Ford, eds., *Housing for an Aging Population: Alternatives* (Toronto: University of Toronto Press, 1981), pp. 11-22.

[7] Note that this ratio can be calculated as a ratio of population numbers or population percentages. To see this, note that:

$$POP \equiv POPY + POPW + POPE$$

where *POPY* denotes the young population (aged 0 to 14 years); *POPW* denotes the working-age population (aged 15 to 64 years); *POPE* denotes the elderly population (aged 65 years and over); and *POP* denotes the total population, so that:

$$1 \equiv \frac{POPY}{POP} + \frac{POPW}{POP} + \frac{POPE}{POP} .$$

Note that (*POPY/POP*) and (*POPE/POP*) are presented in Figure 4-2. The dependency ratio can be calculated as:

$$\frac{POPY + POPE}{POPW} = \frac{(POPY/POP) + (POPE/POP)}{(POPW/POP)} .$$

These data are available for Canada from Tables 1-2 (history), 3-9 and 3-10 (future projections).

[8] The peak for Canada occurs in the year 2007 at a dependent proportion of 0.306 and an inverse total dependency value of 2.27.

[9] This interpretation, of course, employs the *current*, not the 1851, definition of the working age.

[10] This is even true of the high fertility assumption—see note b in Table 4-2.

[11] The exception is New Brunswick.

[12] For more details see Economic Council of Canada, *One in Three* (Ottawa: 1980); J-A. Boulet and G. Grenier, "Health Expenditures in Canada and the Impact of Demographic Changes on Future Government Health Insurance Program Expenditures," *Discussion Paper*, no.123 (Ottawa: Economic Council of Canada, 1978); and L. A. Lefebvre, Z. Zsigmond and M. S. Devereaux, *A Prognosis for Hospitals, 1967-2031* (Ottawa: Statistics Canada, 1979).

[13] The figures in 1976 dollars were $4,745 per person aged 65 years and over and $1,909 per person aged 17 years and younger, for a ratio of 2.49. See Canada Treasury Board Secretariat, "Changing Population and the Impact on Government Age-Specific Expenditures" (Ottawa: 1977). See also Ontario Ministry of Treasury and Economics, *Issues in Pension Policy* (Toronto: 1979), p. 14, where, based on estimates of age-related cost by major program, figures in 1976 dollars were $3,975.57 per person aged 65 years and over and $1,858.62 per person aged 14 years and younger, for a ratio of 2.14. However, this latter calculation excludes estimated Canada Pension Plan/Quebec Pension Plan per capita costs.

[14] See R. Clark, J. Kreps and J. Spengler, "Economics of Aging: A Survey," *Journal of Economic Literature*, vol.16 (September 1978), p. 922.

[15] For empirical evidence and further information, see Statistics Canada, *Income of Individuals by Sex, Age, Marital Status and Period of Immigration*, Catalogue No. 94-760; and idem, *Canada's Elderly* (Ottawa: 1979).

[16] This should *not* be interpreted as support for inflation, since the argument is predicated on the losing group being subject to "money illusion"; that is, only concerned with maintaining their nominal budget rather than their real (inflation-adjusted) budget.

[17] See note 7 above.

[18] See, for example, Ontario Ministry of Treasury and Economics, *Issues in Pension Policy* (Toronto: 1979), p. 14. Note that when $\omega=1$, this definition reduces to the numerical dependency ratio.

[19] Note that the proposed formula has been defined in terms of young person equivalents; it could have just as easily been defined in terms of elderly person equivalents, in which case *POPY* would be weighted by $(1/\omega)$.

[20] That is, there are no economies or diseconomies of scale.

[21] Note that it could be easily varied if sufficient information regarding the changes in the relative cost of the provision of public services over the projection horizon were available.

[22] Although consistent with the data in Figure 3-1, this statement is a little misleading, since the programs actually in place in past history were not the current programs that are the basis for these calculations.

[23] The minimums are: for $\omega=1$, 0.963 in 1982 and 1983; for $\omega=2$, 0.982 in 1982; and for $\omega=3$, 0.992 in 1981.

[24] Assuming that no changes are made to existing public programs. The indexes reach 1.0 in 1992 for $\omega=1$, 1987 for $\omega=2$, and in 1984 for $\omega=3$.

[25] For further details on the Ontario index, see Foot, *Public Policy and Future Population;* and idem, "Population Aging in Ontario."

259

Chapter 5

[1] See, for example, W. Clark, M. S. Devereaux and Z. Zsigmond, *The Class of 2001* (Ottawa: Statistics Canada and the Canadian Teachers Federation, 1979).

[2] See, for example, Statistics Canada, *From the Sixties to the Eighties: A Statistical Portrait of Canadian Higher Education* (Ottawa: 1979); and Science Council of Canada, *University Research in Jeopardy: The Threat of Declining Enrolment* (Ottawa: Science Council of Canada, 1979).

[3] Two points should be kept in mind when interpreting these rates. First, unlike births and deaths, which occur throughout the year, enrolments represent the number of students in the school system at the commencement of the school year. Consequently, the enrolment rate is a ratio of one stock to another rather than a ratio of a flow to a stock. Secondly, in Canada the school year commences in September and school enrolments are usually measured in October. Since almost all population measurements are centred on the census date of June 1, it is customary to relate October enrolments to the previous June populations rather than to the subsequent June populations. An alternative (and probably superior) measure would be the estimated September populations.

[4] It may not exactly equal 100 per cent in practice for a number of reasons, which are outlined below (see also note 15 below).

[5] Note that this approach is quite different from the transition probability approach to enrolment analysis, where the probability of transition from one level (grade or year) to the next level (grade or year) is calculated for each age-sex group. In this latter approach, the enrolment in any particular year is directly related to enrolment in the previous year—rather than being indirectly related through the population of the previous year.

[6] Elementary and secondary enrolments are combined in this study because the results of this study are in close agreement with existing work in the area (see note 1 above). Post-secondary enrolments are divided to permit a more detailed examination of the existing work in this area (see note 2).

[7] Currently, the compulsory starting age is 6 years in Nova Scotia, Quebec, Ontario, Alberta and the Northwest Territories and 7 years in all other jurisdictions. See Statistics Canada, *Elementary-Secondary School Enrolment*, Catalogue No. 81-210, for further details.

[8] For example, Nova Scotia, Prince Edward Island, New Brunswick, Alberta and the Northwest Territories fit into this system. British Columbia and the Yukon Territory have seven and five respectively, while Saskatchewan has eight and four respectively. Newfoundland and Quebec have the fewest total number of years, at six and five respectively, while Ontario has the greatest total number of years, at eight and five respectively.

[9] A student may leave upon attaining his/her 15th birthday in Prince Edward Island and British Columbia, must complete the school year in which his/her 15th birthday occurs in Newfoundland, Quebec and the Northwest Territories, may leave upon attaining his/her 16th birthday in Nova Scotia, New Brunswick, Ontario, Saskatchewan and Alberta, and must complete the school term in which his/her 16th birthday occurs in Manitoba and the Yukon Territory.

[10] See note 8 above.

[11] Note that since these numbers are an approximation calculated by dividing *total*

enrolments (for *all* ages) by the population aged 5 to 14 years, numbers in excess of 100 per cent are possible.

[12] Recall that Ontario has the highest number of years of elementary-secondary education.

[13] These calculations are biased upward, since they include some students (aged 18 years and over) in the numerator that are not included in the denominator. For example, the enrolment rate for 5-to-19-year-olds in Ontario is around 88.7 per cent.

[14] Rates for the open-ended age classes (5 years and under, and 20 years and over) were calculated by dividing by the population of the contiguous age class (5 and 20 years respectively).

[15] There are also other reasons for this discrepancy, such as the existence of illegal residents whose children attend school but who avoid census enumeration. In general, all reasons for census underenumeration of the young will be applicable to this point.

[16] The results for the remaining seven projections can be inferred from these by using the information provided in the previous chapter.

[17] For this reason the detailed results are not presented here.

[18] See also D. K. Foot, "A Troubled Future? University Enrolments in Canada and the Provinces," in D. M. Nowlan and R. Bellaire, eds., *Financing Canadian Universities: For Whom and By Whom?* (Toronto: OISE Press, 1981), pp. 37-63.

[19] These include CEGEPs (Quebec), CAATs (Ontario), junior colleges, other institutes of technology, schools of nursing, teachers' colleges, and other vocational schools that are clearly post-secondary in their course offerings.

[20] No data on part-time non-university post-secondary enrolments are available.

[21] Note that the elementary-secondary enrolment rate for Quebec was much lower than for Ontario and most other provinces (see Table 5-4).

[22] Note, however, that such stabilization has apparently been achieved through gradually declining male rates offsetting the gradually rising female rates.

[23] In these cases, 1979-80 data were not available at the time of the study.

[24] These results implicitly assume that new immigrants adopt the enrolment rate behaviour of Canadians. This is probably not a realistic assumption in the short run but may become so as time passes.

[25] At 1979-80 enrolment rates, this figure is 630.3 thousand students.

[26] Actual total enrolments for the 1979-80 academic year were 590,996; enrolments with average enrolment rates (Table 5-13) were 1.4 per cent higher at 599,360.

[27] Of course, movements in enrolment rates may also affect the actual outcome. For an examination of the sensitivity of enrolments to enrolment rates, see Foot, *"A Troubled Future?"*

[28] In 1978-79 Quebec enrolments accounted for 55 per cent of this total (see Table 5-13).

[29] See Foot, "A Troubled Future?" p. 45.

[30] That is, an increase of 4.8 per cent over 1979 levels, followed by a 17.1 per cent decrease. Ibid., p. 52.

[31] Thus extending the declines in elementary-secondary enrolments unchanged to the post-secondary system. See, for example, the Science Council of Canada, *University Research in Jeopardy*, p. 37.

[32] See Foot, "A Troubled Future?" p. 45.

Chapter 6

[1] This definition is analogous to the birth and death and interprovincial migration rates of chapter 3 and the educational enrolment rates of chapter 5.

[2] In Canada the labour force survey does not cover Indians on reserves or residents of the Yukon and Northwest Territories. These groups are also removed from the relevant source populations.

[3] For a review of many of the issues involved, see, for example, Department of Finance Canada, *Participation Rate and Labour Force Growth in Canada* (Ottawa: Department of Finance Canada, 1980).

[4] Five specific age groups for each sex within each province are considered. Aggregation over these ten groups then provides a total labour force for the province, and aggregation over the provinces provides a total labour force for Canada.

[5] Note that there is the implicit assumption that new entrants adopt the traditional labour force attachment patterns established by their peers.

[6] Note that the residents of the Yukon and Northwest Territories have been removed from the source population estimates in Table 6-1, but that inmates of institutions and Indians on reserves have not. Hence the estimated participation rates are biased downwards slightly.

[7] Note that the change in definition from a lower age of 14 to 15 years artificially raised the participation rates slightly in 1951. See note b in Table 6-3 for further details.

[8] Note that there is no direct linkage between these data and census data, since the questions are somewhat different. Hence there can be a difference between the census labour force and the survey labour force. From the 1971 figures in Table 6-5 it can be deduced that the difference is of the order of one-half of 1 per cent.

[9] Again the reader is reminded of the inherent differences between the census results and the survey results. A comparison of Tables 6-1 and 6-6 for 1971 shows a discrepancy of 0.8 of a percentage point or about 1.4 per cent.

[10] Over the decade of the 1970s the figures were approximately two-thirds and one-third respectively. See D. K. Foot, *A Challenge of the 1980s: Unemployment and Labour Force Growth in Canada and the Provinces* (Toronto: Institute for Policy Analysis, University of Toronto, 1981), p. 10.

[11] See notes 2 and 6 above and the associated text.

[12] Recall that the remaining seven alternative scenarios in chapter 3 are largely combinations of the assumptions incorporated into the first seven.

[13] Or the 2.2 per cent of the 1970s—see Foot, *A Challenge of the 1980s*, p. 19.

[14] The reader is reminded that the use of *average* (1975-79) participation rates and adjustment factors introduces a discontinuity in 1979. The projected labour force in 1979 is 10.947 million persons under the assumed conditions, compared to an actual labour force of 11.207 million persons (see Table 6-5).

[15] In the population futures of chapter 3, 77.75 per cent of immigrants are assumed to be of age 15 years and over, and 71.9 per cent are between 15 and 64 years of age. These are greater percentages than in the Canadian population (see Tables 1-2 and 3-13 to 3-15).

[16] This reduction is primarily registered in Ontario, where average annual labour force growth is reduced by at least one-quarter.

[17] At the provincial level the results are a little different—see Table 6-8.

[18] For a review of current Canadian manpower planning models, see D. K. Foot,

Labour Market Analysis with Canadian Macroeconometric Models: A Review (Toronto: Ontario Manpower Commission and Centre for Industrial Relations, University of Toronto, 1980).

[19] For a historical overview see Table 6-2. The labour force sex ratio decreased from 6.56 in 1911 to 1.91 by 1971. In 1976 the labour force sex ratio was 1.66, and in 1979 it was 1.54. Note that all of these results occurred under conditions of increasing female participation rates and decreasing male participation rates.

[20] In 1979 the actual labour force sex ratio was 1.54. With average 1975-79 participation rates, the *estimated* 1979 labour force sex ratio is 1.62. This demonstrates the impact of increasing female participation rates over this period.

[21] Projection 3 peaks in 2010, Projections 1, 5, 6 and 7 in 2011, Projection 2 in 2013, and there is no peak in Projection 4.

[22] The increases over the estimated 1981 labour force are 43.2, 88.8, 53.2, 2.4 and 10.1 per cent respectively.

[23] For more detailed information, see Foot, *A Challenge of the 1980s.*

[24] Department of Finance Canada, *Participation and Labour Force Growth in Canada* (Ottawa: Department of Finance Canada, 1980); and F. Denton, C. Feaver and B. Spencer, *The Future Population and Labour Force of Canada: Projections to the Year 2051* (Ottawa: Economic Council of Canada, 1980).

[25] Provincial participation rates were derived from the national rates (Table 6-14), using historical differences by age-sex groups. Provincial labour forces are then a product of the province-specific participation rates and source populations.

[26] For a review of these developments, see Department of Finance Canada, *Recent Changes in Patterns of Productivity Growth in Canada* (Ottawa: Department of Finance Canada, 1980).

[27] Reported in Foot, *Labour Market Analysis*, p. 57.

[28] This figure is obtained from empirical estimates of the relevant parameters of macroeconomic production functions for Canada, where the growth in real output over any period can be expressed as a weighted average of the growth in the labour input and the growth in the capital input, together with the rate of technical change over the period, with weights of two-thirds, one-third and one respectively.

[29] That is, $4.5 - .67(1.2) = 3.7$ per cent per annum. This approximate calculation assumes that the impact is linear over the relevant range.

[30] See note 26 above.

Chapter 7

[1] See, for example, J. E. Pesando and S. A. Rea, *Public and Private Pensions in Canada: An Economic Analysis* (Toronto: University of Toronto Press for the Ontario Economic Council, 1977); L. O. Stone and M. J. MacLean, *Future Income Prospects for Canada's Senior Citizens* (Toronto: Butterworths for the IRPP, 1979); Economic Council of Canada, *One in Three: Pensions for Canadians to 2030* (Ottawa: Canadian Government Publishing Centre, 1979); and reports by the federal task force on pensions and the Royal Commission on the Status of Pensions in Ontario.

[2] See, for example, Stone and MacLean, *Future Income Prospects*, p. 14 and chap. 4.

[3] See Economic Council of Canada, *One in Three*, for an elaboration of these concepts.

[4] Hence the title of the Economic Council of Canada study above.

[5] For more details see Statistics Canada, *Pension Plans in Canada, 1976*, Catalogue No. 74-401 (Ottawa: 1978).

[6] See the discussion in chapter 6.

[7] See J-A. Boulet and G. Grenier, "Health Expenditures in Canada and the Impact of Demographic Changes on Future Government Health Insurance Program Expenditures," *Economic Council of Canada Discussion Paper*, no.123 (October 1978); and L. A. Lefebvre, Z. Zsigmond and M. S. Devereaux, *A Prognosis for Hospitals* (Ottawa: Statistics Canada, 1979).

[8] These include both physicians' services and hospital services.

[9] See F. T. Denton and B. G. Spencer, "Health Costs When the Population Changes," *Canadian Journal of Economics*, vol. 8 (February 1975), pp. 38-48; and Boulet and Grenier, "Health Expenditures in Canada," p. 49. For example, the hospitalization needs of persons aged 75 years and over are six to seven times those of ages 5 to 14 years. See Lefebvre, Zsigmond and Devereaux, *A Prognosis for Hospitals*.

[10] Note that in these calculations, pregnancy costs are shifted from women in the childbearing age groups and attributed to children 1 year of age and younger.

[11] That is, between 1981 and 2001, for a weighted average increase of 12.8 per cent.

[12] This represents an overall increase of 24.4 per cent.

[13] From current levels around 40 per cent, to 45 per cent in 2001, and 60 per cent by 2031.

[14] See, for example, the CANDIDE model of the Canadian macroeconomy described in P. S. Rao, "Macroeconomic Effects of Demographic Variables: Evidence from CANDIDE Model 2.0," *Economic Council of Canada Discussion Paper*, no.193 (March 1981).

[15] For a review of these policies see L. B. Smith, "Housing Assistance: A Re-evaluation," *Canadian Public Policy*, vol.7 (Summer 1981), pp. 454-63.

[16] See Statistics Canada, *Household and Family Projections for Canada and the Provinces to 2001* (Ottawa: Information Canada, 1975).

[17] Ibid., p. 55. Family growth rates show a similar decline—see p. 71.

[18] The same compositional changes in future housing needs are also anticipated in the U.S. See T. C. Marein, "The Effects of Declining Population Growth on Housing Demand," *Challenge* (November-December 1976), pp. 30-33.

[19] For further information see B. T. Wigdor and L. Ford, eds., *Housing for an Aging Population: Alternatives* (Toronto: University of Toronto Press, 1981).

[20] See, for example, A. Blumstein, J. Cohen and H. D. Miller, "Crime, Punishment and Demographics," *American Demographics*, vol.2 (October 1980), pp. 32-37, on which much of this section is based.

[21] In general, Canada is a slightly younger population than the U.S., so these profiles might be somewhat delayed. In the U.S. the racial difference in the population is also incorporated into the model.

[22] See Statistics Canada, *Urban Family Expenditure, 1976*, Catalogue No. 62-547 (Ottawa: Information Canada, 1978).

[23] See, for example, P. Boyle and J. Murray, "Social Security Wealth and Private Saving in Canada," *Canadian Journal of Economics*, vol.12 (August 1979), pp. 456-68.

[24] J. P. Aubry and D. Fleurant, "Simulation Analysis of a Model Based on the Life-Cycle Hypothesis," *Bank of Canada Technical Report*, no. 18 (February 1980).

264

[25] But see B. Robey and M. John, "The Political Future: The Demographics of Politics," *American Demographics*, vol.1 (October 1980), pp. 15-21.

[26] The impact of demography on productivity performance is one notable example. See R. Clark, J. Kreps and J. Spengler, "Economics of Aging: A Survey," *Journal of Economic Literature*, vol.16 (September 1978), pp. 927-30, for a brief review.

Appendix

[1] See Statistics Canada, *Population Projections for Canada and the Provinces, 1972-2001*, Catalogue No. 91-514 (Ottawa: Information Canada, 1974), especially pp. 59, 79; and idem, *Population Projections for Canada and the Provinces, 1976-2001*, Catalogue No. 91-520 (Ottawa: 1979), especially pp. 29, 46.

[2] An evaluation of the first series mortality projections was made in light of the actual mortality trends during the subsequent years (1971-76). This involved comparing actual to projected life expectancies in 1971 and the actual to projected number of deaths during the period 1972-76. "Overall, the projections showed only slight deviations from the observed trends. Consequently, it was decided to adopt the original mortality projections (for the second series)." Statistics Canada, *Population Projections 1976-2001*, pp. 19-20.

[3] See Statistics Canada, *Population Projections 1972-2001*, p. 21; and K. S. Gnanasekaran, "Revised Mortality Projections for Canada and the Provinces, 1971-1986," Background paper (Ottawa: Statistics Canada, 1979), p. 6.

[4] See ibid., p. 46; and Statistics Canada, *Population Projections 1976-2001*, p. 25, respectively.

[5] The last set of numbers in each case is selected to develop a hypothetical scenario with zero net international immigration, needed by demographers for theoretical and policy studies.

[6] Defined as the sum of net gains plus net losses.

[7] See, for example, R. A. Easterlin, "What Will 1984 Be Like? Socioeconomic Implications of Recent Twists in Age Structure," *Demography*, vol. 15 (November 1978), pp. 397-432.

[8] See W. P. Butz and M. P. Ward, "The Emergence of Countercyclical U.S. Fertility," *American Economic Review*, vol. 69 (June 1978), pp. 318-28.

[9] These assumptions largely reflect the results of curvilinear trend regressions on provincial data since the early 1960s, although some upward adjustment was included in the data for the 1990s in some cases.

[10] This is described in some detail in Statistics Canada, *Technical Report on Population Projections for Canada and the Provinces, 1972-2001*, Catalogue No. 91-516 (Ottawa: Information Canada, 1975).

[11] See Statistics Canada, *Population Projections 1976-2001*, p. 19.

[12] See Gnanasekaran, "Revised Mortality Projections," for further details.

[13] An implication of this procedure is that actual *reductions* in survival were ignored.

[14] Again any reductions were ignored. See note 13 above.

[15] The three decadal averages are 154.5, 136.6 and 130.0 thousand respectively.

[16] The 1976-79 average was 108.1 thousand, using an estimate of 81.6 thousand for calendar year 1979.

[17] Alternatively, it could be argued that this is a natural consequence of the reduced levels of immigration in the late 1970s, when relatively fewer immigrants were selected by labour market criteria.

[18] A preferred approach might be to relate it to the specific age-sex structure of each province as it changes over time.

[19] See D. K. Foot and W. J. Milne, "Public Policies and Interprovincial Migration in Canada: An Econometric Analysis," *Institute for Policy Analysis Working Paper*, no. 8126 (August 1981).

[20] The reader is referred to Statistics Canada, *Technical Report*, chap. 7, for a discussion of the assumptions for the first series of Statistics Canada projections.

[21] For a fuller discussion of these assumed patterns, see D. A. Norris and J. Perrault, "Migration Projections for Canada and the Provinces, 1976-1991," Background paper (Ottawa: Statistics Canada, 1979), p. 40-49. Note that this is accomplished by adjusting the in-migration proportions *only* (see Table A-7).

[22] They may be obtained from the author upon request. The corresponding Statistics Canada assumptions can be found in Norris and Perreault, "Migration Projections," Tables A.5.1 to A.5.8. (The author wishes to express his appreciation to Mr. R. Raby of Statistics Canada, who made the single-year-of-age data available for this study.)

The Canadian Institute for Economic Policy Series

The Monetarist Counter-Revolution: A Critique of Canadian Monetary Policy 1975-1979
Arthur W. Donner and Douglas D. Peters

Canada's Crippled Dollar: An Analysis of International Trade and Our Troubled Balance of Payments
H. Lukin Robinson

Unemployment and Inflation: The Canadian Experience
Clarence L. Barber and John C.P. McCallum

How Ottawa Decides: Planning and Industrial Policy-Making 1968-1980
Richard D. French

Energy and Industry: The Potential of Energy Development Projects for Canadian Industry in the Eighties
Barry Beale

The Energy Squeeze: Canadian Policies for Survival
Bruce F. Willson

The Post-Keynesian Debate: A Review of Three Recent Canadian Contributions
Myron J. Gordon

Water: The Emerging Crisis in Canada
Harold D. Foster and W.R. Derrick Sewell

The Working Poor: Wage Earners and the Failure of Income Security Policies
David P. Ross

Beyond the Monetarists: Post-Keynesian Alternatives to Rampant Inflation, Low Growth and High Unemployment
Edited by David Crane

The Splintered Market: Barriers to Interprovincial Trade in Canadian Agriculture
R.E. Haack, D.R. Hughes and R.G. Shapiro

267

The Drug Industry: A Case Study of the Effects of Foreign Control on the Canadian Economy
Myron J. Gordon and David J. Fowler

The New Protectionism: Non-Tarriff Barriers and Their Effects on Canada
Fred Lazar

Industrial Development and the Atlantic Fishery: Opportunities for Manufacturing and Skilled Workers in the 1980s
Donald J. Patton

The above titles are available from:

James Lorimer & Company, Publishers
Egerton Ryerson Memorial Building
35 Britain Street
Toronto M5A 1R7, Ontario